Union Organization and Activity

- How have unions responded to the decline of membership and power that began in 1980?
- Have unions been able to use New Labour legislation to recover lost membership?
- What are the pros and cons of union–management partnerships in the public sector?

Union Organization and Activity is the second book in the innovative Future of Trade Unions in Britain series. Featuring substantial and original research on union strategies, this book offers readers a detailed analysis of the opportunities and problems faced by unions in using the new trade union recognition law. Offering fresh research on unions strategies this is a book that will enrich policy debates with much needed evidence. Topics covered include:

- organizing campaigns across different sectors and their relative successes and failures
- public sector unions' strategies including the use of partnership agreements
- the structure of trade unionism as a potential barrier to union revitalization
- costs and benefits for employers of recognizing unions.

Written by key thinkers in the field of industrial relations, *Union Organization and Activity* highlights the conditions under which organizing and partnership are likely to appeal to union members and employers and thus has important policy implications for all parties to industrial relations, unions, employers and government.

John Kelly is Professor of Industrial Relations at the London School of Economics and also Professor of Industrial Relations at Birkbeck College, London. **Paul Willman** is Professor of Management Studies at Oxford University and Editor in Chief of *Human Relations*.

The Future of Trade Unions in Britain
The Centre for Economic Performance

This groundbreaking new series on trade unions and employment relations is the result of the largest research grant ever awarded by the Leverhulme Trust, and the three series titles both analyse and evaluate the nature of unionization in Britain. With a multidisciplinary approach, the series brings together experts in the field of employment relations to offer three of the most informed, broad ranging and up-to-date studies available. Essential reading for anyone studying or working professionally with employment relations in Britain.

Representing Workers
Trade union recognition and membership in Britain
Edited by Stephen Wood and Howard Gospel

Union Organization and Activity
Edited by John Kelly and Paul Willman

Union Organization and Activity

Edited by John Kelly and
Paul Willman

Routledge
Taylor & Francis Group

LONDON AND NEW YORK

First published 2004
by Routledge
11 New Fetter Lane, London EC4P 4EE

Simultaneously published in the USA and Canada
by Routledge
29 West 35th Street, New York, NY 10001

Routledge is an imprint of the Taylor & Francis Group

Typeset in Sabon by
HWA Text and Data Management, Tunbridge Wells
Printed and bound in Great Britain by
The Cromwell Press, Trowbridge, Wiltshire

British Library Cataloguing in Publication Data
A catalogue record for this book is available from the British
Library

Library of Congress Cataloging in Publication Data
Union organization and activity / edited by John Kelly and
Paul Willman. – 1st ed.
    p.   cm.
Includes bibliographical references and index.
  1. Labor unions–Organizing. I. Kelly, John. II. Willman, Paul.
  HD6490 .O7U54 2004
   331.87–dc22   2003023750

ISBN 0–415–28738–3 (hbk)
ISBN 0–415–28739–1 (pbk)

Contents

List of figures   viii
List of tables   ix
List of contributors   xi
Foreword   xii
Acknowledgements   xiv
List of abbreviations   xv

1   **Introduction**   1
     PAUL WILLMAN AND JOHN KELLY

     Union membership in Britain 1975–2002 1
     Agency, action and outcomes 4
     The book 5

2   **Union mobilization and employer counter-mobilization
     in the statutory recognition process**   7
     SIAN MOORE

     Introduction 7
     Method 9
     The statutory procedure 9
     Employer intervention in the statutory procedure 12
     Employer behaviour in the workplace 16
     Union organizing 21
     Conclusions 29

3   **Union organizing**   32
     JOHN KELLY AND VIDU BADIGANNAVAR

     Introduction 32
     Mobilization theory 33
     Method 34

Case 1: organizing research workers 35
Case 2: organizing in a marketing agency call-centre 38
Case 3: organizing Amazon warehouse workers 44
Conclusions 49

4   **Equity and representation in the new economy**   51
    DIANE PERRONS

    Introduction 51
    The new economy, social and gender divisions 52
    The new economy, the state and locality: re-regulation and
        deregulation 53
    A local case study: Brighton and Hove 55
    Conclusion 70

5   **Structuring unions: the administrative rationality of**
    collective action   73
    PAUL WILLMAN

    Introduction 73
    The shape of things 74
    Reactions to membership loss 76
    Organizational issues 80
    Conclusions: revitalization? 86

6   **Public service unionism in a restructured public sector:**
    challenges and prospects   89
    STEPHEN BACH AND REBECCA KOLINS GIVAN

    Public service trade unionism 91
    WERS and the public sector 93
    Public sector modernization 96
    Union responses to public service restructuring 98
    Conclusions 107

7   **Labour–management partnership in the UK public sector**   110
    VIDU BADIGANNAVAR AND JOHN KELLY

    Introduction 110
    Methods: settings, procedures and questions 112
    Results 116
    Partnership and industrial relations 123
    Discussion and conclusions 126

8   The end of the affair?: the decline in employers' propensity
     to unionize   129
     ALEX BRYSON, RAFAEL GOMEZ AND PAUL WILLMAN

     Introduction 129
     Determinants of union presence 130
     Theory 132
     What has happened to voice regimes? 136
     *Decline in workplace unionization, 1984–98: compositional
        change or employer choice? 139*
     *What do unions have to do to persuade non-union employers
        to choose union voice? 141*
     Conclusions 144
     Appendix 146

9   Beyond New Unionism   150
     FRANCES O'GRADY AND PAUL NOWAK

     Unions today 151
     New Unionism 153
     The shift toward organizing 153
     Breaking out 157
     Beyond the workplace 159
     Employers 160
     Government 161
     Conclusions 162

10 Conclusions   164
     JOHN KELLY AND PAUL WILLMAN

     Bibliography   170
     Index   180

Figures

1.1 Agency, process and outcomes 5
2.1 The statutory recognition process 15
5.1 Union growth mechanisms 83
5.2 Performance indicators 85
8.1 Likelihood of union or non-union voice based on cross-classification of employer, union and worker preferences 131
8.2 Voice regime choice: the decision tree 134
8.3 The firm's make or buy decision under three possible cases 136
8.4 Voice regime choice in Britain: 1984 and 1998 137
8.5 Management attitudes to union membership at their workplace in 1998 141
8.6 Management 'in favour' of membership in non-unionized private sector 143
8.7 Probability that management is not averse to union consultation, non-unionized workplaces in the private sector 145

Tables

1.1 Trade union membership and unemployment in
Great Britain 1975–2002   2
2.1 The case studies   10
2.2 The relationship between union membership and
support for unions in CAC ballots   12
2.3 CAC ballots and reasons for balloting where the union
had over 50% membership on application   13
3.1 Issues of concern to contract researchers   36
4.1 Housing composition in Brighton and Hove   57
4.2 Gender, care and unionization   57
4.3 Pay and age characteristics   57
4.4 Work satisfaction, job security and work–life balance   58
5.1 Union numbers and membership 1990–2002   75
5.2 Size distribution of UK unions   75
6.1 Public service trade union membership trends, 1992–2002   90
6.2 Key comparisons of public and private sector union presence
and activity, by percentage of workplaces, 1998   94
6.3 Collective bargaining coverage   94
7.1 Comparing direct worker involvement and influence in
partnership and non-partnership NHS Trusts   116
7.2 Comparing direct worker involvement and influence in
partnership and non-partnership magistrates' courts   117
7.3 Union outcomes in two NHS Trusts   117
7.4 Union outcomes in two MCCs   118
7.5 Perceived effectiveness of union representation amongst
workers in two NHS Trusts   119
7.6 Perceived effectiveness of union representation amongst
workers in two MCCs   120
8.1 Union and non-union voice arrangements in unionized
workplaces, 1984–98   138

8.2   The decline in workplace unionization, 1984–98   139
8.3   Contribution of change in composition and within-group
       change to workplace unionization, 1984–98   140
8.4   Linear estimation models for union voice   148

Contributors

Stephen Bach is a Senior Lecturer in Management and Employment Relations at the Management Centre, King's College, London.

Vidu Badigannavar is a Lecturer in Industrial Relations at the University of Kent at Canterbury.

Alex Bryson is a Principal Research Fellow at the Policy Studies Institute and a Research Associate in the Centre for Economic Performance, London School of Economics.

Rebecca Kolins Givan is a Research Officer in the Centre for Economic Performance, London School of Economics.

Rafael Gomez is a Lecturer in Management in the Interdisciplinary Institute of Management, London School of Economics.

John Kelly is a Professor of Industrial Relations at the London School of Economics and in the School of Management, Birkbeck College, London.

Sian Moore is a Senior Institute Researcher at the Working Lives Research Institute, London Metropolitan University.

Paul Nowak is Director of the New Unionism Project, at the Trades Union Congress.

Frances O'Grady is the Deputy General Secretary of the Trades Union Congress.

Diane Perrons is a Senior Lecturer in the Department of Geography and the Environment and a Fellow of the Gender Institute, both at the London School of Economics.

Paul Willman is the Ernest Butten Professor of Management Studies at Oxford University and a Research Associate in the Centre for Economic Performance, London School of Economics.

Foreword

Profound changes have taken place during the last quarter of a century in both employee representation and voice. Union membership has declined by over five million, the closed shop is almost extinct, half the present workforce has never belonged to a union and now, in the private sector, only one worker in five is a member. Simultaneously there has been a big move away from representative voice to direct voice. Representative voice occurs via a recognized trade union or works council. Direct voice bypasses these intermediate institutions. Instead, management and employees communicate directly with one another through, for example, team briefings, regular meetings between senior management and the workforce, and problem-solving groups such as quality circles.

The Leverhulme Trust realised that these alterations in industrial relations required more attention and initiated a research programme on the Future of Trade Unions in Modern Britain. This research is being carried out in the Centre for Economic Performance and the Industrial Relations Department at the London School of Economics, and includes colleagues from other institutions like King's College London, Oxford and Sheffield Universities and the Policy Studies Institute. The team are very grateful to the Leverhulme Trust for this financial support. In particular the successive directors, Barry Supple and Sir Richard Brook, have greatly helped us with their wisdom and flexibility.

Programme research is organized around a number of themes: membership; interaction with employers and the state; adapting to change; performance outcomes; and public sector and public policy (see http://cep.lse.ac.uk/future_of_unions). The various outputs are being distilled into a trilogy published by Routledge. The first volume, edited by Howard Gospel and Stephen Wood was published in 2003 and focused on trade union recognition and membership. It analysed the reasons for the decline in membership, what unions do for younger workers and women, the willingness to unionize among non-union workers and the impact of new laws governing trade union recognition and information and consultation.

This second volume edited by John Kelly and Paul Willman, deals with union organization and activity. It covers organizing campaigns, union structures, representing workers in the new economy, and interactions with employers including social partnership. The team much appreciates the cooperation and input from Francesca Poynter and Rachel Crookes of Routledge in bringing this volume to fruition. Volume 3, to be edited by Sue Fernie and myself, will present different approaches to the future of unions and examine performance outcomes. The approaches include organization theory, social movements and standard economic analysis. The performance outcomes cover economic and industrial relations performance in both the public and private sector.

David Metcalf
Director, Leverhulme Trust Programme on Future of
Trade Unions in Modern Britain

Acknowledgements

This book is based on research conducted as part of the Leverhulme funded research programme on the Future of Trade Unions in Modern Britain based at the Centre for Economic Performance, London School of Economics. We would like to thank the Leverhulme Foundation for their financial support for the programme and the Centre for Economic Performance for administrative support.

The editors would also like to thank Francesca Poynter and Rachel Crookes at Routledge for their help in compiling this volume.

Abbreviations

ACTU	Australian Council of Trade Unions
AEEU	Amalgamated Engineering and Electrical Union (now AMICUS)
AMO	Association of Magisterial Officers
ATL	Association of Teachers and Lecturers
AUT	Association of University Teachers
BALPA	British Airlines Pilots Association
BMA	British Medical Association
BWRPS	British Worker Representation and Participation Survey
CAC	Central Arbitration Committee
CBI	Confederation of British Industry
CCT	Compulsory Competitive Tendering
CHI	Commission for Health Improvement
CIPD	Chartered Institute of Personnel and Development
COHSE	Confederation of Health Service Employees (now UNISON)
CWU	Communication Workers Union
DTI	Department of Trade and Industry
ERA	Employment Relations Act (1999)
GPMU	Graphical, Paper and Media Union
HRM	Human Resource Management
IiP	Investors in People
IPA	Involvement and Participation Association
ISTC	Iron and Steel Trades Confederation
JCC	Joint Consultative Committee
LFS	Labour Force Survey
MCC	Magisterial Courts Committee
MPO	Managerial and Professional Officers (now part of GMB)
MSF	Manufacturing, Science, Finance (now AMICUS)
NAHT	National Association of Head Teachers
NALGO	National and Local Government Officers Association (now UNISON)

NASUWT	National Association of Schoolmasters and Union of Women Teachers
NLRB	National Labor Relations Board
NUPE	National Union of Public Employees (now UNISON)
NUT	National Union of Teachers
OECD	Organisation for Economic Cooperation and Development
PAT	Professional Association of Teachers
PFI	Private Finance Initiative
PPP	Public-Private Partnership
RCN	Royal College of Nursing
SHA	Secondary Heads Association
SIC	Standard Industrial Code
TELCO	The East London Communities Organisation
TGWU	Transport and General Workers Union
TUC	Trades Union Congress
ULR	Union Learning Representative
USDAW	Union of Shop, Distributive and Allied Workers
WERS	Workplace Employee Relations Survey
WIRS	Workplace Industrial Relations Survey

Chapter 1

Introduction

Paul Willman and John Kelly

There is a very broad picture to be drawn about union organization in Britain across the last twenty-five years. More or less independent of the measure of union organization one takes – and we will discuss several below – there is less of it than there was in 1979. The task for the academic analyst may thus be seen as documenting the decline and attempting explanations for it and, indeed, much of this type of activity has taken place. However, the attempt to explain the decline in union organization has itself indicated the complexity of the phenomenon and the information loss which results if one fails to disaggregate the process of change in trade union organization.

The year 1979 is often seen as a watershed in this matter, with a change of government from one broadly collaborative with trade union organizations to one distinctly hostile coinciding with the beginning of a long period of decline in membership and density. In subsequent years, increasingly hostile legislation on union organizing and activity went along with membership loss and density reduction. However, the pattern of change is complicated and there are a number of dimensions of union organization and activity to be considered. We begin by describing the broad pattern of change.

Union membership in Britain 1975–2002

Union membership in Britain climbed rapidly during the 1970s, fell from 1980 and began to rise again, albeit briefly, at the end of the 1990s. Part of the explanation for the turnaround in membership after 1979 was the sharp rise in unemployment which began that year (see Table 1.1). A large component of the unemployment growth was the shakeout of labour in the heavily unionized manufacturing sector: in 1979 there were just over seven million employees in the manufacturing industry but by 1992 the number had fallen below four million (Blyton and Turnbull 1998: 49). Employment expansion occurred primarily in private services where union density has always been far lower than in manufacturing or the public sector. In addition, government policy towards unions became extremely hostile from 1979, measured for example by its legislative programme to curb union power,

Table 1.1 Trade union membership and unemployment in Great Britain 1975–2002[a]

Year	Membership (000s)	Unemployment (%)
1975	11,656	3.5
1979	13,212	4.5
1984	11,064	10.9
1988	10,387	8.8
1992	8,929	9.8
1996	7,938	8.3
1997	7,801	7.2
1998	7,852	6.3
1999	7,898	6.1
2000	7,781	5.7
2001	7,750	4.9
2002	n/a	5.2

Sources: Union membership: Certification Office for Trade Unions and Employers' Associations, Annual Reports. Unemployment: data supplied by Jonathan Wadsworth, Centre for Economic Performance, LSE.

Note
a Claimant count for 1975, 1979 and 1984, thereafter the ILO count is used.

and remained so until the election of the Labour Party in 1997. The legal duty on employers to recognize and bargain with a union representing the majority of its workforce was abolished in 1980.

As well as sectoral shifts in employment, changes to employer policy within sectors became important. In general, employer policy towards union recognition became much tougher and the owners of new plants, in particular, became increasingly reluctant to deal with unions. For example, 59 per cent of workplaces opened in the 1970s had union recognition for collective bargaining within ten years; the comparable figure for workplaces opened in the 1980s was just 34 per cent and for the 1990s it was 27 per cent (Machin 2000: 635; Bryson *et al.*, this volume). Some employers actively sought to remove unions altogether: in the mid-1980s the incidence of derecognition was running at approximately 25 cases per year but by 1992 this number had leapt to 72 per year before then tailing off to just seven cases in 1998 (Kelly 1996: 89; Gall 2003a: 11). Some of the causes of decline were endogenous to unions themselves. Unions devoted few resources to organizing and recruitment: at the start of the 1990s almost half the TUC unions with 3,000 or more members did not even have a national recruitment officer (Kelly and Heery 1994: 48).

However, by the early years of the following decade, the situation had changed significantly and in ways that should have favoured a significant resumption of membership growth. Unemployment had begun to fall again from 9.8 per cent in 1992 to reach just 5.2 per cent in 2002 (see Table 1.1). Job losses in manufacturing continued throughout the 1990s albeit at a slower rate than in previous years but public sector employment actually rose by 149,000 between 1998 and 2000, primarily in health and education (Bach and Winchester 2003: 294). The union recognition provisions of the Employment Relations Act (ERA 1999) came into effect in June 2000 and their passage through parliament was associated with a sharp rise in the number of new recognition agreements, from 108 in 1997 to 668 in 2001 (Gall 2003a: 11). Very few cases have gone to the Central Arbitration Committee (CAC) – just 233 between June 2000 and May 2003 – suggesting that in the first few years of its operation the new law has not triggered substantial employer resistance (Wood *et al.* 2003; Moore, this volume). Finally unions themselves now devote more resources to organizing than ten years ago: 62 per cent of unions now have a national recruitment officer and a substantial minority of unions have sent trainees through the TUC Organizing Academy, created in 1997 (Heery *et al.* 2003: 59).

It is impossible to make an exact prediction about the effect of this set of circumstances on union membership. There is no agreement either about the impact of any one of these variables on union membership or about the relative weights that can be attached to each of them (cf. Dunn and Metcalf 1996 and Freeman and Pelletier 1990 on the impact of legal changes). But what we can reasonably say is that the environment and union policies changed to such a degree in the late 1990s that between 1997 and 2002 unions should have returned to membership growth. Membership did increase in 1998 and 1999 but these gains were wiped out in the following two years.

It will be a central concern of this volume to discuss why union recovery has been so limited. Some of the factors may be environmental, but some may be internal to unions. In the findings from the British Worker Representation and Participation Survey (BWRPS) there is evidence to suggest that there is a demand for representation among non-members that unions do not meet (see Gospel and Willman 2003). Data from the Workplace Employee Relations Survey (WERS) on the reduction in union density under collective bargaining indicates that union services are not always sought when they are readily available. Other evidence on the union wage differential indicates that the instrumentality of unions may have declined over recent years (Blanchflower and Bryson 2003). In short, there is at least a case for arguing that some of the reasons for reduction in many measures of union organization may be endogenous.

However, because of this complexity in the factors which influence measures of union organization and the range of measures themselves, we need some form of framework for the analysis of union organization and activity. This framework must deal with the influence of the three major institutional actors in industrial relations – government, employers and unions. It must also consider a wide range of measures of union organization and activity.

Agency, action and outcomes

Our approach here is as follows. First, we identify three broad agents of impact on union organization and activity. These are employers, government and unions themselves, the main actors in industrial relations. They often act in concert or at least the consequences of their actions are interactive. However, their actions impact union organization and activities in ways which are conceptually and temporally distinct.

Second, we turn to the dimensions of union organization and activity which may be characterized as the set of dependent variables we are seeking to explain. Three are identified, as follows:

1 Resources; what are the key resources available for trade unions to organize members, by which we mean the broad processes of recruitment, mobilization and retention?
2 Processes; how do unions, in this broad sense, organize?
3 Outcomes; what are the consequences of union organization?

We know that there is no simple relationship between the dimensions. For example, take resources and outcomes. Unions may have large resources in terms of existing membership and financial resources but be unable to secure a union wage differential. Or take the example of processes and outcomes. Unions may become involved in large-scale recruitment activity but secure few members. A final example, of imbalance between resources and processes, comes from France, where large-scale union action can be mobilized on the basis of very low levels of membership and participation.

The agents may affect the dimensions in very different ways. Governments may provide unions with resources for organization through legislating to allow check-off or time off for representatives. They may afford processes, such as the current recognition provisions. They may even guarantee outcomes, such as the provisions of the old Fair Wages resolutions or the National Minimum Wage. Similarly, employers may provide the resources which sow the seeds of permanent organization by provision of facilities or information, may give recognition and bargaining opportunities as processes and may give up wage premia as a result of bargaining. Here, as with the government as agent, it may be that concession is a better word for provision but it remains the case that factors which affect these agents' propensity to concede or provide will be vital for union organization. Unions themselves act as agents specifically in making decisions about resources and implementing mobilization processes which may generate organizational outcomes. As with governments and employers, these acts may have positive or negative impacts.

We have attempted a schematic summary of theses issues in Figure 1.1. The cell entries are examples not comprehensive lists. Our purpose is to show that the organizational data which, for example, are trawled by WERS,

Dimension		**Agent**		
		Government	Employer	Union
	Resource	Check off legislation Time off for representatives	Facilities provision information	Finances Expenditure decisions Participation levels
	Process	Recognition Provisions	Recognition Bargaining success	Campaign Dispute Service provision
	Outcome	Schedule II Fair wages Resolutions Minimum wage	Wage premium procedures	Membership Density Collective agreement

Figure 1.1 Agency, process and outcomes

represent different phenomena with different implications for union organization. Specifically, an abundance of resources will not generate organizational
processes in all cases and these processes are not always successful in
generating outcomes. A full understanding of the past and an accurate
prediction of the future trend of union organization and activity in the UK
depends on an understanding of the complex interactions of agency and
dimension.

The book

The chapters in the book focus on different aspects of agency and dimension.
In Chapter 2, Moore offers the first major examination of the operation of
the statutory recognition procedure. Here the government acts as agent to
secure union recognition as an outcome by offering a statutory route. On
the positive side for trade unions, not only does this route work much of the
time, but the legislation appears to cast a shadow raising the overall level of
voluntary recognition. However, the process also allows contest between
the mobilization resources of the union and those – often greater – of the
employer directed at avoiding unionization; in some cases, the greater
resources prevail.

Organizing resources are a central concern of Kelly and Badigannavar
and Perrons in the next two chapters. In Chapter 3 Kelly and Badigannavar
use case studies of successful and unsuccessful organizing campaigns to
illustrate the difficulties in mobilizing employees. Employer hostility is an

important determinant of outcomes, but by no means the only one. Perrons' Chapter 4 on the 'new economy' highlights some of the difficulties unions have in organizing outside their traditional strongholds. She shows, first, the diverse and complicated nature of work in the new economy and, second, some of the difficulties unions have in offering services and representation to such employees.

In Chapter 5, Willman focuses directly on union agency. He argues that the form of conglomerate union structure which has come to dominate the set of large unions is poorly designed as a platform for revitalization. In fact, it represents a defensive and risk-averse response to decline leading to a situation where some of the barriers to renewed union growth are internal to unions' own structure.

The next two chapters focus on developments within a traditional union stronghold, the public sector. Bach and Givan, in Chapter 6, examine the ways in which public sector reform initiatives influence the processes of union restructuring. Here government acts as direct employer and its agency has clear effects on organizing outcomes. Difficult questions face public sector unionism and, as Badigannavar and Kelly show, partnership initiatives at local level may not offer much help. Their matched-pair analysis of workplaces with and without such agreements illustrates the limited transformative power of partnership and the range of contextual variables which can influence organizing outcomes.

Bryson, Gomez and Willman focus on the employer as agent in Chapter 8. Most employers want some form of voice mechanism in the workplace but increasingly they choose the non-union option. This chapter models the employer choice of voice mechanism in terms of its cost and the risks involved. Although on some measures of cost and risk, the union voice option should be more attractive, there are very strong cohort effects showing a preference for non-union voice. On the positive side, WERS data show that there is, among non-union employers, indifference rather than widespread hostility to union voice.

In Chapter 9, O'Grady and Nowak offer an insider assessment of the strengths and weaknesses of the TUC's New Unionism initiative and map out a number of ways in which unions can progress the New Unionism project. The book finishes off with a concluding chapter by the editors.

Chapter 2

Union mobilization and employer counter-mobilization in the statutory recognition process

Sian Moore

Introduction

The statutory recognition procedure, introduced under the Employment Relations Act (ERA) in June 2000, is succeeding in providing union recognition where the majority of the workforce wants it – *in most cases*. Yet recognition ballots held under the procedure are proving an area of uncertainty, with unions losing over a third of ballots ordered by the Central Arbitration Committee (CAC) in the first three years. In this chapter I explore the roles played by union organizing and employer behaviour in the outcome of statutory recognition ballots.

In the United States there is an extensive literature on determinants of union success and failure in National Labor Relations Board (NLRB) certification elections. These largely empirical analyses consider a range of factors predicting election outcomes, including the political, social and economic context; procedural factors; bargaining unit demographics; company and union characteristics and employer tactics (for examples see Cooke 1983; Farber and Western 2002; Lawler 1984). Wood and Godard have characterized the US system of recognition as 'based on a largely adversarial model' (1999: 214) and in the previous volume of this series Kochan (2003: 169) argued that opposition to unions in the UK 'pales in comparison to the deep anti-union culture that historically and currently pervades US management'. The history of the CAC procedure so far and specifically the proliferation of voluntary recognition agreements in the shadow of the law (TUC 2002a, 2003), probably bears this out. Yet the case studies of recognition ballots at the heart of this chapter demonstrate that a number of employers have adopted the type of anti-union tactics used in US elections. The orientation of the employer towards the union, but more explicitly, whether employers are willing to turn opposition into counter-mobilization (Kelly 1998), is crucial in UK recognition ballots. Counter-mobilization is underpinned by an ideological opposition to unions and involves the deployment of substantial resources against the union (and a preparedness to risk productivity in doing so) and the polarization of the workplace (Cohen and Hurd 1998), introducing conflict not only between management and workers, but also between workers themselves.

In both the UK and US more recent consideration of unionization has shifted away from structural determinants and onto unions themselves as actors shaping their own destinies. Bronfenbrenner and Juravich (1998) have emphasized the key role of union organizing strategies in NLRB election campaigns and the particular importance of 'rank-and-file intensive tactics'. They find that union organizing tactics can significantly influence the chances of winning NLRB elections:

> ... union tactics as a group play a greater role in explaining election outcome than any other group of variables, including employer character-istics and tactics, bargaining unit demographics, organizer's background, and election environment. This suggests that union strategies not only matter in determining election outcome but that they may matter more than many other factors.
>
> (Bronfenbrenner and Juravich 1998: 21)

Mobilization theory provides a dynamic and comprehensive explanation of workers' collective agency. This includes the effectiveness of union organization, yet also asserts the importance of social processes and structural factors including the legal framework and national and international product market competition and labour markets. It allows for counter-mobilization by the employer. Theories of union instrumentality suggest that workers' desire for unions will reduce if they begin to doubt that the union will resolve their grievances or start to believe that it may even increase their frustrations (Charlwood 2003). The case studies below show that whilst in the statutory procedure some employers were able to alter union supporters, and even members', perceptions of union instrumentality and to raise the perceived costs of unionization too high for some workers. Yet other employers were unable to change workers' calculations or were unwilling to invest the level of resources required to do so. Variation in workers' perceptions of the cost of unionization can also be explained by structural considerations, for example the labour market. Another mitigating factor is the existence and character of the activists involved. For Kelly 'the whole process of collectivization is heavily dependent on the actions of small numbers of leaders or activists' (1998: 44), who are key to promoting group cohesion and identity, in persuading workers to take collective action and in defending such action in the face of counter-mobilization. The case studies presented in this chapter show that a number of activists were prepared to face the threatened costs of collective action.

The chapter begins by looking at the operation of the statutory procedure. The next section focuses on employers, determining (1) how far the design of the legislation allows employers to intervene in the procedure to encourage ballots; and (2) their behaviour in the workplace. It then draws some conclusions about the impact of employer tactics on ballot results. The following section concentrates on unions, exploring (1) how far they have adopted organizing tactics; (2) how they have used their rights of access to the workplace during the ballot period; (3) the role of activists in sustaining support for recognition and countering employer mobilization; and (4) the perceived costs of unionization in cases which go through the statutory process. The section concludes by considering how far union tactics affect ballot outcomes.

Method

The chapter focuses upon the 64 recognition ballots ordered by the CAC in the first three years of the operation of the statutory procedure – June 2000 to May 2003. It is based on three main sources. First, there are CAC reports and where employers are named it is on the basis of these data. Second, the chapter draws upon a survey of the 64 CAC recognition ballots, referred to throughout as 'the ballot survey'.[1] This survey took the form of a questionnaire to the union officer responsible for the ballot, administered by post, telephone or face-to-face interview. It provides the basis for cross-sectional analysis of the factors that may influence election results. The survey represents a comprehensive source of information on employer behaviour before and during ballots; CAC reports include such evidence in some, but not all, cases.

Third, more in-depth investigation is provided by case studies of eight ballots. These are based upon publicly available CAC reports; access to union documentation from the CAC process, and semi-structured interviews with union officers, organizers and activists. In four of these cases the union secured sufficient support to gain recognition, but in the other four the union lost the ballot. Three of these ballots were unsuccessful despite the fact that on application to the CAC the union had a majority of its proposed bargaining unit in membership; in the fourth case votes for recognition in the ballot fell below the original membership figure. These cases have been selected in order to highlight the factors that can lead to the haemorrhaging of union support during the statutory process. Table 2.1 summarizes the characteristics of the case studies, which are anonymized to protect the identity of union activists.

The chapter is based upon CAC and union sources – there is no primary data from employers. In largely reflecting union perceptions of employer behaviour and calculations of the costs of unionization it was not possible to be on both sides of the contested terrain.

The statutory procedure

It appears that the political and legal framework is influential in workers' ability to organize collectively (Freeman and Pelletier 1990; Towers 2003). The context of this research is the introduction of government support for

Table 2.1 The case studies

Case study	Sector	Ownership (parent)	Sites covered by bargaining unit	Company employees (in UK)	Bargaining unit	Membership of bargaining unit on application	Support in ballot (% of bargaining unit)	Proportion of women workers in bargaining unit	Proportion of Black/minority ethnic workers in bargaining unit	Proportion of manual workers in bargaining unit
Fastwon	Service	US	110	10,000+	500+	Under 30%	75%+	Under 10%	60%+	100%
Mediwon	Manufacturing	UK	1	500–999	100–199	30–50%	51–74%	50–60%	50–60%	100%
Cablewon	Manufacturing	Owner-manager	1	100–249	100–199	Under 30%	41–50%	50–60%	Under 10%	100%
Woodwon	Manufacturing	Owner-manager	1	Under 50	Under 50	51–74%	51–74%	Under 10%	Under 10%	100%
Satellost	Service	Multi-national	1	10,000+	400–499	Under 30%	40% or under	50–60%	Under 10%	None
Autolost	Manufacturing	UK	1	10,000+	100–199	51–74%	40% or under	Under 10%	Under 10%	100%
Englost	Manufacturing	US	1	1,000–1,499	50–99	51–74%	40% or under	Under 10%	Under 10%	100%
Banklost	Service	European	1	Under 50	Under 50	75%+	40% or under	60%+	60%+	None

recognition. The Labour government's intention was to introduce a mechanism for union recognition where a majority of the workforce is in favour, but that it should be used as a last resort, its existence encouraging the conclusion of voluntary agreements. The history of the statutory procedure so far suggests that it has stimulated an increase in voluntary recognitions in the shadow of the law (Wood *et al.* 2003) and in the first three years relatively few (233) distinct applications for recognition were made to the CAC.[2] Unions have been successful in securing recognition in 60 per cent[3] of cases where there has been an outcome, although there are indications that it is getting harder. In 23 cases (11 per cent), the CAC has awarded statutory recognition without a ballot, whilst in another 41 (20 per cent) the union has won a recognition ballot. In 59 cases (29 per cent), the union has withdrawn the application and secured a recognition agreement with the employer (a 'semi-voluntary' agreement). These cases suggest a pragmatic response by employers once the threat of the CAC is invoked.

Recognition ballots

Unions have lost over one-third (36 per cent) of ballots ordered by the CAC, despite the fact that on application the union either had a majority of the bargaining unit in membership or had demonstrated to the CAC that a majority of the bargaining unit was likely to support recognition. The TUC had campaigned for a procedure in which recognition would be automatically granted where a union could show that it had a majority within the bargaining unit (TUC 1995). This principle was subsequently reflected in the government's White Paper, *Fairness at Work*:

> A simpler procedure should apply where employees are actually already members of a trade union. Where over half the workforce is in union membership already, so that they have clearly demonstrated through membership their desire for the union to bargain for them, then recognition should be automatic without a ballot.
>
> (Department of Trade and Industry 1998: Paragraph 4.18)

Yet following lobbying from the Confederation of British Industry (CBI), the final legislation requires the CAC to order a ballot if the union does not have over 50 per cent of the bargaining unit in membership, but *also* gave it discretion to call a ballot if there is a majority in membership using the following criteria:

- the CAC panel deems it is 'in the interests of good industrial relations' to hold a ballot
- the CAC is informed by a significant number of union members that they do not wish the union to represent them for collective bargaining

- the CAC has evidence which leads it to doubt that a significant number of union members want the union to bargain on their behalf or
- union membership has declined and the union no longer has a majority in membership.

Under pressure from employers the government also added a threshold to the recognition ballot – a union must secure not only a majority of those voting, but also 40 per cent of those eligible to vote.

Employer intervention in the statutory procedure

In general the CAC has operated on the principle that union membership does not necessarily reflect support for recognition in the bargaining unit. For example, in the case of the airline pilots' union, BALPA's application for recognition at easyJet:

> The Panel, drawing on its industrial relations experience, recognizes that there will be individuals who prefer not to join a trade union although supporting recognition, or whose union membership is conditional upon recognition, and that support for recognition may thus be greater than the level of union membership.
>
> (TUR1/73[2001] CAC decision 12 June 2001)

Table 2.2 shows that this has been borne out in over two-thirds (69 per cent) of cases, where the proportion voting for recognition exceeded union membership on application. Yet in just under a third (31 per cent or 20 cases) the proportion voting in favour was below the membership level as verified before the ballot. This means that membership levels or density (through changes in the bargaining unit) fell during the procedure and/or that union members abstained or voted against recognition in the ballot.

Table 2.2 The relationship between union membership and support for unions in CAC ballots

	Ballot won	Ballot lost	Total
Proportion voting for recognition exceeded union membership on application[a]	40 (98%)	4 (17%)	44 (69%)
Proportion voting for recognition below membership on application[a]	1 (2%)	19 (83%)	20 (31%)
Total	**41 (64%)**	**23 (36%)**	**64**

Note
a Or after revalidation if bargaining unit changed

CAC figures show that having a higher proportion of the bargaining unit in union membership on application is not related to ballot success. In fact the mean percentage membership was significantly higher for unsuccessful ballots (44 per cent compared to 35 per cent for successful ballots; $t = -2.53$, $p < 0.05$). This is an unexpected result since the statutory procedure is premised on majority membership. It suggests that once a case is in the procedure, a number of contending forces come into play introducing uncertainty. The prospect of such uncertainty encourages employers to intervene in the procedure to ensure there is a ballot. They may do so either by eroding the union's majority so the CAC has to order a ballot; or if it still has a majority, by providing evidence to persuade the CAC to invoke one of the discretionary criteria upon which it may order a ballot.

Of the 64 ballots ordered by the CAC in the first three years of its operation, 46 were required because the union did not have a majority of the bargaining unit in membership on application. Eighteen ballots have been held in cases where the union, on application to the CAC, was verified by the case manager through a membership check as having a majority in membership (Table 2.3). Of these 18, four were ordered because changes to the bargaining unit (either agreed or determined by the CAC) meant that the union no longer had a majority in membership.

Table 2.3 CAC ballots and reasons for balloting where the union had over 50% membership on application

Reason for ballot	Ballot won	Ballot lost	Total
Union had 50%+ on application			
In the interests of good industrial relations	4	1	5
The CAC was informed by a significant number of union members that they did not wish the union to represent them		1	1
The CAC had evidence which led it to doubt that a significant number of union members wanted the union to bargain on their behalf	1		1
Union agrees to a ballot	1	2	3
Changes to bargaining unit means union no longer had a majority in membership	1	3	4
Fall in union membership means union no longer had a majority in membership	1	3	4
Total	**8 (44%)**	**10 (56%)**	**18**
Union did not have 50% on application	**33 (72%)**	**13 (28%)**	**46**
TOTAL	41 (64%)	23 (36%)	64

In four other cases a ballot was ordered because union membership had fallen and the union had lost its majority whilst the case was in the procedure. Whilst the loss of membership or density in a bargaining unit may be due to labour turnover, to recruitment into the bargaining unit, to redundancies or to members' resignations, each of these occurrences themselves may be the result of employer calculation. One example is the case of the GMB and Richmond Mirrors (TURI/191 [2002]. The company recruited new staff into the bargaining unit, which diluted the union's membership from 52 per cent to 39 per cent. The CAC report includes the concern of the union officer at this rapid recruitment in the light of the adverse trading conditions described by the company in their correspondence with the CAC and the redundancies that had been made in September of three union members.

If the employer has not been able to undermine the union's majority he may attempt to provide information to the CAC to invoke one of the discretionary criteria upon which it may order a ballot. Banklost is the small UK headquarters of an international bank. On application to the CAC the union had over 75 per cent membership amongst the predominantly female clerical and administrative workforce. The CAC ordered a ballot after it received letters from employees, including from union members, stating they did not wish the union to conduct collective bargaining on their behalf. The union submitted to the CAC that this had been done under pressure from management.

In the US, the ability of employers to prolong the recognition process has been part of concerted campaigns to undermine unions (Wood and Godard 1999: 231). Such delays may frustrate and demotivate union members and supporters, whilst allowing the employer to legitimately campaign against the union at a time when the union may have limited or no access to the workforce. In the UK there are time limits for every stage of the procedure, but there is also the facility for the parties to request extensions, which the CAC may encourage in order to promote agreement (Figure 2.1). In the case of Banklost, the senior manager had rejected all informal approaches from the union for discussions on voluntary recognition, but once the statutory procedure was invoked, he then changed tactics. He reacted to the union's formal letter under the legislation on day nine of the ten day 'first period' allowed for the employer response, by saying he wanted to meet with the union to discuss recognition and asked for an extension of the procedure. The union officer was convinced that the employer had no intention of concluding a voluntary agreement and the union finally referred the application to the CAC four months after its formal approach. In retrospect the officer believed the union did not move fast enough:

> There was never a case when a deadline was set and the employer did not find an excuse to put it back ... the union made mistakes by allowing delays because it wanted to be constructive, which gave management time to work on members.

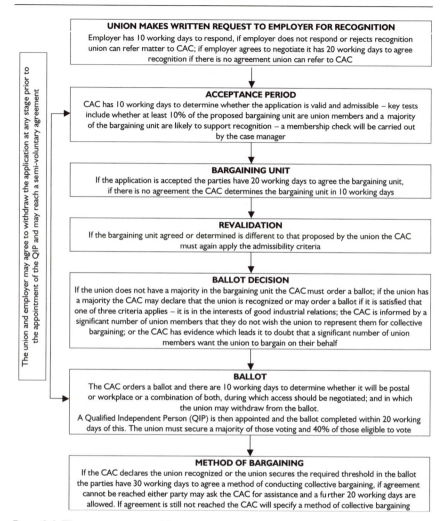

The union and employer may agree to withdraw the application at any stage prior to the appointment of the QIP and may reach a semi-voluntary agreement

UNION MAKES WRITTEN REQUEST TO EMPLOYER FOR RECOGNITION
Employer has 10 working days to respond, if employer does not respond or rejects recognition union can refer matter to CAC; if employer agrees to negotiate it has 20 working days to agree recognition if there is no agreement union can refer to CAC

ACCEPTANCE PERIOD
CAC has 10 working days to determine whether the application is valid and admissible – key tests include whether at least 10% of the proposed bargaining unit are union members and a majority of the bargaining unit are likely to support recognition – a membership check will be carried out by the case manager

BARGAINING UNIT
If the application is accepted the parties have 20 working days to agree the bargaining unit, if there is no agreement the CAC determines the bargaining unit in 10 working days

REVALIDATION
If the bargaining unit agreed or determined is different to that proposed by the union the CAC must again apply the admissibility criteria

BALLOT DECISION
If the union does not have a majority in the bargaining unit the CAC must order a ballot; if the union has a majority the CAC may declare that the union is recognized or may order a ballot if it is satisfied that one of three criteria applies – it is in the interests of good industrial relations; the CAC is informed by a significant number of union members that they do not wish the union to represent them for collective bargaining; or the CAC has evidence which leads it to doubt that a significant number of union members want the union to bargain on their behalf

BALLOT
The CAC orders a ballot and there are 10 working days to determine whether it will be postal or workplace or a combination of both, during which access should be negotiated; and in which the union may withdraw from the ballot.
A Qualified Independent Person (QIP) is then appointed and the ballot completed within 20 working days of this. The union must secure a majority of those voting and 40% of those eligible to vote

METHOD OF BARGAINING
If the CAC declares the union recognized or the union secures the required threshold in the ballot the parties have 30 working days to agree a method of conducting collective bargaining, if agreement cannot be reached either party may ask the CAC for assistance and a further 20 working days are allowed. If agreement is still not reached the CAC will specify a method of collective bargaining

Figure 2.1 The statutory recognition process

Employers have challenged unions at every possible stage of the procedure and raised extraneous legal points with the apparent intention of not only defeating the union procedurally, but also of delaying the process. Autolost is a large Midlands-based automotive parts and accessory manufacturer, established following a management buy-out involving union derecognition. The union's proposed bargaining unit covered operatives on one of its five UK sites. Here the employer was represented by a series of barristers who engaged in extensive litigation. The employer not only challenged the composition of the bargaining unit, but claimed that because the union had merged with another since the application, the CAC did not have authority to deal with the case. When this argument failed it then claimed the union had transgressed its own rulebook in granting membership at reduced rates, which led the CAC to order a ballot. Had this measure failed, the employer had submitted a number of letters from the workforce calling for a ballot. This litigation meant the case was in the CAC procedure for a year, from the submission of the formal letter requesting recognition to the ballot result.

Intervention in the procedure can thus undermine the union, particularly if it leads to delay, dilutes the union's majority or persuades the CAC to call a ballot. Yet although intervention may reflect the level of employer hostility to the union, it can also be regarded as legitimate behaviour encouraged by the design of the procedure. In other cases employers may not engage with the procedure at all, but seek to undermine union support in the workplace, and it is to this behaviour that I now turn.

Employer behaviour in the workplace

There is variation in the extent to which employers are willing to go to prevent unionization even once in the procedure. In some cases employers appear to be using the statutory machinery to test majority support for recognition amongst the workforce and may adopt a neutral stance throughout the procedure and the ballot. In the case of the Amalgamated Engineering and Electrical Union (AEEU) and Honda (TUR1/129[2002]), the company committed itself to remain 'neutral' during the ballot process. The union was allowed full access to the workforce and secured majority support for recognition in the ballot.

At the other end of the scale, the case studies show that a number of employers are prepared to actively organize against unionization in the workplace and to invest whatever is necessary to defeat unions. Such behaviour is admissible because the only part of the statutory procedure where employer behaviour is the subject of any regulation is within the ballot period. In the case of AMICUS (the union created by the merger of the AEEU and Manufacturing, Science and Finance Union [MSF]) and Black and Decker the CAC panel recognized that workers' decisions to join unions are not made freely, but subject to employer influence, yet at the same time acknowledged the rights of employers to engage in campaigns prior to the ballot period.

> It was agreed by both parties over the course of the hearing that since September 2002 the Company regularly communicated to its workforce through monthly briefing meetings, visits from US managers, and other opportunities to present its views that union recognition would produce no added value to the Company and that it wished to address workers' concerns by other means. We do not believe that this was done in an intimidating fashion, and recognize that the Company has the right to communicate its views in this way to its employees. However, we believe that such a consistency of message and communication will have

influenced the willingness of workers to join or remain in the Union. We note that the Union had no comparable opportunity to present its views ...

(TUR1/215[2002] CAC decision 6 February 2003)

The union had reported to the CAC that US managers had stated that recognition could prejudice the long-term viability of the site, whilst 'individual managers had threatened workers within the bargaining unit that if the union gained recognition the site would be shut down'.

US studies have identified a number of employer tactics which influence the outcomes of recognition ballots. These include the use of outside consultants, captive audience meetings, letters to workers, supervisor one-to-ones, the dismissal or promotion of activists, redundancies, changes in benefits or pay increases, media campaigns and anti-union committees (Bronfenbrenner and Juravich 1998). The case studies and ballot survey show that all of these have been adopted to different degrees by employers in CAC recognition ballots, although one tactic not included by Bronfenbrenner and Juravich is the threat by the employer to close or relocate the workplace.

Threats to close or relocate

Satellost is a huge multi-national media corporation renowned for its anti-unionism. The CAC application covered sales staff working in a call-centre in Scotland, one of three sites in a division of the corporation employing around 10,000 workers. The employer countered with an explicit threat to relocate. Following the union's complaint to the CAC about this threat, in a statement resonant of US consultants (Logan 2002), the company openly conceded:

> ... staff were also briefed that 'if anything occurs within sales in Scotland which jeopardizes our competitive edge, then we will look at alternative operational models to deliver'. We were upfront with staff and told them that exploratory talks had already started. This is a statement of fact. It is not a statement that we will close if the union is granted recognition.
>
> (from union documentation of CAC application)

The clear perception of the workforce was that they had to choose between the union and the company and between the union and their job: 'to be pro-union meant you were against the company, you were for or against' (activist at Satellost). Some activists were told by other workers 'you are going to cost me my job' and one was threatened with violence. Division within the workforce was encouraged by the large numbers of long-term temporary workers not included in the bargaining unit, who were told they would not be made permanent if the union secured recognition. As a consequence these temporary workers put pressure on permanent workers during the campaign.

At Autolost a number of workers wrote to the CAC complaining that a meeting had been held in which a manager told the workforce to 'think very carefully which road you are going down'. As one worker stated 'many employees saw it as a veiled threat to move the contract and their jobs with it'. The existence of the nearby non-unionized sister site lent credibility to rumours of relocation:

> The informal rumour mill was working – team leaders and supervisors were sending out messages that the contract would be moved elsewhere [to the other site] and the company would rationalize the business and close the site if recognition was secured – this was what lost the ballot.
> (Union officer at Autolost)

Englost is a US-owned multi-national producing engine technology with five UK factories at the time of the application. The bargaining unit covered production workers in one factory in the north west. Although it was never formally stated that the workplace would close, workers were informed in briefing meetings by senior executives brought over from the US that the corporation would not look kindly upon the site being unionized and there would 'definitely be long term consequences'. Prior to the ballot supervisors were telling workers, 'I've heard they are going to shut the place if the union comes in – but I haven't said anything'.

In six of the eight case studies the issue of the relocation or outsourcing of production became salient. Yet in the successful ballots the threat of closure did not become a decisive issue. There is variation in the explicitness of such threats and in the three unsuccessful ballots illustrated above the threats of relocation were perceived by the workforce to be credible (see p.26).

The use of supervisors

As the case studies have shown, supervisors, or team leaders, can be crucial in identifying union support, soliciting or disseminating information on the shop floor and in particular as the source of rumours or whispering campaigns from which the employer can then disassociate himself. In five of the eight case studies, union officers and activists reported that management used supervisors or team leaders against the union. In Englost it was clear to workers that supervisors were being briefed by management: 'they would all disappear from the shop floor at the same time and within 24 hours would come out with the same line'.

One-to-ones and captive audience meetings

In Bronfenbrenner and Juravich's (1998) analysis the use of 'supervisor one-to-ones' is considered as one employer tactic. Yet in UK campaigns, the use of supervisors and one-to-ones appear to be separate, since calling workers in for individual talks on union membership or recognition is more likely to be done by more senior management or human resources staff. At Englost, the employer used both captive audience meetings and one-to-ones. US executives first addressed a series of mass meetings in the company canteen. The company then held seven meetings of about 12 people, each chaired by a US manager, asking what people thought about joining the union. Activists reported that workers were reluctant to voice their real feelings and felt intimidated. Subsequently, either the plant manager or the local human resources manager took people individually into their office and asked what they felt about unions and if they would be joining. In a further individual meeting, the minutes of the company's communications meetings were placed on the table and people were told to have a look and then asked if they wanted to raise any issues.

Victimization

In the US, anti-union consultants stress the 'chilling effect' that the victimization of union activists can have on organizing campaigns (Logan 2002). In the UK, Part VIII of the statutory procedure makes it unlawful to subject workers to detriment or employees to dismissal for recognition-related activities. Yet in the case of Banklost, the two main union activists were made compulsorily redundant on economic grounds and offered compensation well above any previous company payment and higher than an Employment Tribunal award. In these circumstances the union officer felt unable to pressurize them to reject the offer, but stated that, 'this was a killer point because the union was seen as unable to defend their key people – that's when we lost it'.

Woodwon is a small owner-managed company making and renovating furniture and based in two units on one site in the south east. The owner sacked a union supporter for using waste materials for his own purposes, despite the fact that it was customary for workers to do this as long as it was not in the employer's time. A union officer represented the member, using the opportunity to be seen on company premises and to expose the lack of adequate disciplinary procedures. The worker was subsequently dismissed and lost his internal appeal, perhaps not surprisingly because the case was heard by the owner's wife! The union then filed an Employment Tribunal claim on the grounds of dismissal for trade union activities and the company settled on a favourable basis. The main union activist was particularly affected by the victimization:

> My back got right up, I decided the fight was on. The sacking worried people, but the workers were strong-minded, the sacking hardened them, they were fighters, we said if you want a fight you've got it, we will go down fighting – this shocked the employer.

The impact of the victimizations was different at these two small workplaces, although it is possible that the effect would have been more damaging at Woodwon had it been the main activist who was sacked.

Bargaining unit size

It has been argued that size of bargaining unit is negatively associated with ballot success, with larger employers more willing to commit increased resources to avoid unionization. By contrast the greater communication, cohesiveness and conformity amongst workers in smaller units may be more conducive to building union support (Cooke 1983; Lawler 1984).

The CAC ballot survey shows a significant *positive* relationship between bargaining unit size and ballot outcome, with the mean size of the bargaining unit in successful ballots being 362 compared to 130 for unsuccessful ballots (t = 2.21, p<0.05). The case study of Banklost suggests that the ability of employers to pressurize workers is greater in small bargaining units based in single workplaces, although in Woodwon employer pressure seems to have encouraged rather than weakened worker cohesion.

The CAC procedure appears to discourage larger bargaining units across multiple sites, since it is harder for unions to build sufficient membership simultaneously across a number of workplaces. However, there are exceptions to this rule. Fastwon is a large national fast-fit automotive repair service which at the time of recognition was owned by a US-based multi-national car manufacturer. Here the union achieved a substantial victory in a bargaining unit covering over 100 workplaces in the south east. This was attributed by the union to the fact that executive management was largely insulated from the strength of union support in the workplaces, leading it to underestimate union chances in the ballot. Possibly as a result of this calculation it did not actively intervene against the union once it had lost the argument over the bargaining unit.

The impact of employer tactics

The ballot survey shows that half of the employers (51 per cent) used at least two anti-union tactics[4] and that there is a significant relationship between such tactics and ballot outcomes. Employers had adopted at least two anti-union tactics in nine out of ten (86 per cent) of unsuccessful ballots, but had done so in under a third (31 per cent) of successful ballots. The mean percentage voting for recognition was 18 percentage points lower for employers using two or more tactics compared to those using either one or no tactics (40 per cent compared to 58 per cent, t = −4.60, p<0.01). In terms of individual tactics, the actual dismissal of union activists; employer one-to-ones and captive audience meetings all show a highly significant relationship with voting figures. The chilling effect of firing activists is clear:

unions won only one (Woodwon) of the eight ballots where this occurred. Direct communication between employer and workers also appears to be effective. However, threats to relocate or close do not have a significant effect on ballot outcomes. The case studies suggest this is because there is variation in how explicit and how credible workers perceive such threats to be. In eight cases (under one in five ballots) it is known that the employer used a consultant or legal advisor with a reputation in union avoidance, but there is no significant relationship between use of such a third party and ballot outcome. However, this finding should be interpreted with care: in other cases union officers suspected the employer was being advised, but had no evidence.

The combination of employer tactics used at Englost provoked a worker to write to the union:

> all these actions by the company intimidated a lot of people ... I feel I have to anonymously speak out on behalf of all the people who had previously joined the union of their own free will. Due to the intense pressure and the 'would not be in the company's and the employee's interest' statements by management a number of people reluctantly decided to vote against union recognition.

Union organizing

For Bronfenbrenner and Juravich (1998) the effectiveness of union strategies in NLRB elections depends upon the comprehensive adoption of specific organizing tactics. In particular they emphasize a rank and file approach, focusing on personal contact, leadership development and internal and external pressure tactics. The adoption of the organizing model by UK unions, symbolized by the establishment of the TUC Organizing Academy, has now led to a literature on UK organizing (Heery et al. 2000a). Classic organizing campaigns have a participative or mobilizing dimension through a representative organizing committee, comprised of workplace activists, which plans tactics, identifies organizing issues, maps the workplace and becomes involved in one-to-one recruitment. There is generally reliance on paid lead organizers to oversee campaigns and foster activism amongst the workforce. Campaigns may also be characterized by: attempts to raise the profile of the union through actions such as badge wearing and petitions; the identification of levers, allies and pressure points to discourage employer opposition; and the development of community support extending the campaign beyond the workplace.

Recognition ballots under the procedure may encourage an organizing approach as they are by definition adversarial. Since the benefits of winning may be perceived as higher for the union as compared to other types of campaigns, unions may invest significant resources into organizing. The statutory requirement on the employer to provide access to the workforce facilitates the sort of personal contact with workers highlighted in the organizing model. In two of the successful case studies, campaigns were run by organizers trained at the TUC Organizing Academy along the lines of the organizing model. In the other six cases, elements of the model were used, but not systematically, and campaigns were run by full-time officers, occasionally assisted by organizers. In the two successful cases union membership at the time of application was under 30 per cent. However, union officers were vindicated in their belief that whilst they could not recruit a majority into membership (due to high labour turnover, and in the case of Cablewon, also intimidation), they would still be able to mobilize a majority in a ballot. In both cases support for the union was demonstrated via a petition. In the case of Fastwon this was done through an intensive operation in which a team of 14 organizers and officers visited all 110 sites in the organization twice over a period of around five days, in which they aimed to meet every employee. An element of surprise meant that it was not until the end of the period that the employer realized what was happening and tried to prevent access. The union secured 80 per cent support in the ballot.

Cablewon covers production workers at one of the owner-manager's two factories in South Wales, which are part of the cable and plastics industry. Here US organizing methodology was reflected in the use of house calls during the campaign, and there were also attempts to place outside pressure on the employer. The union used the local media and also involved the local MP in a number of activities, including leafleting the workplace during the ballot, a tactic designed to neutralize employer opposition. The case studies provide no examples where unions have mobilized other local trade unionists or the wider community in support of the recognition campaign, although the ballot survey shows that it has been done, and it is possible that such solidarity would break down the isolation sometimes experienced by activists. All union officers stressed the huge commitment in terms of resources that these statutory recognition claims demanded.

Access during the ballot

The UK statutory process allows the union access to the workforce during the period of the ballot. A Code of Practice encourages the employer to allow the union one meeting of at least 30 minutes for every ten days of the access period and, where appropriate, to hold union 'surgeries', organized in working hours 'at which each worker would have the opportunity, if they wish, to meet a union representative for 15 minutes on an individual basis or in small groups of two or three' (DTI 2000: Paragraph 31). The original requirement in the government's *draft* access code for the allocation of one day for surgeries provoked strong opposition from employers during consultation and was subsequently diluted (Moore *et al.* 2000).

The CAC may order employers who are breaching their duty to allow reasonable access to take steps to do so and can award recognition without a ballot if an employer fails to abide by such an order although such a case has not yet arisen. The access period represents the only part of the recognition procedure where the employer's behaviour is subject to some regulation and union officers have emphasized its value – 'the strongest bit of pro-trade union legislation', according to the officer responsible for Fastwon. Here a highly detailed access agreement was negotiated based upon surgeries rather than mass meetings. It was agreed that two union officers would be allowed two visits to each workplace to meet all employees for the purposes of conducting surgeries of one or two employees for up to 20 minutes, in working time and on work premises. In addition one brief visit per workplace was allowed to encourage the return of ballot papers. The access agreement specified not only the location, but also the size of union notice boards and included a duty on workplace managers to display materials circulated by the union, a measure considered by the union officer to have key symbolic value.

Interviews with union officers have confirmed the value of surgeries, in many cases over and above larger workplace meetings. In the case of Woodwon, the union was largely able to dictate the access arrangements because the employer 'had no idea'. As well as a mass meeting, the union officer held face-to-face meetings with every employee for 15 minutes in working time in a private but central space in the factory. This enabled the union to have a visible presence in the workplace and instilled confidence into members. The officer felt that the surgeries were 'key' and more important than the mass meeting, allowing members to express concerns and the officer to provide reassurance.

Mediwon covers one of three factories in the manufacturing division of a large UK-owned group operating in the international healthcare market. Here the union officer believed that the 'surgeries were the most important thing', allowing workers to raise a range of issues, which they could not have done in a mass meeting. For example, the union picked up a number of cases of repetitive strain injury and was subsequently able to push for risk assessments. In this case the company had allowed surgeries in order to restrict mass meetings to one. The officer felt the employer made a tactical mistake here and he 'would have surgeries any day'.

In three of the four case studies of unsuccessful ballots there were no union surgeries. In Englost, the employer traded surgeries for longer mass meetings and the ballot survey shows that this tactic has been adopted by employers in other campaigns. Again in Autolost the employer refused the union's request for surgeries and the union decided that to resort to the CAC for mediation would further delay the procedure. In the case of Satellost a third access agreement was negotiated with the assistance of the CAC allowing the union small group meetings of 30 minutes in working time on the premises. The union reported that these were arranged so that all the activists were seen together, whilst team managers were spread throughout the meetings.

If employers have already created a climate of fear before the ballot, then access can be compromised. The officer responsible for Banklost stated that by the time of the ballot 'the damage had already been done' and the employer was able to remain neutral throughout the ballot period. In Englost, workers would telephone the officer outside working time to get basic information rather than be seen to approach the union noticeboard set up as part of the access agreement. In this case the company had agreed to pay workers for attending two mass meetings, each covering two shifts provided they were 'in normal working hours'. However, the union failed to pick up the fact that for one shift the meeting would be outside normal working hours so that 'only half the workforce turned up, the early shift had been told they wouldn't be paid for attending the meeting and were not encouraged to stay'.

The importance of activists

The development of a group of activists is seen as central to both the US and UK organizing models, with 'the involvement of activists in the development and running of campaigns through a representative "organizing committee"' an indicator of union effectiveness (Heery *et al.* 2000a: 40). In none of the case studies were the activists referred to formally as 'an organizing committee'. Organization in the cases of Woodwon and Cablewon was characterized by regular meetings open to all members in a local pub or club after work. In the cases of Fastwon and Mediwon, meetings tended to be between activists and union organizers or officers. At Banklost, in the early days of the campaign, regular meetings were held with members in a nearby pub and virtually all of them attended. As time went on it became impossible to hold meetings, as members became suspicious of each other, some alleging that certain individuals had been sent by management to listen. Similarly, in the case of Autolost, there were regular weekend meetings at a local working men's club, but union activists realized that details of the campaign were getting back to management.

The absence of union activists in the workplace makes it virtually impossible for the union to win. At Englost, the only activist left his job during the campaign and although subsequently a few members rang the local union officer, they were reluctant to put themselves forward as union representatives. The original activist felt the union would have had a better chance if he had stayed: 'I had a different perspective on things, they were easily swayed and there was no-one else who could put the arguments inside the company'. Union officers stressed the importance of securing a spread of activists throughout the workplace. In Satellost the inability of the union to attract activists on all shifts was seen by them as a key weakness.

It is not just the existence of an activist group that is important. What emerged most strongly from the case studies was that the union has to have a visible presence in the workplace. Activists are key to ensuring such a presence because they are prepared to be identified as union leaders and are able to instil confidence in other workers to declare their membership. Such commitment can be difficult to secure: in the case of Satellost the activists felt under surveillance by management:

> It was an underworld that couldn't be discussed, if someone was talking to you about the union you wouldn't know … I was very cagey because that person could quite easily stab you in the back and go to their manager … that is the culture.

Similarly in Woodwon the key activist described organizing as: 'like being in the French Resistance … We would pass round these little notes to secretly arrange meetings in dinnertime'. At Autolost, following the victimization of activists at another division within the company, the union said it didn't want martyrs and told activists not to engage in any union activity in company time or approach anyone they didn't know. At Banklost, where employees were under intense pressure, union members did not want their membership known by management. The union officer conceded he used 'questionable tactics' in writing letters for members saying that they had resigned their membership 'to get them off the hook with management'. When the company ran its own internal ballot on recognition, which had to be completed by hand, the union reluctantly advised members to vote against, so that members could not be identified: 'probably a very dodgy tactic and difficult decision'.

In contrast, at Cablewon, the activists insisted that union members should declare their membership by wearing badges and stickers in the workplace. At Woodwon, union membership was not open until a non-union member inadvertently brought into work a CD which included the Strawbs' hit song 'Part of the Union'. When it was played the main activist produced his union membership card and held it aloft which encouraged other members to do the same: 'this broke the ice, everyone saw the funny side and it got round the other site'.

When a supervisor at Mediwon confronted one of the activists on the issue of speaking to people about the union in working time she would tell her to 'mind her own business' or that she had been given time off to do it. Such confidence is infectious. This activist remembered a point in the campaign when the company had sent an anti-union letter to workers' homes. When her colleague decided to return it in person to management, the activist assumed that she would want her to go with her. In fact the colleague stated that 'she was going to do this for herself', telling them she 'had enough of this trash through her door – she didn't want it'.

Where union activists are active on employee representative bodies this can help provide the union with a presence in the workplace and give activists some protection. In Mediwon it was the Works Council representatives who became frustrated with this body, joined the union and then became the core of activists behind the recognition campaign. In contrast at Autolost, a non-elected body was used to oppose recognition and a similar forum was set up at Satellost to which management appointed employees thought to be anti-union.

Perceived costs of unionization

As the cases studies demonstrate, employers attempted to raise the costs of unionization either by threatening to close or relocate the workplace, by creating an environment in which anyone identified with the union was seen as vulnerable to dismissal or by actually dismissing union activists with lasting effects. Threats to close or relocate workplaces varied in their explicitness and credibility. Not surprisingly they can appear more credible if made by multi-national corporations. At Cablewon, the owner manager cut back on (compulsory) overtime during the campaign in an attempt to demonstrate that orders were low, but could not sustain this position. On the other hand, at Satellost, work had recently been outsourced to India and there were call-centres nearby where the company also outsourced work during busy periods. The credibility of threats to relocate was underlined by continual reference to the proprietor's history of transferring production in the newspaper industry.

Calculations of the cost of unionization were informed by workers' experience of the local labour market and the possibility of finding satisfactory alternative employment. In the case of Satellost, the flexibility of working hours increased the perceived costs of job loss: one activist reported that workers with dependants, particularly single parents, told him they just could not afford to lose their jobs. At Banklost, the employer was based in a small and highly specialist job sector where a reputation as a union activist would be potentially damaging. On the other hand in the case of Fastwon, where the business is based on the provision of a service to the customer on the premises, threats of closure or relocation were less credible. The fact that the centre managers were also union members appears important because they were prepared to stand up to threats of dismissal or discipline:

> Fastwon staff are sought after, the industry is so easy you can walk out of here and walk in somewhere else ... the company threats were hearsay and were not carried out, no-one was ever disciplined, they had nothing to fear, if they got the sack they could get a job elsewhere – it was a win–win situation.

In the three successful ballots where threats of closure were made, activists effectively countered them. Preparing the workforce for the likelihood of such threats ('inoculation' in organizing parlance) was an important part of campaigns based upon organizing principles. At Cablewon:

> a lot of people were afraid because he had always said he would shut the place down if there was a union, but he's been there for 20 years, it's his bread and butter so he's not going to ... where's he going to go?

In Mediwon, the activists responded to the company's threats of closure by stating that there were always such rumours: 'if they are going to take it abroad they'll do it anyway ... but a lot were frightened about their jobs, some pulled out and then within six months of recognition rejoined'. The union officer for Woodwon responded aggressively to rumours of closure, writing a letter to the company stating if it didn't stop making threats the union would take it to court for harassment. The union activist reported that threats 'were going round every week', but since they knew the firm was profitable they did not believe them: 'but we just humoured them, pretended to agree, and didn't react to them ... it's what your brain can take, it's just intimidation, some people let themselves be intimidated, it does get to you after a while'.

The case studies support the argument that to make a difference, activists must be seen to challenge the employer, engage in arguments for recognition with other workers (to act as what one organizer defined as 'persuaders') and stand up to intimidation. Or as Rundle expresses this, activists must 'take risks on behalf of their desire for a union' (1998: 229). When employers raised the costs of unionization in recognition ballots a number of the activists interviewed were prepared to stand up to the threat of collective job loss and to run the risk of personal job loss. Their motivations for unionization went beyond instrumentality and were also informed by ideological frameworks, albeit the 'abstract ideologies that circulate within the labour movement' (Kelly 1998: 29). As one of the key activists in Mediwon stated:

> I was probably worried about my job, but I thought if I could make a difference in there while I was there, even if I left all well and good ... when you get to my age you just don't care really.

The main activist in Woodwon said:

> I will not be intimidated, as far as I'm concerned everyone's equal, it's the way I was brought up. ... It's not about winning and losing it's about what's right, it's better to lose on your terms than win on someone else's, I wanted what was right ... at the end of the day it's a self-respect thing.

The ballot survey

The ballot survey suggests no significant association between the outcome of ballots and the degree to which the recognition campaign was run in line with the 'organizing model'. This finding, however, might reflect the fact that the measure of organizing used was not sufficiently defined in terms of the comprehensive adoption of specified organizing tactics. Neither is there any significant relationship between the use of organizers trained at the TUC Academy and ballot success. Heery *et al.* (2000a) have concluded that within UK unions, the use of the methods and principles associated with the organizing model is uneven, and in many cases, rather than invest in specialist resources, generalist full-time officers have been encouraged to adopt organizing methods. This finding is also suggested by both the case studies and the ballot survey, and it appears that the specific circumstances of CAC ballots facilitate the use of organizing methods and reliance on full-time union officers.

The survey does confirm the importance of union surgeries in recognition ballots. There is a significant relationship between union success and surgeries with the mean percentage voting for recognition 13 points higher where surgeries were held (55 per cent compared to 42 per cent, $t = 2.87$, $p<0.01$). Surgeries allow the union the sort of personal contact that has been identified as highly important in organizing campaigns. There is no relationship between ballot outcome and the use of larger workplace meetings held in the ballot period. Both union access during ballots and the holding of surgeries have been highly contested. There is a significant association between employers using two or more anti-union tactics and the presence of union surgeries: surgeries were held in 40 per cent of ballots where employers adopted at least two anti-union tactics compared to 77 per cent where they did not. The ballot survey shows that in other cases where surgeries have been agreed, employers have been able to undermine them by insisting they are held outside working hours or by locating them away from the workplace or communal areas. In the case of The Video Duplicating Company (TUR1/192[2002]) the union walked out of the surgeries and complained to the CAC when the company attempted to hold them in a room with an active security camera.

The ballot survey also shows a significant association between the number of workplace activists and the ballot outcome. Where the number of activists was above the sample media of four, the mean percentage voting for recognition was 11 points higher (54 per cent compared to 43 per cent, $t = 2.51$, $p<0.05$). There is no relationship between the ratio of activists to workers and ballot outcome, which may confirm the evidence from the case studies that union success is based upon a *small* number of activists and that it is their character and resilience that is important. In all but two of the 12 ballots where the union has won in the face of two or more anti-union tactics, unions have had an above average number of activists; in one of the exceptions organizers were used in addition to activists and the other case was one of the rare cases where the union extended the recognition campaign beyond the workplace and built solidarity amongst local workers and the community.

Conclusions

> I went into this expecting a level playing field; I never expected dirty tactics.
>
> (Activist from Satellost)

For unions, recognition ballots represent an uncertain terrain where membership and support is fragile. There is no clear relationship between union membership in a bargaining unit and the result of recognition ballots, but the adoption by employers of anti-union tactics is related to the outcome of ballots. The proliferation of voluntary agreements is testimony to union organizing and the pragmatism of employers in an altered political and legal context (see Chapter 3). Yet this chapter shows that in a minority of cases employers transform opposition to unionization into counter-mobilization. A number of the tactics used by UK employers are reminiscent of those advocated by anti-union consultants in NLRB elections and these, in particular the *actual* dismissal of activists, do influence ballot results.

At the same time the eight case studies that form the basis of this chapter confirm the importance of union tactics, in particular personal contact with the workforce, borne out in the association between the use of union surgeries in the access period and ballot success. Above all, it is essential that unions have a group of activists embedded in the workforce, who are able to create a visible presence for the union and are prepared to take risks in challenging the employer or its representatives during counter-mobilizing campaigns. This vindicates the re-emphasis in the labour movement on organizing and the importance of research on union organizing strategies as part of any model of unionization. Yet placing the explanatory burden on union activity is to ignore the wider economic, social and political context in which the recognition legislation was introduced. *Fairness at Work* indicated government ambiguity on the promotion of collective bargaining as a model for industrial relations, acknowledging that many employers and employees would continue to choose direct relationships without the involvement of third parties. The design of the statutory procedure reflects the influence of employers, specifically in the discretion the CAC has to order ballots where a union has a majority in membership. It allows for employer intervention in the process, whilst granting unions no rights of access to the workforce until the ballot period (although unions may be granted minimal access before the ballot following the review of the ERA). The case studies described in this chapter raise the issue of what constitutes legitimate employer behaviour. Despite protection for individuals against detriment and dismissal for engaging in recognition related activity, redress via an Employment Tribunal generally comes long after recognition campaigns are dead. It is clear from the evidence in this chapter that a minority of employers are prepared to pay the price of compensation to rid themselves of activists. The absence of effective legal redress has led the TUC in its response to the government's review of the ERA to argue:

> ... existing protection against detriment is not adequate and greater protection is required. This could take the form of an unfair labour practice which makes conduct of this kind unlawful and enforceable by the union, rather than the individual employee. Interim relief should be available, as it is for cases of discrimination on grounds of union membership, so that the action of the employer may be stopped immediately.
>
> (TUC 2003: Paragraph 79)

In a number of other countries legislation exists outlawing specific anti-union conduct and such legislation can be seen as 'an integral and necessary feature of any procedure designed to facilitate trade union recognition' on the basis of majority support (Ewing *et al.* 2003: 59).

The success of the statutory procedure lies in its shadow effect, the conclusion of voluntary agreements in the shadow of the law. Yet this outcome is dependent upon the perceived effectiveness of the statutory process. In the first three years of its operation most cases that went into the statutory procedure resulted in recognition. But if the law or the CAC cannot respond to the minority of employers who attempt to undermine the objectives of the legislation, its overall and long-term effectiveness may be compromised.

The government's aim of fairness at work based upon balancing the rights of employers and workers ignores the reality of workplace relations following decades of employer ascendancy and the fundamental tenet that the employment relationship is unequal. Ultimately this balance of forces means that employers can raise the costs of collective action too high for many workers. The absence of adequate legal redress apparently means that employers can dismiss union activists and are free to state quite openly during CAC ballots that they will consider moving production in the event of union recognition. The deregulation of global markets and the experience of manufacturing communities in the past 20 years mean the threat by a multinational to relocate investment has credibility. In this context the resilience of those few activists who 'take risks' in the face of counter-mobilization cannot be underestimated.

Acknowledgements

I am extremely grateful to those union officers and union activists, who generously gave their time to talk to me. I would also like to thank Helen

Bewley, Celia Dignan, Keith Ewing, Gregor Gall, John Kelly, Sonia McKay, Paul Willman and Stephen Wood for helpful comments and advice on previous versions and Simon Gouldstone for clarifications on CAC data.

Notes

1   This is a sub-sample of a survey of all CAC cases conducted by Sian Moore and Stephen Wood as part of research on recognition under the Leverhulme Future of Unions Programme. The response rate for the ballot survey was 94 per cent, although data on membership and voting figures for the missing cases can be provided from CAC reports.

2   Wood *et al.* estimate that statutory and 'semi-voluntary' (or 'semi-statutory') agreements comprised just over 10 per cent of all new recognition agreements.

3   Of CAC cases where there had been an outcome by the end of May 2003 and where information is known.

4   Defined as use of supervisors; one-to-ones; captive audience meetings; victimizations; redundancies involving union members; threats of closure/relocation.

Chapter 3

Union organizing

John Kelly and Vidu Badigannavar

Introduction

In 1998 aggregate trade union membership in Britain increased for the first time in almost twenty years. The rise of 51,000 was followed by a similar increase in 1999 – 46,000 – but heavy job losses in the following years contributed to renewed membership decline and by early 2002 total membership had fallen back below its 1997 level (Certification Office).[1] This brief and modest recovery of membership was disappointing for trade unionists themselves but it was surprising for analysts of the union movement. A conventional way of thinking about union membership trends argues they are a function of five factors: the business cycle, workforce composition and the policies of the three main actors we identified in Chapter 1, unions themselves, employers and the state (Metcalf 1991). Both unions and the environment in which they operate have changed significantly in recent years in ways which arguably should have led to a more substantial increase in membership. Unemployment is lower in 2003 than in the 1990s; unions now devote more resources to organizing than in the early–mid-1990s; employer derecognition of unions began to abate from 1992–3 onwards; and the union recognition law came into effect in June 2000 (see Chapter 1). Why then was the recovery of membership in Britain so modest in the period 1998–2002? This is a difficult and complex question which embraces a range of issues, including the limitations of the recognition law identified above, the attitudes and behaviour of employers and the commitment of unions to organizing, to name only a few (Chapter 8 this volume; Gall 2003a, 2003b; Heery *et al.* 2000a, 2000b, 2003). This chapter explores one part of the answer to that question by examining problems that arose within a number of recent union organizing campaigns. Measured by the number of additional members recruited into the union and retained for a significant period, all three campaigns were fairly unsuccessful. By explaining where these campaigns went wrong from the union standpoint we may be able to enhance our understanding of the limited membership gains of recent years.

In the first part of the chapter we draw on mobilization theory to set out a number of possible explanations for recent membership trends, focusing in particular on the dynamics of organizing campaigns. We next introduce the three main case studies that will comprise the focus of our discussion and evidence from these cases is then presented in the remaining parts of the chapter.

Mobilization theory

According to mobilization theory it is not simply dissatisfaction at work which triggers unionization, but a sense of injustice, a breach of legal or collective agreement rights or of widely shared social values (Kelly 1998). Such rights could be either procedural – the right to a fair hearing on a disciplinary charge – or substantive – the right to overtime pay for example. In a workplace where there is no union presence, such grievances must be felt by substantial numbers of workers in order to generate a shared sense of group identity. Workers who identify with one another in this way are more likely to share a sense of grievance and to feel their grievance is legitimate. They are also more likely to form a cohesive group that can withstand managerial pressure against the formation of a union. Before getting to that stage, however, workers must either attribute blame for their problems to an agency, normally the employer or the government, or must feel the employer or government can remedy them. Attributions for injustice which focus on impersonal forces such as 'the market' or 'global competition' are disabling (regardless of their validity) because they fail to provide a target for collective action. For example, Javeline (2003) found that Russian workers who believed the government was to blame for non-payment of wages were far more likely to protest than workers who believed it was the result of 'economic forces'. Finally people must have a sense of agency (or efficacy), i.e. the belief that collective organization and action can make a difference. In the US literature on union membership, perceived union instrumentality, the belief that the union will be effective, is one of the best predictors of whether a worker will vote for or against a union in a certification election (Clark 2001).

These sets of beliefs, known as 'collective action frames' (Klandermans 1997: 17), are necessary but not sufficient for workers to join unions. There must also be a collective organization that can provide the resources necessary for such action; a leadership willing and able to mobilize members for action; a balance of power favourable to such action; an opportunity structure, i.e. channels through which demands can be placed, such as bargaining structures; and minimal costs, e.g. state or employer repression, associated with collective organization and activity (Kelly 1998; Tilly 1978). The logic of social movement theory is that the fortunes of labour movements therefore depend *inter alia* on the scale of injustice at the workplace, the attitudes of employees towards management and the effectiveness of union organization and action. People's beliefs about these issues will in turn depend on the actions and rhetoric of union leaders and their opponents. They will also be influenced by the structural conditions that shape union power, in particular the state of labour and product markets (unemployment and competition respectively) and the forms of legal regulation of union activity.

Method

Mobilization theory could offer a variety of explanations for the limited recovery of union membership in Britain since 1997. For example, unions may have devoted too few resources to organizing. Or the legal provisions of the ERA may allow employers too much freedom to campaign against trade unionism (both of these factors have proved problematic in the USA, see Bronfenbrenner *et al.* 1998). In this chapter we want to focus on the characteristics of organizing campaigns themselves, rather than the number of campaigns. In particular, given our aim is to shed light on the barriers to membership recovery, we concentrate on three campaigns that were relatively unsuccessful, though in different ways.

In order to select case studies for research we first considered the distribution of non-union members in relation to union presence and we would argue it is useful to distinguish three groups: first, there are free-riders, non-members in companies covered by union recognition who benefit from collective agreements. Metcalf (2001: 26) estimates this group comprised as many as three million people in 1999. Second, there are workers in non-union firms, but in sectors of the economy where union density is moderate to high, a group which also numbers approximately three million. Car workers employed by Honda before it recognized the AEEU in December 2001 would be a good example (manufacturing union density was 27 per cent in 2001 [Brook 2002: 348]). Third, there are non-union workers in very weakly-organized sectors of the economy, such as hotels and restaurants (union density in 2001 was 5 per cent) or business services (2001 union density was 11 per cent) (Brook 2002: 348). The case studies we report in this chapter map onto these three groups of non-unionists. The first is a study of an organizing campaign amongst university research workers. These are employees on fixed-term contracts, normally of between one and three years' duration, whose principal terms and conditions are regulated by national collective bargaining between the Association of University Teachers (AUT) and the university employers' organization. However, across the university sector as a whole the union estimates that less than 10 per cent of these workers are AUT members (AUT website at www.aut.org.uk). The second case comes from a non-union call-centre in Bedford. Union density is estimated to be around 25 per cent amongst the UK's half million call-centre employees, with heavy concentrations in centres owned by banks and utilities companies (LRD 2001). Our third case study was the Amazon on-line distribution company, a US-owned non-union firm. Union density in the retail and wholesale distribution sector is low (approximately 12 per cent in 2001 [Brook 2002: 348]), although one-fifth of workplaces with twenty-five or more employees had union recognition in 1998 (Cully *et al.* 1999: 92). The research focused on manual workers employed in a major warehouse and distribution centre in Slough.

Case I: organizing research workers

The AUT campaign in a Welsh university began in spring 2002. National union membership in January 2002 was 44,051 a figure that reflected nine years of continuous growth. The union's core membership, as reflected in its name, is university academic staff. It also recruits amongst administrative, computer, library and research staff and conducts annual, national negotiations on pay increases, pay scales and some working conditions for all these grades of university staff. In the case of research workers, recommendations on bargaining issues are produced by a national committee for Fixed-Term Staff which holds its own annual meeting and reports to the national executive committee. Density levels are very low amongst research workers. One reason is that in 2001 almost all of them – 94 per cent – were on fixed-term contracts, compared to just 17 per cent of academics (AUT 2002: 7). National data suggests that density amongst temporary workers is a little over half the figure for permanent staff (19 per cent as compared with 30 per cent [Brook 2002: 347]). The AUT identified research workers as a target recruitment group on two grounds: first, they are already covered by national collective agreements and might therefore be familiar with some of the achievements of the union; and second, because of the temporary nature of their employment contracts they might be expected to have a strong sense of job insecurity that could lead them to take up union membership.

The Welsh campaign involved the local union committee, consisting mainly of academics and academic-related staff, as well as a TUC Academy-trained organizer. The union held a series of meetings beginning in April 2002 and running into the summer and distributed literature aimed at the university's 130 researchers. We conducted a total of eleven interviews, with the two key organizers and with several members of the local committee. In addition we distributed in June 2002 a questionnaire survey to all 130 researchers and obtained 46 replies, a response rate of 35.4 per cent. The questionnaire was designed around the variables specified by mobilization theory and for the most part used five point scales: employment issues of concern to employees and any current grievances; beliefs about who was responsible for these or who could remedy them; level of trust in management and perceptions of managerial fairness; beliefs about the costs and benefits of joining a union; reasons for joining or not joining the AUT; knowledge of the local campaign and of AUT achievements on behalf of research workers; and standard demographic variables – age, sex, ethnicity, tenure and pay.

At the start of the AUT campaign there were no more than five or six union members. By November 2002 the number had only increased to fifteen. On the other hand the union had created a functioning research workers' committee based around four or five key activists and was involved in negotiations with the university management. As the union already enjoyed national recognition for research workers it was not surprising to find there was no opposition to the campaign from any level of university management. Further evidence on managerial attitudes emerged during interviews. It was reported by some researchers that the university used to offer very generous maternity leave and pay for permanent staff but only the legal minimum for fixed-term staff. Recent legislation has outlawed such discrimination and when the union brought this fact to management's notice, the situation was immediately rectified and the same maternity provisions offered to all staff.

The key question here is why a reasonably well resourced campaign with a dedicated organizer yielded such a small increase in membership. The first clue to this outcome emerges in questions about issues of concern at the workplace (Table 3.1).

There was no single issue that dominated employee concerns and no issue that was of concern to a majority of respondents. Nor was there evidence of a great strength of feeling about these particular issues. Asked whether they received 'adequate information from their employer on key employment issues', 62 per cent disagreed. But when asked whether 'management decisions concerning my employment matters are fair' 83 per cent agreed they were. This impression of a relatively contented workforce was reinforced when we asked about blame for any employment problems. Recall that one of the preconditions for workers to join a union is the belief that management is either to blame for their work-related problems or has the capacity to deal with them. Respondents were asked to agree or disagree with the following statement: 'My employer is unable to provide me with better terms and conditions mainly due to external pressures'. Seventy-seven per cent of respondents agreed with this statement, a view which implies there is little the union can do. On the other hand the few who did join the union clearly felt there were many issues on which the university could take action. According to one senior researcher who had recently joined the union:

Table 3.1 Issues of concern to contract researchers (N = 46)

Issue	Percentage
Pay	44
Employment security	39
Lack of consultation	29
Lack of voice	29

Source: AUT questionnaire survey.

The University simply acts like a warehouse. They provide us with a roof over our head and electricity cables coming out of the walls ... that's where their responsibility ends. It is left entirely to the researchers to identify sources of funding, write proposals and secure grants to extend their contracts. There needs to be more support from the University to ensure adequate funding and continuity of employment. The union should take up this issue.

Respondents seemed unsure whether the union would make a difference to the workplace. Asked whether they would have more say at work if more people joined the union, 73 per cent agreed, but when asked if management would treat everyone fairly if more were in the union, opinion was more divided: 59 per cent agreed but a significant minority of 41 per cent disagreed. Perhaps as a result of the AUT's campaign, two-thirds of respondents were aware of the university working party on career management for research staff. On the other hand, almost three-quarters were unaware that the AUT had secured significant improvements in terms and conditions of research staff at other universities, including transfer of staff from fixed-term contracts to open-ended permanent contracts.

The organizing campaign itself had certain deficiencies. During interviews the union reps acknowledged they had yet to establish proper communication channels with their target members and relied on occasional emails rather than regular union meetings or newsletters. The campaign itself was campus-wide and spread across all departments. However, most of the 130 contract researchers were in physical sciences with very few in social sciences: there were 40 research staff in the Biology Department alone. A concerted effort to organize this large group of members in a single department, if successful, could have raised union density amongst research staff to over 33 per cent. Instead the union was trying to recruit across the university and consequently spreading its resources thinly.

Overall this evidence suggests that one of the key problems faced by the union is that it has not yet constructed a strong sense of grievance amongst its target membership at the university. Moreover to the extent that there are employment problems felt by staff, there appears to be little conviction that university management can do much about them and uncertainty about exactly what the union can do. This picture is borne out by responses to a direct question to respondents asking those who thought they would *not* join the union (N = 16), why this was the case. The most common answer was that membership fees were too high (60 per cent) followed by the view that 'the union does not achieve anything' (50 per cent). Forty per cent cited the temporary nature of their employment as a reason for not joining and the same percentage said 'people doing my job don't join a union'. One interviewee reported that some professional workers at the university think that unions are for manual workers not for them. The perceived lack of effectiveness was mirrored in the reasons cited by those who thought they would join (or in a few cases, were already members). Ninety-three per cent of this group thought that greater membership levels would increase the union's effectiveness whilst 90 per cent expressed a 'belief in what the union stands for'. Theoretically this degree of ideological conviction is double-edged. On the one hand it suggests a potentially high level of commitment to the union and one of the known consequences of such commitment is union participation, in various forms (Clark 2001). It may be this degree of commitment which lay behind the union's ability to create a functioning committee based around a small number of enthusiastic activists over summer 2002.

On the other hand, the argument from mobilization theory is that a viable, membership-based union organization will be almost impossible to construct on the basis of ideological conviction alone. Potential members will join only if they have a strong sense of grievance, if they feel the employer is to blame or can remedy their grievance and if they feel the union can make a difference. These critical perceptions do not as yet appear to have taken root amongst a majority of the predominantly non-union workforce and consequently the union has made very little progress in building its membership.

Case 2: organizing in a marketing agency call-centre

In this case the Graphical Paper and Media Union (GPMU) ran a successful organizing campaign and recruited a majority of the workforce, eventually securing recognition. Yet within a few months of the agreement being signed, membership had dropped significantly and the union was in a precarious position. We interviewed the two lead union reps who initiated the organizing campaign (one of whom has since left the company) as well as the current union rep and three former union reps (two of whom are still at the company). We also interviewed the union full-time officer with responsibility for the campaign.

The company was set up by two individuals in 1991 and currently employs 150 workers at its Bedford site and about 100 workers in London. One of the original owners raised funds for Bill Clinton's Democratic election campaign in the US and wanted to do the same for the Labour Party. Both owners are Labour supporters and the company was set up to raise funds for the party, which remains one of its largest clients. Throughout the 1990s it branched out into fund-raising for charities and established an image of itself as a socially responsible company, working for 'good causes'. By 2003 it was raising funds for many of the UK's leading charities, including Oxfam, the World Wildlife Fund and Greenpeace. Because of this profile, union reps believed the company attracted people sympathetic to these kinds of movements and who were therefore committed to their work. The company also provided flexible working patterns which suited many women workers, particularly young mothers and single parents, as well as students. Approximately 70 per cent of the Bedford employees were women and 90 per cent of the employees were white Caucasians. The working atmosphere was described by one rep as 'friendly and relaxed'. Measured by financial turnover, it is the twelfth largest agency of its kind and has won several business awards.

The impetus for the union organizing drive was twofold: a change in top management, with the departure in late 2000 of one of the company founders; and a decision by the remaining owner to transform the company's business strategy and focus more on the commercial sector where there was believed to be a bigger market and higher returns. To effect this shift in strategy, the owner recruited a number of managers from the commercial sector and created what one union rep described as a 'layer of bureaucracy who cared only for profits'. There were two new call-centre managers, a Human Resources manager, as well as new operations managers and supervisors. Most of these new recruits had a background in the commercial sector but lacked experience of charity fund-raising. The new management team began to transform both the way employees interacted with clients as well as the culture of the organization. First, they developed a tighter system of control over work. Staff used to have considerable freedom over how they spoke to clients and according to one union rep had developed strong social norms about how to perform their work. For example, he reported that staff often took a sympathetic view of the financial situation of pensioners and tried not to 'hard sell' them into making large donations. The new management imposed a system of control, familiar from other call-centres (Taylor and Bain 2003). There were prepared 'scripts' for each campaign which had to be read out by staff and strictly adhered to. Staff calls began to be recorded and the time spent on each call was strictly monitored. Several staff complained that requests to go off-line and visit the toilet were treated unsympathetically, managers asking 'if they really wanted to go to the toilet'.

Second, reps reported increasing pressure from managers to raise the flow of income by 'pushing each donor as hard as possible' to get more out of them. This was said to have caused resentment, especially in the cases of pensioners whom staff had previously been reluctant to pressure into giving large donations. Third, the company imposed a strict dress code on workers, and made it compulsory for all men to wear ties. Several workers, including current union reps, protested that it was sometimes too hot to wear a tie and as they were not dealing with the client face-to-face their mode of dress was immaterial. Union reps believed that labour turnover began to increase in response to these changes but the company was able to recruit quite easily from local populations of young workers, single parents and women wanting part-time work.

Although there was staff resentment at these changes and the fact that they were imposed without consultation, let alone negotiation, it would take several more instances of such behaviour to generate a sense of grievance sufficient to induce collective action. Two events proved to be critical: one was a work restructuring project and the second was a change in shift times. One component of the restructuring exercise focused on the procedure for daily work allocation. The prevailing system of allocation was that staff were assigned a quota of calls at the beginning of each shift. From time to time however staff had worked through their quota before the end of the shift and had to be assigned an additional set of calls. This second allocation was carried out during a regular, paid half-hour break, but to save on costs, the company decided to make it an *unpaid* break. Some of the more experienced workers did suggest that the management could simply allocate more calls to all workers at the beginning of the shift so that the second allocation was redundant but they were told to accept this change to their contractual terms or quit their jobs. According to one union rep, 'people were really frightened … they realized that the management could change their jobs at will or their jobs could simply disappear. They felt very helpless on their own'. However, from the standpoint of mobilization theory we can see that this fear of management is double-edged because it suggests workers attributed their problems to managerial action, an essential precondition for collective action.

The second issue involved the abolition of a whole shift (10 am to 3 pm) which was primarily staffed by women, many of whom were single parents with childcare responsibilities. Few of these workers could have switched to another shift because of their family commitments. Thus the very flexibility which had originally attracted some workers to the company was now being removed. One senior activist summed up events this way:

> The company in the process of becoming bigger, became more petty, more rule oriented, regimented … it was a process of social control and we were not controllable. So we reacted by mobilizing to form a union.

The organizing campaign

In the wake of these events, several employees, one of whom had a union background in a local authority, decided to contact a union. They first approached the TUC and were then directed to the GPMU and the General, Municipal and Boilermakers' Union (GMB). The activists chose GPMU for two reasons; the union had its headquarters in their home town of Bedford, and one of the activists knew some of the senior union officials.

The organizing campaign was led by a core group of four activists, different in many respects from their peers. They were older than the average employee in the workplace, mostly men, in a predominantly female workforce, who had previously worked in unionized settings and had either belonged to a trade union or to the Labour Party. The campaign was described by the leading union rep as a 'clandestine venture'. Many early discussions between activists and workers were 'snatched conversations' that took place in relatively private locations, such as toilets, or in the company car-park. Most of the workforce were young and had virtually no previous exposure to unions, a fact reflected in the type of questions they asked. One rep quoted a worker who said to him: 'What are unions, what do they do? My father tells me they [unions] did not allow the dead to be buried.' Organizing this group of workers was therefore an uphill task for the activists. However, there was sufficient discontent with managerial treatment of staff and with their lack of voice, that the union activists, assisted by the union full-time official, steadily increased membership. As early as November 2000 one of the lead activists wrote to the management saying that workers would like to have an independent union to represent their views.

The company response to the organizing drive was complex and comprised three elements; first, managers launched a campaign to persuade workers and activists that a union was unnecessary. The CEO wrote to the union reps reminding them of the various mechanisms developed by the company to inform and consult staff, including monthly briefing groups, a system of team leaders and a joint problem solving group – the Performance Management Working Party – set up to explore ways of improving call-centre performance. As the union continued steadily recruiting members through late 2000 and into 2001, these mechanisms do not seem to have been effective. Second, the company sought to pre-empt union and worker demands for representation by creating its own structure – a staff forum known as the 'Callers Committee'. The union response was to engage the company in serious discussion. Asked at one meeting about the best ways to improve communications inside the firm the majority of staff present suggested an independent union!

Third, in early 2001, the call-centre management, led by the Operations Manager, drew up a 'hit list' of ten union activists whom they wished to dismiss. The union activists acquired a copy of this list through a sympathetic line manager and immediately passed it to GPMU full-time officials. They in turn informed the company's CEO that they were in possession of the list and were going to pass it on to Labour Party headquarters, which, by implication, meant that the company could lose a major client. At about the same time one of the leading union activists was threatened with dismissal by the Call-Centre Manager on the grounds of gross misconduct. (This threat was issued just three hours after the activist had written to the CEO asking for a meeting to discuss union recognition.) A few days later, a second union activist was disciplined for using 'strong language' against a manager. At the appeal hearing, attended by the CEO and the Call-Centre Manager, union activists accused the company of victimizing them because of their trade union activity and demanded disciplinary action against the Operations Manager who had drafted the 'hit list'. Two days later, the Operations Manager was dismissed. Union interviewees reported that many staff were delighted at her departure as the Operations Manager was widely regarded as the 'main orchestrator of bile against the union'. Her dismissal also had a more profound and enduring effect, in demonstrating the power of the union to bring about significant change. Subsequently a number of young workers joined the union and many more were reportedly more sympathetic.

By summer 2001 the union had recruited 70 out of 120 workers at the Bedford site. Senior management had finally come to accept that they could not avoid recognition and that an anti-union image would harm their business interests. Given that the union had secured well over 50 per cent membership, some activists wanted to go through the statutory route and win legally binding recognition. Management and union agreed, however, on a voluntary ballot for a union-designated bargaining unit with the result to be binding. On a turnout of over 70 per cent, the union won a resounding 93 per cent 'Yes' vote in favour of recognition. Management then began negotiations with GPMU full-time union officials and the recognition agreement was signed in October 2001.

After recognition

The organizing campaign appeared to represent a significant victory for the union. It had secured a high level of membership amongst a young, female, mobile workforce; maintained union support in the face of employer counter-mobilization; won a recognition ballot with an overwhelming majority; and obtained a recognition agreement. Less than two years later, however, the union's membership had fallen from 70 to around 30 (June 2003) despite employment growth to 150 and it had failed to negotiate a collective agreement on any issue. How had this happened?

The overarching factor was the way in which union and management interactions eroded the effectiveness of the union. Since most workers join unions for instrumental reasons, the continuing attachment of new members will be highly sensitive to perceived union effectiveness. During an organizing campaign a union without bargaining rights will rarely have an opportunity to demonstrate its effectiveness to current and potential members. Consequently it will be union action in the immediate post-recognition period that is likely to have a critical impact on worker perceptions of union instrumentality. Yet from the time of the recognition agreement the union repeatedly failed to overcome managerial intransigence and demonstrate its effectiveness. The recognition agreement itself was fairy minimal. Described by one union activist as 'hollow', the agreement was a two-page document that merely conformed to the minimum requirements laid down in the Employment Relations Act (1999). It states the management will negotiate over basic pay, hours of work and holidays and will *discuss* procedures for discipline and grievances. Other things being equal, however, this factor alone would probably not have proved critical because narrow agreements can be built on and improved. But it became clear in the months after the agreement that the employer's post-recognition strategy was consistent with the key recommendation of US union busters: go through the motions of negotiation but agree to little or nothing (e.g. Levitt and Conrow 1993). As one union activist said, 'the management's concept of negotiation is simply saying no to everything', despite the fact that a series of major pay problems had occurred since October 2001.

The first of these was a management proposal to change the handing-in day for weekly timesheets from Thursday to Sunday. There would be a one-off loss of four days' pay for some workers which the company said would be made up when they left the firm. Union reps pressed unsuccessfully for immediate payment but management refused to make any concessions or even to meet the union for negotiations. A second issue involved a pay error. A one-off payment of between £200 and £500 was inadvertently made to a number of workers who were not entitled to receive it (as well as to those who were). When the mistake was discovered shortly afterwards the union proposed the money be paid back in instalments but management insisted on immediate repayment and deducted the sums from the next month's pay cheques. Third, when the union submitted its first ever pay claim early in 2003, the company rejected it and refused any annual rise on the grounds that 'we already pay our workers above market rates so workers should not expect a pay rise every year' (interview with union rep, 12 June 2003). What the company did offer was a new performance measurement and remuneration system, shown to the union shortly before pay talks were due to begin. The management insisted that it would not negotiate the principles of the new system, despite the fact that some higher paid workers would be worse off as a result of its implementation. The union reps were highly critical of the system, one of them alleging, on the basis of his own experience, that,

> Only those who are in the good books of management get rewarded. If you ask too many questions and create waves then you get nothing.
> (Interview with union rep, 6 June 2003)

This continuous refusal on the part of management to engage in meaningful negotiation resulted in acute frustration amongst union reps and employees. Although it probably reinforced the sense of grievance and antagonism to management which had fuelled the organizing campaign, it simultaneously undermined employee perceptions of union effectiveness. One result, already noted, is that union membership dropped from about 70 out of 120 at the time of recognition to its current (June 2003) level of around 30 out of 150. Membership loss comprised three elements: union members who quit the firm; resignations among existing union members still in the firm, particularly over the union's failure to deal with the 'loss of four days' pay' issue; and a failure to recruit new employees. According to union reps, new employees were reluctant to join because they didn't see what the union was doing for them and therefore saw no benefit in membership.

The impact of managerial intransigence was compounded by problems amongst the union's own leadership. The small cadre of activists which had built the union was depleted by the loss of three of its members: two resigned from the firm to take up jobs elsewhere and a third resigned her union post early in 2003, frustrated with the intransigence of the employer. In addition the union's full-time official who had been highly supportive throughout the campaign left the GPMU for another union. Those leaders who remained in the firm were unable to develop an effective strategy to overcome the reluctance of the employer to negotiate in good faith.

The final twist to this story is that union reps believe management is now thinking of the ultimate solution to union presence: closing the Bedford site and transferring work to its non-union London site. The lease on the Bedford site expires in December 2003, but despite the fact that management is in talks with the leaseholder, the company has recently created a hundred more 'caller seats' at its London office (interview with union rep, 7 August 2003). Should this move come about it will expose a further weakness in the union campaign, namely its concentration on just one site of a multi-site company

Given the management of this company wished to remain union-free, it could have pursued a more aggressive approach, taking the issue to the CAC perhaps or hiring anti-union consultants. Instead it adopted a much more sophisticated strategy. It voluntarily recognized the union on the basis of a minimal agreement, conceded virtually nothing in negotiations and thereby gradually eroded perceived union effectiveness, thus contributing to membership decline.

Case 3: organizing Amazon warehouse workers

Amazon was launched in 1995 in the US and is now one of the world's largest e-retailers with subsidiaries in a number of countries, including Britain, France and Germany. Five years after launch it recorded world sales of US $2.6 billion but it wasn't until 2001 that the company went into profit (Gibson 2003; Spector 2000). The British subsidiary turned a £2 million loss in 1999 into a £378,000 profit in 2000 (Amazon UK 2002). Amazon employs over 4,000 people in the US and a total of approximately 1,000 in Britain, France and Germany. The company management, both in the US and in Britain, is strongly anti-union as American and British unions began to discover when they launched organizing drives early in 2000 (Greenhouse 2000a, 2000b; Milne 2000). According to the UK managing director, 'we don't currently believe that having our employees represented by a union would best allow us to achieve [our] goals' (Milne 2000). The Amazon campaign was launched by the GPMU in May 2000 and was eventually wound up early in 2002 without a recognition agreement. Data for this case study was collected from interviews with three key individuals: the union's Head of Organizing, the Amazon organizer and the leading lay activist within Amazon itself. In addition we secured access to correspondence between the union and the company and attended a union training session for organizers.

According to the GPMU organizer assigned to the campaign, Amazon was targeted by the union for several reasons. It is a large employer and therefore a successful organizing campaign could yield a substantial number of new members. Its warehouse in Slough employed 250 core workers and as many as 700 seasonal workers during peak times such as Christmas holidays. In May 2000 when the organizing drive began there were approximately 150 casual workers making a total labour force of around 400. In addition, Amazon is a well known and high profile non-union firm and the GPMU General Secretary was keen to secure recognition in companies such as this and raise the union's profile still further within the distribution industry. Finally, and despite its return to profitability after a huge loss in 1999, the company paid its warehouse staff a basic hourly wage of £5 in late 2000, on a par with checkout operators in retail stores.

The GPMU leadership has always firmly supported the TUC Organizing Academy. In the three years 1998–2000 seventeen of the Academy's 104 trainees were sponsored by the GPMU, a figure exceeded by only two other unions (Iron and Steel Trades Confederation [ISTC] and Union of Shop, Distributive and Allied Workers [USDAW]) (Heery et al. 2000b: 402). However, its approach to Amazon did not begin with an organizing drive but with a letter to the management and a request for a meeting. The calculation here was that in the light of the ERA (1999) recognition provisions some employers have been willing to meet the union and amicably discuss arrangements for a ballot. In the case of Amazon this belief turned out to be a serious miscalculation. The employer did agree to a meeting and talked to the GPMU representatives but no decisions or actions emerged. A further approach by the union in summer 2000 led to a management rejection of any further contact on the grounds that it was now involved in discussions with two other unions, the Transport and General Workers Union (TGWU) and the GMB. A few phonecalls by the GPMU organizer quickly established that this claim was simply untrue. Consequently in August 2000 the union began 'cold leafleting' the warehouse. At this stage in the campaign the union had no internal contacts and had not been approached by any Amazon employees about grievances over working conditions. The organizers were therefore pleasantly surprised when their literature elicited a positive response, especially from the lower grade, lower paid ethnic minority workers. Within a few weeks, a nucleus of four vocal activists had emerged and was starting to recruit inside the warehouse.

The internal organizers framed the key issue in terms of racial discrimination within the promotion system, pointing out that ethnic minority workers were disproportionately concentrated in lower grades within the company. By December 2000 the union had managed to recruit approximately 120 workers out of a total non-managerial labour force of around 400. On the face of it this suggests the internal activists had constructed a highly appropriate 'collective action frame', capable of mobilizing substantial numbers of workers. But in terms of workforce composition, the racial discrimination frame had a serious downside: almost all of the union's membership came from the ethnic minority half of the Amazon labour force but very few from the white half of the workforce. For this reason the leading external organizer tried to frame the key grievance in union leaflets in terms of 'favouritism' rather than 'race discrimination' so as to 'avoid putting off the white workers from joining the union' (interview, 25 February 2002). At this point it seemed that the management had inadvertently supplied the union with an additional issue. Over the busy Christmas period workers put in a substantial amount of overtime but as late as March 2001 many were still owed overtime payments. The reasons for the delay in payment are not clear but delay itself became another issue in the organizing drive as the union sought to consolidate and increase its membership in readiness for a secret ballot.

The company meanwhile had begun its own counter-mobilization against the union, deploying a wide range of tactics in what ultimately proved to be a sophisticated and successful strategy. Shortly after the organizing drive began it relocated its warehouse forty miles away to Milton Keynes. Whilst this was a move that had been planned many months previously the management may have hoped that some or all of the key internal organizers would quit their jobs rather than follow the company to its new location: they didn't. The next response by the employer was to try and curtail the leafleting of workers as they entered and left the warehouse. At one point the union organizer was even told by a warehouse manager that he should stop leafleting around the company car park as 'he could be run over by speeding cars' (interview with GPMU organizer, 25 February 2002). Its second response was to transfer into Milton Keynes an experienced HR manager from Glasgow. Starting late in 2000 the new manager soon began to implement a classic US-style anti-union campaign, based around five key elements: leadership style, supervisory activity, rewards, coercion and new forms of employee representation (see Levitt and Conrow 1993).

First, he spent far more time than his predecessor in the warehouse itself, meeting workers one-on-one and expressing interest in their views and concerns. According to the leading internal union organizer, this new managerial style impressed some union members who took it as a sign that working conditions might improve (interview, 24 July 2002). Second, the new manager appointed, and organized training for, a new tier of supervisors (known as Leads) whose prime function was to continue the one-on-one discussions with workers about the costs of joining a union. Evidence from

US organizing drives shows that supervisory discussions with workers are a potent force in reducing the size of the pro-union vote (Bronfenbrenner and Juravich 1998). Third, one of the themes reiterated throughout this period was that 'unions have no right to come and ask for higher pay for you, only you can come and ask us and we will give you more money' (interview, 24 July 2002). During spring 2001 the new management awarded no less than three pay rises including payment of the long-overdue Christmas 2000 overtime premia. One of the union organizers subsequently argued that the union had perhaps not done enough to influence worker beliefs about the causes of the pay rises and attribute them to union pressure rather than managerial benevolence. Fourth, rewards to workers for staying non-union were complemented with threats made against those who showed strong pro-union sympathies. This coercive side of the employer campaign came to a head in May 2001 when the leading internal union organizer was suspended for allegedly refusing to carry out a work assignment, despite the fact that he was on light duties because of a certified medical problem. In the argument that ensued about a particular work assignment he was asked to leave the premises but refused to do so until threatened with police eviction. The company's internal disciplinary panel dismissed him on 2 July 2001. Ironically the internal appeal panel, which met on 25 July 2001, agreed he should not have been asked to perform the duties requested of him but upheld his dismissal because he 'refused several reasonable requests ... to leave the premises' (Amazon to 'Internal Organizer' [name withheld], 3 August 2001).

Fifth, the management decided to create a rival body to the union, a staff consultative forum, a familiar anti-union technique and one used by call-centre management in the previous case (see also Bronfenbrenner and Juravich 1998; Fantasia 1988: 126–8). Workers were invited to put forward nominations and the election date was fixed for 12 and 13 September 2001. The union responded to the ballot announcement by asking management to postpone it until talks on recognition had been completed. When management refused, the union was faced with a strategic dilemma. Should it try to undermine the legitimacy of the ballot by refusing to participate and urging workers not to vote, but continue the campaign for full recognition and bargaining rights? Or should it nominate its own candidates and seek to win a majority on the consultative forum, an outcome that would create a dilemma for management? The union leadership responded to this strategic dilemma with a strategic error: it tried to pursue both options. Initially it was sufficiently confident of membership support that it argued for a boycott, and conducted this campaign with some style. In the pre-election period workers were invited to deposit their ballot papers in toilet bowls that had been placed outside the warehouse by the union organizers. This was a piece of symbolism designed to illustrate the union's contempt for the balloting process and the ballot papers. The act of destroying ballot papers in public should have created a high degree of cohesion amongst the workers, strengthening their antagonism to the employer and building their commitment to the union. However, it soon became clear that relatively few workers were participating in the boycott and by implication therefore a substantial proportion would participate in the ballot. Very late in the day the union proposed its own slate of candidates and although a few were elected, their numbers fell well short of a majority. The union therefore ended up with the worst of all worlds: it had failed to carry through either a successful boycott or a successful election campaign.

By autumn 2001 the union and its campaign were in serious trouble: it had been defeated in the consultative forum ballot; membership had dropped back to around 25, from its peak of 120; high labour turnover was constantly eroding the union's base; one of the leading internal activists had been dismissed and the union's lawyers advised that an application for unfair dismissal to an Employment Tribunal was unlikely to succeed (interview, 12 December 2001). Towards the end of the year the union formally abandoned the Amazon campaign and diverted its resources elsewhere.

The Amazon campaign illustrated three of the key factors identified by mobilization theory as critical to organizing success. First, the central issues in the campaign need to be framed in ways that can maximize worker support, weaken internal opposition and place management on the defensive. Since the union recruited overwhelmingly from the ethnic minority rather than the white half of the workforce, we may infer that issues were not framed in a way that could transcend racial divisions amongst the workers. Second, one of the employer responses to union organizing drives, familiar from the US, is to offer rewards in the course of the organizing campaign and argue that unionism is therefore unnecessary. Such actions raise an interesting attribution problem: do employees attribute such pay rises to the employer or to the union? As we noted earlier, one of the organizers suggested the union could have been more effective in persuading workers that pay rises ultimately stemmed from union presence and activity not the employer. Third, the responsibility for framing issues, initiating tactics and responding to employer counter-mobilization normally rests with a small group of union leaders both inside and outside the workplace. In the Amazon case, it is clear that the union leadership made a number of errors in its conduct of the campaign. One of the organizers subsequently admitted that the initial approach to the employer was premature on two counts. First, the union had not yet built up a significant membership and, by implication, was not ready to confront the employer if that proved necessary (as it did). Second, the union's approach effectively served 'advance notice' on the employer and gave management plenty of time to prepare what turned out to be a sophisticated anti-union campaign. Also, the leadership was forced to do a *volte face* on its boycott of the company ballot when it became clear there was insufficient worker support. For all these reasons then the Amazon campaign ultimately ended in failure.

Conclusions

We began this chapter by noting that union membership had not risen as much since 1997 as some commentators had hoped or expected and set out a number of possible explanations for this fact. In part this outcome is a reflection of the resources devoted by unions to organizing but that is far from being the whole story. By drawing on mobilization theory the three case studies in this chapter were able to throw light on four issues that can arise in organizing campaigns. These are: changing worker attitudes, maintaining pro-union beliefs in the face of employer counter-mobilization, promoting union effectiveness in the face of employer reluctance to bargain in good faith and the regulation of employer behaviour.

The AUT organizing campaign amongst research workers was a good example of 'infill recruitment', where there is already a union presence and workers are covered by a national collective agreement. Some commentators have suggested that recruitment amongst these groups of workers is a more sensible use of union resources and one that is likely to yield better results as compared to 'greenfield recruitment' (Metcalf 2001). The AUT campaign suggested, however, that workers in these types of settings may be difficult to organize for reasons identified by mobilization theorists. They may not have a strong and widely-shared sense of grievance; even those with a sense of grievance may not believe that any problems they experience can be remedied by the employer; and they may not believe the union is capable of making enough impact to justify payment of an annual membership fee.

The call-centre case reinforced the salience of these variables: workers with a shared sense of grievance, who were antagonistic to management and believed the union could make a difference voted overwhelmingly for the union, as mobilization theory would predict. What the call-centre and Amazon cases also demonstrated however was the fragility of worker beliefs. In the former case the employer's reluctance to negotiate in good faith starved the union of any evidence for its effectiveness and thus began to erode worker beliefs in the power of the union. In the Amazon case, employer concessions on pay and other issues were not, in general, attributed to union pressure thereby increasing union membership still further. Rather they appeared to have the opposite effect as workers began to drift away from the union. Both cases therefore underline the enormous effort involved in both changing worker attitudes and sustaining attitude change in the face of employer actions.

The call-centre case also shows that creating collective organization, winning a ballot and securing a written agreement from the employer are not sufficient to ensure a viable union presence. The employer who negotiates in bad faith presents the union with an acute dilemma. Acting as if the collective bargaining machinery represents a real 'opportunity structure' – the union strategy in the call-centre – is unlikely to shift the employer's position. What other options does a union have in such circumstances? It could have offered a partnership arrangement under which the union would supply benefits to the employer (see Chapter 7). This might have elicited a positive response or it might simply have signalled union weakness to the employer and reinforced the hostility it was supposed to erode. Alternatively the union could have imposed costs on the employer through some form of collective action until meaningful negotiations took place. This approach would have required the local union leadership to mobilize its membership around an appropriate issue and confront the employer. Used in conjunction with external pressure through the Labour Party collective action might have, and might still, produce a revival of the union. In either case the union would have required organization across both company sites.

Finally, both the call-centre and the Amazon cases underline the significance of employer anti-union campaigning. Under the recognition provisions of the ERA (1999) the employer is free to set up a rival, employee representative body and to offer financial inducements to workers to remain non-union. Both measures were used by Amazon management and, as in the US, both proved highly effective in disorganizing the union campaign. If the recognition law is to assist the spread of union representation then, contrary to the Labour government's view (DTI 2003a), there will need to be much tighter regulation of employer behaviour.

Note

1   Figures from the Labour Force Survey, based on responses from individuals rather than unions, do not show quite the same picture. Both LFS and Certification Office data agree that membership began to rise in 1998 but was falling by 2001. On the other hand, LFS data found that aggregate membership in autumn 2000 was still 197,000 higher than the autumn 1997 level whilst the Certification Office reported the December 2000 figure to be 22,000 *less* than December 1997.

Chapter 4

Equity and representation in the new economy

Diane Perrons

Introduction

In recent years there have been contradictory tendencies towards re-regulation and deregulation in the labour market. The former is associated with the adoption of national and supra-national employment legislation, guidelines and programmes for enhanced social rights, gender equality and work–life balance. The latter, however, is associated with the development of more deregulated and individualized workplaces in the new economy, which makes their implementation more difficult.

Some accounts of the new economy stress new information and communications technologies (ICT), knowledge work and the scope for productivity increases (Castells 2001; Coyle and Quah 2002) while social theorists, such as Ulrich Beck (2000) and Richard Sennett (1998), emphasize deteriorating working conditions, increasing insecurity, and individualization associated with the demise of traditional systems of social support including trade unions and state welfare policies. This chapter briefly outlines a theorization of the new economy, which links these contrasting interpretations, foregrounds social divisions and explains why these social divisions are likely to take a gendered form. This framework then provides the context for an empirical investigation of working conditions in new media, refuse collection and care work in one local labour market, Brighton and Hove on the south coast of England. These sectors have been chosen because they reflect contrasting dimensions of the new economy. New media is an archetypal illustration of the popular understanding of the new economy, defined in terms of ICT technologies. Refuse collection and care work, although more usually associated with the old economy, are nevertheless characterized by new working patterns consistent with gloomier interpretations of the new economy. Both have been affected by fragmentation, casualization and the increasing use of agency workers, as a consequence of deregulation, privatization and market testing. Moreover, these three sectors are organically connected, as the long hours worked by knowledge workers leave little time for social reproduction, making them increasingly dependent on publicly

provided or marketized personal and collectivized services. Given this inter-
pretation of the new economy, it is not 'ironic' to find that some of the
fastest growing occupations in the 1990s were in the caring services such as
nursery nurses, hairdressers and housekeepers as well as in sectors linked to
the knowledge economy such as computer system managers, software
engineers and computer programmers.[1] Finally, I consider how employees
perceive the role of trade unions and how trade unionists have responded to
and perhaps could do more to respond to these changing circumstances,
possibly through new forms of organization at the local level.

The new economy, social and gender divisions

The conceptualization of the new economy developed here goes beyond
optimistic interpretations resting on new information and communication
technologies, the dot.com boom, and highly skilled knowledge workers
moving seamlessly from job to job to expand their portfolios. It also goes
beyond the rather universalistic and pessimistic accounts which refer to
deteriorating working conditions, the 'corrosion of character' (Sennett 1998)
or increasing risk and insecurity in the 'brave new world of work' (Beck
2000). The former characterization has been undermined by the economic
downturn and by falling stock market values, especially of dot.com companies,
while the ideas of the portfolio worker and increasing job insecurity, lack
empirical substantiation. Doogan (2001), for example, has demonstrated
that there has been an increase in long-term employment in both the UK and
in continental Europe. Green (2003) has shown that overall job security has
not fallen either in the UK or the USA in the decade leading up to 2001,
though there has been a striking expansion of fixed-term contracts in the
public sector, and temporary employment in the private sector (Nolan and
Slater 2002). In this chapter I consider the new economy to be something of
a new era whose effects are pervasive but also differentiated, which makes
measurement through aggregate statistics difficult (see also Castells 2001;
Coyle and Quah 2002; Quah 2003). This perspective is elaborated elsewhere
(Perrons 2003a) but is briefly summarized below as it provides the framework
for the empirical investigation.

For Quah (1996, 2003) the hallmark of the new economy is the increasing
significance of knowledge, weightless or dematerialized goods, collectively
termed 'bitstrings' whose economic properties should theoretically tend
towards equality but in practice tend towards widening income inequalities
and social divisions. Knowledge goods are infinitely expansible, that is they
can be replicated at very low cost, and they are non-rival; thus one person's
consumption does not prevent another's. These properties should tend to
generate greater equality. However, knowledge goods are also characterized
by increasing economies of scale, thus large firms tend to dominate the market
and having done so they create a range of related products locking consumers

into their particular brand: Microsoft would be a good example. A further property is the superstar effect, which refers to consumers' preferences for products of greater renown even though they may be barely distinguishable from competitors. Given their weightless nature there are few constraints on market size so these producers capture an increasing share of the market.[2] As knowledge goods become more important in the economy therefore, social and spatial inequalities correspondingly increase. Quah (1996) suggests that people accept widening inequalities because of higher levels of social mobility in the new economy, which raise individual expectations of becoming rich. In practice, work is typically coded by ethnicity, sexual orientation, class and gender, the last two forming the main foci of this chapter. Thus rather than being random, the predicted widening social divisions are likely to reinforce existing structural inequalities in the labour force.

Work in which the working class, women and ethnic minorities are typically over-represented, especially care work or work in personal or collective services, has very different, almost completely opposite, economic properties from knowledge goods. In general these services are not infinitely expansible or non-rival but are inherently technologically unprogressive, productivity increases are difficult to achieve and wages tend to be low (Baumol 1967). For example, although a professional childcare worker can care for more than one child simultaneously there is a fixed and relatively small limit to the number of children each carer can supervise, thereby constraining productivity, income and earnings (Folbre and Nelson 2000). Similarly, despite developments in transport technology and refuse bins, each bin or bag has to be wheeled or carried from the doorstep to the refuse lorry, which constrains productivity. Costs can only be reduced by increasing the intensity of work, for which finite natural limits remain, or else by lowering wages, which, in the case study below, is achieved by employing agency workers, paid at two-thirds the hourly rate of regular employees. The arguments in this section have been abstract and largely reflect market logic, but all markets operate within social and political frameworks and institutions and correspondingly are open to modification by prevailing cultural norms, political and social pressures, including state legislation and action by trade unions, and therefore need to be explored empirically.

The new economy, the state and locality: re-regulation and deregulation

A succession of measures has been introduced to regulate the labour market, enhance equality, promote work–life balance and protect the rights of trade unionists in the UK, partly to comply with the EU employment guidelines and regulations. These rights are, however, to exist within 'a flexible and efficient labour market' (DTI 1998), characteristics which are assumed to be enhanced by deregulation and privatization which in turn make worker organization more difficult, though as the case study will show, not impossible.

The minimum wage came into effect for the first time in 1999 and EU Directives were enacted into UK legislation on Working Time (1998), Parental Leave (1999) and Part-time Work (2000). Further legislation to enhance equality including the amendment of the Race Relations Act (2000) and the Employment Equality (Sexual Orientation) Regulations to combat homophobic discrimination came into force in 2003 to comply with the EU Employment and Race Directives. Trade union rights have also been improved under the statutory recognition procedure in the Employment Relations Act (1999), which gives a right of recognition in firms of more than 20 employees. Legislation to enhance flexible working and promote work–life balance has also been introduced under the Employment Act (2002), such that from April 2003 'parents of children aged under six or disabled children aged under 18 have the right to apply to work flexibly and their employers will have a duty to consider these requests seriously' (DTI 2003b).

Some of the EU Directives have been implemented rather reluctantly and in minimal form. For example the government tried (but failed) to restrict the Parental Leave Directive to children born after the legislation became effective, rather than to all children under eight years old. Moreover, the UK is the only country to allow individuals to opt out of the Working Time Directive resulting in the longest average working hours in the EU (TUC 2002b). Similarly, the UK, along with the Danish, Irish and German governments, has opposed the EU Temporary Agency Worker Directive which would have given agency workers the same rights as their permanent colleagues in relation to pay, holidays, and all forms of family related leave.

Likewise, the DTI promotes flexible working through a variety of initiatives, including a Work–Life Balance Campaign launched in 2000, and argues that such practices contribute to business efficiency by simultaneously increasing productivity, staff commitment and retention as well as equal opportunities, while reducing absenteeism (DTI 2003c, 2003d). However, the reality is rather different. In practice the flexibility agenda seems to have more to do with extending the temporal and spatial boundaries of paid work and lengthening working hours rather than allowing people to establish a harmonious balance between paid work and other aspects of their lives, including caring. The IER (2001) survey found that people were allowed to work long hours, especially by working at weekends and during unsocial hours, but only a tiny minority of employers allowed other forms of flexibility, leave arrangements or assistance with childcare.

There has also been a series of measures to enhance equal opportunities for women including amendments to the 1975 Equal Pay Act and proposals to assist parents in work. The National Childcare Strategy (NCS) was introduced in 1998, with further funding and a new Inter-Departmental Childcare Unit to ensure consistent policy in 2002 (Strategy Unit 2002). While there has been a significant expansion in childcare provision, coverage is far from comprehensive (Skinner 2003). One reason for this is that the government's strategy is driven by a number of conflicting motivations. It has been designed to increase the employment rate of women in order to raise competitiveness and productivity but also to tackle child poverty, by raising the employment rate of lone parents. This explains why the government's efforts are concentrated in areas of deprivation, through the Sure Start scheme, with parents in general being left to cope with a range of rather expensive and uncoordinated facilities, largely in the private and voluntary sectors (Skinner 2003).[3] Despite this expansion, little consideration has been given to the terms and conditions of employment for the predominantly female childcare workers, which, with the exception of formally qualified teachers, are well below average: the minimum wage is the only safeguard.

The commitment to childcare provision and legislation, and the development of interactive websites, which provide information and guidance for employers and employees, are significant improvements on previous practice. However, there are contradictory tendencies, including the continuation of privatization and sub-contracting of public sector activities and the Private Finance Initiative (PFI), which aims to increase the role of the private sector in financing public services. The effect of these measures is that workforces formerly linked to local authorities have been fragmented. Some are employed indirectly from employment agencies – a growing trend in the private sector too – and this development has resulted in a multi-tier workforce. In these circumstances workers are effectively individualized; it is difficult for them to organize and for trade unions to organize them and give effect to employment legislation. There are, for example, more than 60 employment agencies in Brighton and Hove and they include multi-national firms, some of whom are dedicated to supplying staff to particular sectors and even specific employers, as well as more general recruitment agencies. Agency workers are regularly employed in the three sectors studied, alongside regular employees.

The case study below illustrates some of the contradictions between the potentially progressive employment legislation and new employment forms associated with deregulation and the emergence of new sectors. The refuse collectors and care workers have experienced various forms of privatization in recent years, while the new media sector is characterized by new small firms and younger workers with little or no experience of trade unions.

A local case study: Brighton and Hove

The local context

Brighton and Hove reflects many aspects of the divided nature of the new economy.[4] The combined effects of the seaside location, cultural image and proximity to London, makes Brighton and Hove a very attractive place to live. Indeed so many celebrities have recently moved to the city that the council has organized house-spotting tours.[5] This creates problems for local people as house prices have risen faster than incomes in recent years and the extent of local authority housing provision is relatively low (see Table 4.1). In 2001, the average price of a one bedroomed flat was four times average gross household income (excluding households with no earned income) and five times average earnings.[6] Thus those on low and even median earnings struggle to pay for housing and cannot generally afford to live in the city unless they have housing association or local authority accommodation. These circumstances have led to union demands for a 'Brighton weighting', similar to London weighting.

The findings below are based on a purposive and largely administered structured survey of 100 employees in new media, care work and refuse collection carried out in 2002, together with 25 follow-up in-depth interviews. Some general characteristics of the survey sample are presented in Table 4.2.[7] The research focused on the terms and conditions of employment, but emphasis was also given to gender divisions, employees' perceptions of trade unions and employee views about what trade unions might do to better reflect their interests.

New media and IT

Brighton and Hove markets itself as one of the fastest growing new media clusters in the EU. Estimates vary, but there are thought to be around 300 small-scale new media firms in the city, employing roughly 3,000 people.[8] This sector is sometimes thought to be gender-neutral but there is marked gender imbalance in the composition of the labour force and in the levels of pay in Brighton and Hove, in conformity with national trends (see Tables 4.2 and 4.3).

The smaller new media companies did not have formal equality policies and as with some of the other companies in Brighton and Hove, interviewees felt that formal policies were not really necessary as 'discrimination was not an issue'. Thus interviewees frequently remarked: 'well this is Brighton', 'we are very laid back', 'there are all sorts here' (ID 502). Nevertheless others referred to the desirability of such policies. Indeed even though working atmospheres can be 'laid back' and apparently egalitarian, gendered patterns of vertical and horizontal segregation are clearly evident suggesting that informality may not be the best way of addressing inequalities (see Gill 2002). Gender segregation cannot be explained by working hours as in contrast to the entrepreneurs and managers, employees usually worked around 37 hours per week, Monday to Friday (Perrons 2003b). Nonetheless employees were expected to respond to the uneven flow of work, characteristic of the sector, whenever necessary. One company, for example, required workers to voluntarily opt out of the EU's Working Time Directive, but rewarded employees for working excessive hours with bonuses such as 'stress busters' at a local

Table 4.1 Housing composition in Brighton and Hove

	National stock (%)	Brighton and Hove stock (%)	Brighton and Hove price per week (£)
Owner occupation	69	65	200[a]
Private rented	10	20	145[a]
Housing association	6	4	69.04
Local authority	15	11	47.75

Sources: Data taken from BHC (2002) and an unpublished report to the Economic Strategy Group.

Note
a Estimated mortgage repayments/rent on an averaged price one bedroomed flat (89K).

Table 4.2 Gender, care and unionization

	% female	% without caring responsibilities	% unionized
New media (n = 46)	32.6	84.8	2.2
Childcare (n = 28)	96.4	67.9	37.0
Refuse collection (n = 27)	37.0[a] and 5[b]	59.3	93.6

Note
a This figure includes the call-centre workers and administration staff; b This figure includes those directly involved in refuse collection and street cleaning.

Table 4.3 Pay and age characteristics

	New media	Childcare	Refuse
Age – modal	25–34	18–24	35–44
Pay £ gross annual earnings			
Mean	26,600	15,299	15,557
Mode	16–22,000	11–13,000	13–16,000
Median	19,420	14,820	14,820
Range	4–56,000	4–35,000	7–35,000

Note
In new media the average female age was 30 and earnings £25,000, the corresponding figures for men were 32 and £27,500. Given the gender imbalance for childcare and refuse collection, the statistics are not gender differentiated.

luxury hotel or bottles of champagne. Such measures reflect a more general pattern of paternalism within the sector, where employees are rewarded with 'treats' or gifts rather than higher overall pay.

Again in contrast to the early media images of dot.com workers, the Brighton and Hove new media workers were not among the elite. They earned only two-thirds as much as those in the highest decile nationally, but were comparatively well paid by local standards, earning 1.5 times local average earnings. The average media worker's pay was significantly higher than the median, indicating that there is a minority of high earners, and the range of earnings was wider in this sector than the others examined. Indeed, companies state that one of the attractions of Brighton and Hove is the relatively low pay in the city, and many employees argued that they could earn more in London but chose Brighton and Hove because of the attractive and alternative lifestyle. The women in the survey earned on average £2,500 per annum less than men.

In common with national trends the sector is characterized by volatility, and freelancers, together with employees and small firms, bear the costs of the economic fluctuations. The employer of a rapidly expanding firm that had survived the dot.com burst and the post-11 September recession commented:

> Unless I can see a year's work in advance, I prefer to call in freelancers or use fixed term contracts, even on projects that involve large teams and large budgets. Big headcounts that cannot be sustained lead to redundancy. We want to treat people as well as we can.
>
> (New media entrepreneur)

Somewhat surprisingly therefore the vast majority of media workers – 69 per cent – were confident that they would be able to stay with their firm if they wanted to in the following year, even though 44 per cent of them had been with their present firms for less than a year (see Table 4.4). One of the larger companies, Digitalreel,[9] which experienced dramatic expansion immediately prior to the survey, subsequently let go half of its staff, but within two days was advertising for freelancers.[10] When demand is high, freelancing enables people to build their career profiles but at other times work in this sector is highly precarious. Compared with employees in other sectors, however, media workers were significantly less satisfied with both the nature of their work and with their work–life balance, possibly because of less predictable working hours and lower job security (see Table 4.4).

Table 4.4 Work satisfaction, job security and work–life balance

% Satisfied or very satisfied	Nature of work	Sense of achievement from work	Job security	Work–life balance
New media (n = 46)	34	61	69	49
Childcare (n = 28)	86	100	86	79
Refuse collection (n = 27)	77	82	96	70

Note
Job security is measured by the percentage who perceived that they could stay with their firm for more than a year.

Despite the precarious conditions, almost universally they saw little role for trade unions. Freelancers, for example, tended to accept market fluctuations as a characteristic of the sector and considered themselves personally responsible for maintaining their marketability by constantly updating their skills. There was a more or less incredulous response to my questions about trade unions such as, 'They were something we learned about at school' (ID 5) or

> You mean *trade* unions? – No, I can honestly say that those two words have never been mentioned all the time I have been here. I suppose trade unions are there to represent the workforce independently of the company but it makes me think about miners and things.
>
> (ID 12)

Following the downturn after 11 September, when another large company, Classic, made a significant proportion of staff redundant, both the redundant and retained employees sought union advice:

> Employees contacted us and the issue was redundancies. But more importantly, the way the redundancies were handled. And it's quite a close knit workforce; they socialize a lot together and basically they were called in one afternoon – called into a room, were given an envelope that said 'Please don't open this, open it when you get home. By the way we have turned your computer off and you're all sacked.' ... And obviously people were coming out crying, in tears understandably. And on the back of this they asked if they could have a meeting.
>
> (ID 907 regional trade union organizer)

Employees in this sector would on average have started their working lives in the late 1980s or 1990s and unless they have worked in the public sector would be unlikely to have had any direct experience of unions[11] so their perceptions were shaped by largely negative and inappropriate images of manual industrial workers in conflict as portrayed in the media (see ID 12 above; see also Diamond and Freeman 2003). Indeed a frequent response to the question about unions was 'you mean the winter of discontent and all that' even though many of the interviewees would have been young children at the time. Images of unions were more positive among employers whose parents were union members, and while they stated that they had 'nothing against unions' they were very unsure about their role in this specific sector. In small firms the lines of communication between employees and managers (often the directors) were direct so employees saw no need for more formal procedures. In larger companies, there was concern that existing unions, such as the print union (GPMU) or the National Union of Journalists, would not be specific enough to represent their interests. Indeed this may be a negative aspect of the trend toward concentration among unions given the emergence of new sectors in the new economy.

In the case of the Classic employees (above), almost all of them decided to join the GPMU, but to conduct negotiations themselves.[12] Specifically they decided to form a partnership agreement with the firm rather than a formal recognition agreement, to which the employers were more hostile. They secured improved conditions including pension contributions, low interest loans to help with the high cost of living in Brighton and Hove and a small pay increase. Nevertheless they continued to seek advice from trade union officials and were prepared to pursue formal recognition if working conditions deteriorated.

The Classic case represents a significant breakthrough in a sector where more generally workers have internalized the philosophy of individualism. One significant factor was the union's use of websites, which provided information and advice. Indeed websites effectively lower the 'sampling cost' of unions (Gomez 2003) among a generation of workers with little direct experience of unions, yet in a workplace where traditional union concerns with protecting employee rights are increasing. In the early days of IT and new media, and even now among the very small companies, work is bespoke, requiring innovative and imaginative solutions, but as time passes, work becomes 'more formulaic' (ID 29) especially in the larger firms so employees are 'less like pioneers at the technological frontier and more like routine white collar workers' (ID 46). Unions have found websites to be more effective than leafleting as employees are highly computer literate but contacts with unions are considered subversive. Although the workers are not really in fear of management, they nevertheless prefer to keep a low profile. Moreover given fluctuating employment, short-term contracts and the use of agency workers, e-contact often provides a more permanent link than personal contact via the workplace.

More generally, as illustrated in Table 4.2, the level of unionization in new media is extremely low, which conforms to the national trends within the sector and with low rates of unionization among young people and new workplaces (Brook 2002). Amongst IT workers in larger, more mixed organizations such as the NHS Trust or Brightex, a major private sector employer in the town,[13] union membership was also low. In the NHS Trust, and in conformity with national trends, IT workers said they had not been asked to join a union. Understandably the main health union (UNISON) focuses on organizing the much lower paid ancillary workers who are increasingly employed through a range of competing agencies, but as the work of IT workers becomes more routine, their receptiveness to union organizing is likely to increase. Consequently, workplace and locally based forms of organization and campaigns around common concerns, for example local pay weighting, or better conditions for agency employees, may prove more effective than more traditional sector-based campaigns. Certainly the alliance between different groups of low paid workers in care and service work proved effective (see below).

In Brightex, unions were strongly discouraged. Instead, the firm continually engaged in consultation with employees in conformity with the EU Directive on Information and Consultation, as one IT employee there noted:

> They do put a lot of emphasis now on employee satisfaction and in our department I think we are about to have a representative that basically gathers information about how we feel about stuff and then passes that on – I'm not sure – to a manager and also a manager's manager. And they have meetings about that. And we also do a survey every year and the results that come out of those are addressed within the department. So, erm, you do get a chance to have a gripe and because it is confidential, especially our team – we've got somebody who is very trustworthy, – so you can say what you think and he'll communicate it effectively.
>
> (ID 52)

But, while superficially providing these workers with a 'direct voice', in practice the questionnaire seems to be designed to elicit the effectiveness of management systems rather than employee well-being:

> It deals with leadership. That is what we usually all grumble about. You know, the quality of the leadership and the decisions that are made. Umm. How you feel that Brightex treats you. And a lot about, you know, do you have the freedom to do your job effectively and do teams work well together and a lot of questions like that. It's a kind of a questionnaire – there is about a hundred of the damn things. 'Do you understand why we do this and that and the other?' 'And do you feel your team leader supports you?
>
> (ID 52)

In Brightex, however, some of the potential conflicts between management and employees are diffused by the widespread use of freelancers, contractors and agency staff and there are several agencies that supply workers solely to this company. For these workers, the agency rather than Brightex deals with day-to-day issues relating to pay or discipline. During the research an employee was sacked for sending an inappropriate email over the firm's intranet system. It was an invitation asking people to come to a party dressed as 'pornstars, prossies, pimps, gimps, flashers, slutty schoolgirls and anything sleazy and cheesy'. It was intended to be ironic and for a friend. The employee commented that:

> A couple of days after sending the email to a friend I got pulled in and told to clear my desk. I couldn't believe it. I then realised I had sent it to

the company's finance director and not my friend who has the same name.

(Brightex employee cited by Rogers 2002)

Whatever the merits of the case, the point here is that she was called in and fired by the agency, not by Brightex:[14] 'None of the managers at Brightex said a peep to me throughout the whole thing' (employee cited by Rogers 2002).[15] Thus the firm itself keeps a distance from disciplinary issues. Indeed it is as if the company has sub-contracted its role as employer. The use of agency workers also allows the firm to vary the size of the workforce in relation to fluctuations in demand, again without getting involved in dismissals. Prior to the survey and during the downturn preceding and following 11 September, the company had restructured and let go most of the contractors (IT agency workers).[16] Moreover, in addition to the use of locally based employment agencies the company was planning to sub-contract both some of their call-centre and PC-based IT work to India and required the Brighton and Hove workers to train up Indian workers. Although this created some tensions, employees felt completely unable to resist such decisions otherwise their multi-national employer would locate even more of their work elsewhere:

> I mean, yes it probably does raise a certain amount of racism – you do hear of certain – you know, 'They're taking our jobs'. But I'd like to think that it's not the fact that they're Indian, it's just the fact that they are obviously another culture – if they had done it with Germany, we would be just as furious ... because it's blatantly obvious that you are training people to do your job, you know. However hard they try and fudge the discussion it's – you know, they get rid of the workforce and then they bring in other people. And because they're cheaper to do your job and you are supposed to train them and they can go and do it and suddenly your job becomes smaller because they are doing – supposedly the mundane side of work. But it does make you think, 'It's only a matter of time before they just displace the whole team.'

(ID 52)

In this case the GPMU also set up an interactive website to assist employees facing redundancy, but nonetheless there is a prevailing sense that it is difficult if not impossible to challenge effectively the decisions of a multi-national firm which can move its operations elsewhere with relative ease. Moreover with contemporary ICT, going international is no longer restricted to large companies. One of the small, dynamic new media companies had also developed a new facility in India, and though there were no redundancies, there were fewer jobs for local employees.

Collective and personal services

Turning to the opposite side of the new economy – collective and personal services – although there is no danger that the jobs will totally disappear, there are constant challenges to the terms and conditions of this already low paid workforce through processes of deregulation, privatization and the use of agency employees. The nature of this work has opposite properties to those of knowledge goods; it is inherently technologically un-progressive, and correspondingly highly labour intensive. It is difficult therefore to obtain cost savings through productivity increases without affecting the quality of the service. Workers in two sectors, refuse collection and childcare, took part in the research.

Refuse collection and street cleaning

Four companies have held the refuse contract in Brighton and Hove since compulsory competitive tendering (CCT) was first introduced in 1988 and, in the last two cases, the companies have seriously underbid the contract. This was possibly because they failed to appreciate the geographical specificity of Brighton and Hove, in particular the narrow streets, high levels of on-street parking and varied elevation, all of which increase costs. As pointed out earlier this work is labour intensive, so obtaining productivity increases is difficult. The different companies tried to maintain profitability by increasing work intensity, but, on each occasion, employees resisted.

The work is organized into routes and each route is covered by a workforce team. Generally the same team is responsible for the same route over a long period. There are differences in the speed of individual workers and in the time taken to complete different routes. One employee reflecting on his colleagues said:

> Him over there, that young un, they call him turbo arse he's such a fast sweeper, a really good worker. The old guy, he's a plodder, plods for miles and miles, but gets it done. But you only need one who does not pull his weight then it's a dead loss – all four of us really go at it. I've got the best round and the best of boys.
>
> (ID 803)

Another employee who had been allowed to work on all the routes, while organizing an employee social club, pointed out that:

> I know about all of the routes – some finish at 11 some finish at 3. Work is task related – you just have to get the route done and they are all different. The last lot [SITA] were trying to even things out.
>
> (ID 802)

Workers are paid by time (37.5 hours a week), but the work to be done is organized by task, so not all workers are working during their paid working hours, i.e. there is some porosity in the working day.[17] The organization of routes and the composition of teams are crucial in determining how much work individual workers actually do, and thus form the essence of bargaining or struggle between the workers and management.

In June 2001, SITA, the French multi-national firm who had held the contract since 1999, made another attempt to reduce costs by rescheduling the routes, which similarly was opposed. The company sacked the workers, who then occupied the site. The sit-in lasted five days, after which the Council terminated the contract with SITA.[18] A new consortium was formed but the workers were not satisfied by the proposals and threatened to take action during the Labour Party Conference, to be held in the city in September. Eventually the local authority took the contract back in-house, calling itself City Clean, and has subsequently operated the service relatively successfully.

There were significant improvements to service delivery in 2001–2, with 70 per cent of the population being very or fairly satisfied with the service, compared to 46 per cent in the previous period (Audit Commission 2002). The workers now report high degrees of work and work–life balance satisfaction (see Table 4.4) and were very complimentary about how the operation was managed. The Audit Commission (2002) also found that:

> In a short period the picture has changed from a poor service provided at relatively low overall cost to a close to average but high cost service.[19] Staff morale and commitment has markedly improved through a series of positive measures and a developing partnership with the GMB union.
>
> (Audit Commission 2002: 27)

More disconcertingly, however, while the Audit Commission concluded that a 'Fair, one star service' was being delivered and was positive about the improvement in industrial relations, it remained concerned by a cost increase of 43 per cent.[20] It recommended that the Council address this issue even though this would 'test' industrial relations.

> [City Clean] has acted effectively to remove some causes of dissatisfaction by harmonizing pay and conditions. It is also including staff and unions more actively in planning service changes and understanding service needs and pressures. This is a positive development but it is being tested and is likely to be further tested *as the Council moves to change working practices, reduce high sickness and overtime rates and achieve essential increases in productivity.*
>
> (Audit Commission 2002: 36, my emphasis)

And it recommended that:

... the Council needs to use the current review as an opportunity to increase the progress of change and make *some difficult decisions about service methods*.

(Audit Commission 2002: 27, my emphasis)

This conclusion is curious and contradictory, because the Audit Commission recognized that the increase in cost was necessary to take account of past underbidding and to cover the costs of harmonizing pay and conditions among workers (see below). The refuse collection service in Brighton and Hove is now among the costliest 25 per cent nationally, but this could well reflect the intrinsically high costs of providing the service in this locality as well as the high cost of living. While national comparisons might provide useful indicators of costs, some workers will have to work harder or experience lower living standards than others to meet the national standards, unless the different circumstances of work are also taken into consideration.

There are some working practices that could be changed. For example the Audit Commission identified a two-hour overlap between the shifts of street cleaners, and there are the variations in the workloads of different routes referred to earlier, but it is difficult to envisage other cost reductions without either increasing the intensity of work or lowering pay as the expected pace of work has to take into account the diversity of employees. Moreover, some employees are already working long hours and still have difficulty even approximating a living wage, as the employee below commented:

I work every day [meaning seven days a week] – well I like it but I have to really because the blokes need the money. I feel sorry for them; they work really hard ... We work really well together, but they earn nothing. That one over there – he would like to get a flat with his girlfriend – but he can't – he can't get the deposit – I don't know what they will do. That's one reason I work every day, for the men, because they need a driver – but I do like my holidays.

(ID 803)

This employee just returned from a holiday in Mombasa, but his relative affluence came from a pension from previous work as a public sector bus driver, not from refuse collection. Nevertheless he was clearly committed to his team and concerned that they could not earn a living wage. Given the prevailing housing costs, refuse collectors could not afford to live in Brighton and Hove, unless they had local authority or housing association accommodation (see Table 4.1).

The Audit Commission suggested that savings might also be made through reducing the number of agency workers, which rather overlooks the financial constraints within which the public sector operates, which in turn makes the flexibility and short-term savings from agency workers attractive.[21] In this case, 20 per cent of employees were agency workers and were paid only £4.75 an hour, with a £20 bonus if they worked five days in a row (compared to an average of £6.50 for permanent employees).[22] In addition they had inferior conditions in relation to holiday, sick pay and pensions.

Despite the differences in pay, the agency employees all belonged to the union, making total membership density over 90 per cent (see Table 4.2). This high density level seemed to be the result of an agreement between the union and either the agency or the employer, rather than a reflection of individual preferences. Agency workers also suspected that the union had opposed their request for permanent status as discussions had been taking place for some time but little progress had been made: 'there is a rumour that it was the union stopping us getting made permanent' (ID 803). More generally however there was a very positive attitude towards the union, particularly around the issue of liaison between management and workforce. Comments such as 'there is supposed to be frequent consultation, there are notices, but it mainly happens through the union' (ID 802), or 'the union does that [consultation] we hear through the union, I'm happy with them' (ID805) were widespread. Tensions sometimes arose because 'they use the union as a go-between – which can impact on relations with colleagues' (ID 804) and, as argued above, the agency workers were not totally convinced that the union represented their specific interests. Overall though employees in the survey attributed the success of the sit-in and the ensuing improvement in working conditions to the union.

Industrial action is more likely to be successful in this sector than in new media or care work because of the collective nature of the workplace and the way that work is organized in teams, both of which are conducive to discussion. In addition there is a higher level of unionization. Industrial power also arises from the Council's low tolerance towards rubbish in a tourist city. On the other hand rubbish collection had only recently been amalgamated on a citywide level (Brighton and Hove were formerly separate towns) so workers did not know each other and were on different kinds of contracts, which also varied because of the succession of private companies. One shop steward, for example, estimated that the employees, currently numbering about 250, were on 47 different contracts. So collective organization and action were never easy and the GMB had to be very active in terms of presenting a 'bigger picture' around which to unite the workforce and gaining support from other unions and from the local population.

So far these workers have been able to defend their conditions, but the Council will have to take note of the Audit Commission report, and when the contract comes up for renewal will be obliged by law to follow 'Best Value' procedures. Best Value was designed to overcome the bias of CCT towards the lowest cost tender. Past experience, as well as what seem to be contradictions within the Audit Commission's report (highlighted above), suggest that national financial comparisons may override practical knowledge of local cost structures, and enforce cost reductions that are difficult to sustain except by imposing more arduous conditions on the employees, so the future is unclear. Nevertheless, the industrial power of the regular workers, their gender composition, degree of workplace contact and level of unionization are fundamentally different from those of the workers in the much more individualized and much more hidden work of caring discussed below.

Care workers

Childcare has expanded in the UK with the development of the National Childcare Strategy introduced in 1998 and is provided in a number of ways: state nursery schools, private nurseries, after-school and holiday clubs, nannies and child-minders. For children between three and five years old, childcare and education have to some extent merged as the government now covers the cost of 2.5 hours a day education whether provided by a state nursery school, whose staff include qualified teachers, or in private nurseries, by staff who have received additional training.[23] For working parents these private nurseries are particularly useful as they provide 'wrap-around care', that is their opening hours are generally between 8 am and 6 or 7 pm and they supply education within this period. By contrast the state nursery schools only provide education for 2.5 hours a day, leaving parents to make alternative arrangements for the rest of the day.

These new arrangements mean that in both the public and private sectors there are people with different qualifications and very varied terms and conditions of employment 'caring' for children in the same environment and as with all activities involving caring it is difficult to fragment the work actually done between employees on the basis of skills. As a head teacher of a nursery school commented:

> We do not have any conflicts but we regret that they don't get more pay. We try to make things better. They [the nursery nurses] don't do any paperwork, which is tedious. They have an equal say in planning and in contact with the children, *there is no difference in the work they do* and I shouldn't really say this but we let them go home early sometimes.
>
> (ID 4, my emphasis)

One of the key concerns of employees is the growing gap between the responsibilities and pay of childcare assistants. The assistants are receiving between £5 and £6 per hour but the work involves being with and talking to children, some of whom have quite complex social problems. As a teaching support assistant commented, 'It's not just picking up the paint pots any more. It's a skilled job on an unskilled wage' (Kelso 2002).[24] Indeed national data confirm that childcare work is one of the lowest paying jobs in the UK, with average gross annual pay being less than £11,000, which is lower than for people working as gardeners or cleaners (Daycare Trust 2001).[25]

Despite these concerns, childcare workers expressed the highest degrees of satisfaction with the nature of work, their sense of achievement and their work–life balance (see Tables 4.3 and 4.4). Low pay, however, remains a key issue,[26] making it very difficult if not impossible to buy housing or even pay an independent rent in the Brighton and Hove area. Indeed one of the employees, who had worked for over 20 years and inherited her parents' apartment, was now thinking of moving out as she was unable to pay the annual maintenance charges.

At the time of the survey employees were not very confident that unions would help resolve this issue. The level of unionization varied, however, between the public and private sectors. All of the teachers and nursery nurses working in crèches and nurseries linked with public institutions, such as the local authority or the university, were members, but the learning support assistants were not, arguing they could not afford the subscriptions. None of the nursery workers or assistants in private sector nurseries belonged to the union.

One key reason for union membership was protection. Employees were concerned about potential litigation from parents in the event of any kind of accident or accusation and the unions were considered a vital support. However, even where there was commitment to unions in general and a history of trade union membership, the unions were still seen as rather distant or 'remote'. Similar to the IT and new media workers, care workers were concerned that the unions would not address their specific concerns. There was also a sense that there was too much rivalry between unions and competition for their 'subs'.

> We had someone from the GMB come to talk to us some time ago and wanted to discuss the benefits of joining GMB rather than UNISON. They were slagging UNISON off and said that the subs would be less and that they would do more for the LSAs [learning support assistants]. But I worked it out and it was still too much.
>
> (ID 6)

She further commented that:

> The grievance I have with the union is that they go on all the time about different treatment [meaning between teachers and the nursery nurses] and then it turns out that the subs are the same and yet we are on roughly half the salary. We were quite disgusted frankly – they are almost paying lip service to our demands. Teachers get double the salary and they are charging us the same.
>
> (ID 6)

Her calculations were factually incorrect, as the union had an earnings-related subscription scale, but even so there was a clear perception that the unions treated nursery workers and learning support assistants as second-class citizens:

> I really feel that the union treat us as second-class citizens as well. The NUT treats their members really well. They have interesting speakers and meet at the top hotels in Brighton and have a lovely buffet and wine. All we had was Hove Town Hall, with tea, biscuits and warm orange squash – and we already feel badly off.
>
> (ID 5)

Between six and nine months after the survey, public sector workers took part in a one day strike (July 2002) as part of the national council workers' pay dispute. The result was a three-year pay deal, with a guaranteed minimum wage rate of £5 per hour. The strength of action and degree of membership commitment was viewed with surprise by the press and delight among union leaders, with newspaper headlines reading: 'Angry women find a voice over pay that doesn't add up' and 'First strike for most of mums' army' (Kelso 2002). A variety of employees including classroom assistants, social workers, carers, librarians and housing officers took part in the strike to highlight the problem of low pay, especially given high housing costs. The refuse collectors also stopped work for the day even though they were not covered by these particular negotiations. This action illustrates that even with a fragmented and individualized workforce, collective action is possible. The private sector nursery workers are not covered by the agreement but they might benefit indirectly if local wages rise as a consequence.

Thus this sector is characterized by quite profound differences in pay and working contracts, probably more so than in the nature of the work and work context, with further differences between those working in or connected to public sector institutions and those in the private sector (see Prism Research 2000).[27] Given the responsibility of the work involved, low pay can only be explained by the technical characteristics of care work, outlined in the first section, and the gender composition of the workforce in a society in which women's work is of low social value. These factors are compounded by the difficulty of organizing workers in small workplaces. Individual nurseries are generally small, caring for between 20 and 40 children, and employing ten or fewer employees even though they are sometimes owned by large companies with multiple branches. In contrast to new media, these workers, especially those caring for the under twos, are less likely to use the Internet in their daily work, so it is less likely to form a way of overcoming their isolation.

Conclusion

This chapter has developed a conceptualization of the new economy that helps to explain widening social divisions that take a gendered form. Although there has been a raft of government initiatives to address employment rights and gender equality, and enhance work–life balance, these measures have done little to tackle traditional forms of gender segregation and inequality and the low pay customarily associated with 'women's work'. Women remain under-represented in new media and over-represented in care work, parts of which are characterized by extremely low pay. When the care workers are compared to the regularly employed, predominantly male, refuse collectors with similar levels of qualifications, they also received lower pay. Both these groups of workers, with the exception of some fully qualified teachers in nursery education, earned less than the workers in new media, and in general were less highly qualified. New media workers were, however, faced with paternalistic employment practices and low job security. In the past their jobs were to some extent protected by their specialist skills but as these are increasingly incorporated into more standardized software their work is becoming more routine and as a consequence they are increasingly subject to cost pressures and their jobs are threatened by relocation to cheaper labour markets overseas.

Despite the generally lower levels of pay, workers in collective and personal services have at least one advantage over the knowledge workers, namely that it would be difficult to disperse their jobs to other locations. Thus, in principle, they have some capacity to challenge the inequalities in the new economy. In practice, however, the average Brighton and Hove new media and IT workers are not earning especially high salaries. Indeed workers in all three sectors faced the difficulty of obtaining a living wage in a city characterized by high housing costs, suggesting grounds for a locally based campaign.

Equalities legislation is also undermined by the increasing use of agency workers, which enables employers to distance themselves from direct relations with employees and adjust to fluctuations in demand. Although agencies claim to follow the legislation, their financial viability depends on satisfying their clients' preferences. In fact, one agency claimed to rebuke employers who asked for 'long legged blondes', but later in the interview prided herself on knowing their clients' preferences and knowing which of their candidates (the people to be placed) could 'take it' (meaning workplace banter of a dubious kind) and which were 'too sensitive' (ID 504), indicating how the role of agencies effectively undermines the equalities legislation.

In contrast, however, to the rather dismal predictions by social theorists (e.g. Beck 2000) and despite falling levels of unionization, it would be wrong to assume that the contemporary individualized and fragmented workforce lacks all power of resistance. During and shortly after the empirical research two instances of industrial action led to positive outcomes. The refuse collectors prevented a further deterioration in their terms and conditions of employment by effectively reversing the tide of privatization and the low paid council workers in the care sector, in the context of a national dispute, secured a minimum wage of £5 per hour. Though the settlement at £5 per hour still reflects the idea that women do not require a living wage. These examples illustrate the continuing power of a well-organized group of workers with a high union density as well as the capacity for traditionally unorganized workers to unite around common themes, with union support. More surprisingly there was one case, in new media, where workers joined a union and formed a partnership agreement with the employer that led to an improvement in their conditions. Thus while the new economy is characterized by widening social divisions, it would be premature to suggest that the role of trade unions in representing workers and challenging these inequalities has altogether disappeared.

Acknowledgements

The author would like to thank the Leverhulme Trust for financing some of the research; the employees and union officials who contributed their time to the study, Róisín Ryan Flood for arranging the interviews; Paul Dinnen, who transcribed the tapes; and participants at the Women, Work and Health Conference in Stockholm in May 2002 and at the Future of Trade Unions dissemination events in 2002 who provided valuable comments on an earlier version of this chapter.

Notes

1   Nolan and Slater (2002) are critical of ungrounded accounts of the new economy, but their account of employment changes is nonetheless consistent with the one presented in this chapter.
2   Another example would be the Harry Potter books; although the end product has a physical form, it can be distributed virtually to printers throughout the globe, thus making J. K. Rowling a global superstar. The difference in earnings between herself and other authors is probably far greater than between those of Charles Dickens and his contemporaries.
3   The lack of coordination makes childcare arrangements especially difficult for parents with children of different ages (see Skinner 2003).
4   The vast majority (88 per cent) of the population of around 245,000 are employed in the service sector with public administration (36,000), banking and finance (32,000) and distribution (20,000) being the most significant and around 30,000 people commute to London (Grogan et al. 2001).
5   Recent arrivals include Cate Blanchett and Paul McCartney.
6   Figures calculated from BHC (2002). The average price of a one bedroomed flat in 2002 was £89,762.
7   Previous in-depth research of 55 new media entrepreneurs and managers carried out in 2000 and updated in 2003 is also drawn upon (see Perrons 2003b).
8   For a more detailed discussion of the new media sector in Brighton and Hove and work–life balance see Perrons (2003b).

9 These company names are fictitious.
10 Own research: interview with personnel manager of the company, plus other interviewees.
11 See Gomez (2003) for an analysis of union membership as an experience benefit.
12 This information rests on the interview with the GPMU official who argued that the issue of union membership was still rather sensitive and I was unable to cross-check with employees.
13 Brightex employs about 3,000 workers in Brighton and Hove, though not all are direct employees.
14 Brightex regarded this incident as an act of gross misconduct and she would also have been sacked had she been a direct employee.
15 In principle the agency could have sent the employee to a different employer but as the agency only supplied Brightex, this was not an option.
16 In this case the ones that were retained tended to be the older workers who were 'the people who were doing the clunky old stuff that nobody learns nowadays' (ID 52).
17 See Palloix 1976.
18 The Council and SITA agreed to terminate the contract in October 2001 and that SITA would pay the Council £3 million compensation.
19 More specifically it now falls in the 25 per cent highest cost services and achieves an average level of service provision compared to other services covered in the Chartered Institute of Public Finance and Accountancy (CIPFA) survey (see Audit Commission 2002).
20 Paradoxically, the overall manager of the service and other managerial staff have remained the same while the companies holding the contract have changed, which confirms the significance of the real material factors in addition to managerial style in shaping industrial relations. With City Clean the manager had more funds with which to run the service, which is crucial, given the nature of the work, and these enabled him to organize it in consultation rather than conflict with the union and employees.
21 See also Nolan and Slater (2002); Rubery et al. (2003).
22 The Council would also have to pay the agency a finding fee of up to £3,000 for every worker made permanent.
23 These nurseries have to follow the National Curriculum and allow OFSTED inspections to qualify for the state support.
24 This quotation comes from a worker taking part in the strike discussed below (see Kelso 2002).
25 The average in the survey in Table 4.3 was higher because some of those interviewed were teachers, and half were in nurseries attached to the public sector but the care assistants in the private nurseries were mainly on the minimum wage.
26 More specifically while a newly qualified teacher would earn a salary equivalent to £9 per hour, nursery nurses at the top of the scale – even those with 20 years experience – would only be earning £7 per hour and the learning support assistants who were often employed directly by individual schools and were not on any fixed pay scale, more in the region of between £5 and £6 per hour, with no pay over the school vacations; assistants in private sector nurseries were generally on the minimum wage.
27 A study of care workers for the elderly and infirm also found systematic differences in the working conditions, pay rates, pension provision and other fringe benefits between workers who remained directly employed by the public sector and those working for private agencies created through the PFI (Prism Research 2000).

Chapter 5

Structuring unions
The administrative rationality of collective action

Paul Willman

Introduction

This chapter describes and explains trends in union structure and behaviour in the UK and makes some predictions about future trends. It differs from some other works on union structure in the following ways. First, it seeks to explain structural developments in terms of strategic issues facing trade unions in Britain. It takes a broadly Chandlerian view of structure in seeing it primarily as a dependent variable, an outcome of certain choices made by unions in response to exogenous and endogenous pressures. However, once chosen, such structures may exert a constraining effect on union behaviour. Second, it takes a slightly broader view of the term 'structure' than exists, for example in Clegg (1976): structure is viewed not simply as external morphology but also as embracing a system of internal exchanges and controls. While there is a clear distinction to be made between issues of structure and of democracy – topics which sustain very different literatures – this chapter will embrace all dimensions of structure as they relate to the 'administrative rationality' of unions, considering the 'democratic rationality' where necessary (Child *et al*. 1973).

There are a number of prevalent structural or structure-conditioning trends in UK unions that require explanation. The most important phenomenon is membership loss. This chapter will not focus directly on the causes of membership loss but rather on its organizational consequences and on the strategic reactions of trade unions. The next most striking phenomenon in the UK is the reduction in the number of unions; this is accompanied by an increase in certain measures of membership concentration and a change in the size distribution. Next comes the prime mechanism for reduction in the number of unions – merger and transfers of engagement – and the key consequence, the growth in conglomeration. Several questions are raised by these trends. First, what are the conditions for continued viability of union organizations? A particular aspect of this question is whether there are significant scale economies in union organization. Second, what are the efficiency and effectiveness properties of different forms of organization? Third, and in conclusion, what are the prospects for union organization? Prior to attempting to answer these questions, we need a short statistical portrait of recent changes in union morphology.

The shape of things[1]

Table 5.1 shows the overall decline in the number of unions and the number of union members in the UK since 1990. The first trend goes back several decades although arguably the rate of decline in this 12-year period is unusually high, with the number of unions going down by a third. As Chapter 1 showed, the second trend extends back to 1979 and is showing signs of deceleration. Whereas membership declined by 18 per cent in the first five years of this period, it declined by only 3 per cent in the last five. Union density also declined; significantly it declined not only in the aggregate but also under collective agreements, i.e. *within* the unionized sector (Millward *et al.* 2000). Although this chapter will focus on the UK, it is worth noting these trends are common to many developed countries (Verma *et al.* 2002).

The concentration figure in Table 5.1 shows no trend, but this is deceptive. The very largest unions (those with more than 250,000 members) increased their share of total membership from 61 per cent to 72 per cent. This continues a trend of membership concentration which also goes back some time (Buchanan 1981). This did not happen because small unions disappeared. Table 5.2 displays one of the more remarkable exotica of UK union structure, with the vast majority of listed (i.e. independent) trade unions very small. This chapter will not concern itself primarily with the Association of Somerset Inseminators but its survival and that of unions of similar size says something about the operation of scale economies in union organization; specifically it indicates that the pursuit of scale economies in union organization is not a precondition for survival but a matter of leadership choice. It is also worth noting that many of these small unions are outside the TUC; since almost all of the large unions are in the TUC, there is a very different size distribution of TUC affiliates and non-TUC unions.

Absorption is the primary mechanism generating both the reduction in the number of smaller unions and the increase in the number with over 250,000 members. There are in fact two phenomena embedded in this statement. First, although unions do dissolve, the main trend is for merger or absorption.[2] Second, membership growth is primarily by absorption rather than recruitment driven; i.e. it is 'market share' trade unionism, redistributing existing members rather than finding new ones (Willman 1989; Willman *et al.* 1993).

In 2001, seven of the 16 unions with over 100,000 members operated primarily in the public sector. The largest five predominantly private sector unions (becoming four by merger at the end of the year) were all conglomerates operating across a range of industries and services. The basis of

Table 5.1 Union numbers and membership 1990–2002

Year	Number[a]	Membership (million)[b]	% of Membership in unions of over 100,000
1990	323	10.04	81.0
1995	256	8.23	79.0
2000	221	7.85	81.5
2002	199	7.78	83.6

Source: Certification Officer's Reports

Notes
a Number of listed unions
b Data from those unions making returns

Table 5.2 Size distribution of UK unions

Size	1993[a]	2001–2[b]
<5,000	224	161
5,000–10,000	21	12
10,001–20,000	12	12
20,001–50,000	19	15
50,001–100,000	8	6
100,001–250,000	11	5
>250,000	9	11

Source: Certification Officer's Reports

Notes
a Year end
b March: Size categories 1993: 0–5,000, 5,001–10,000; in 2001–2: 0–4,999, 5,000–9,999 etc.

conglomeration varied. For example, the TGWU has traditionally sectionalized by trade group. GMB evolved a sectional structure to facilitate absorption of smaller unions in the 1980s which came to overlay the traditional regional structure to form a loose matrix structure. AEEU has preserved the sectional structure which originated in its foundation by merger in 1992 as a basis for merger with Manufacturing, Science, Finance (MSF) in 2002 to form AMICUS. The trend is not confined to the private sector. UNISON's constitution incorporates representation on the basis of occupation, bargaining unit, and gender, giving the member several points of attachment (Waddington 2003a: 224). However, in all cases the key driver is the accommodation of membership diversity generated by merger. Moreover the dominance of conglomerates has been the case for some time (Hyman 2001: 66–115).

All but two of the unions with more than 100,000 members – doctors and nurses – had engaged in merger activity across the decade. Only three – in printing, telecommunications and financial services – remained anything close to industrial unions. We will look at the merger process in more detail below, but it is worth noting here that it is not in any sense a rationalizing process. It does not result in industry, company or location-specific groupings of membership. It does not appear to lead to improvements in financial efficiency or performance (Willman *et al.* 1993). It is emergent rather than centrally planned and merger discussions appear to involve a small number of unions in serial absorption activity. In the 1990s, few unions merged more than once, although several were involved in sets of merger discussions (Willman 1996). However, four large conglomerate unions (AEEU, GMB, MSF and TGWU) were involved in 53 per cent of all absorption transactions.

These trends – membership decline and absorption – are long term. There seems no reason to suspect that they will be reversed in the near future although the rate of change may alter. Several points may be noted. First, it remains the case that employers normally have a choice of union voice suppliers if union voice is their decision (see Chapter 8); even though the number of unions is falling, the emergence of conglomerate forms means that an employer considering recognition can normally choose. Second, in principle the same is true of potential members, although employees will be drawn towards those unions with a presence in their workplace. There remains competition in both markets.

Reactions to membership loss

The pattern of membership loss has varied between unions, both in nature and severity. Generally, as Bach and Givan show in Chapter 6, public sector unionism has stood up better than private. Some 'traditional' industry unions, for example in mining and seafaring, have all but disappeared. However, we know that some broad generalizations are possible. First, membership loss in many sectors has been driven by establishment turnover, to the extent that the age of an establishment is a predictor of union presence (Machin 2000; Willman *et al.* 2003); much membership loss has followed from the loss of bargaining units as establishments have closed. Second, union density under collective agreements has also fallen substantially (Millward *et al.* 2000); this heartland loss is significant since it takes place where unions have their best chance to offer their full range of services. Third, membership loss has generated revenue loss (in most cases) but has had an uneven impact on the financial viability of different unions. Some unions appear to have lost members but improved financial performance because the cost of servicing certain groups may have exceeded revenue (Willman *et al.* 1993) or perhaps because the reaction to revenue loss has been subsequent reappraisal of financial management information systems. Fourth, there is some evidence that union real administrative costs per member have risen, perhaps because unions were not adept at cutting employment levels of union staff following membership contraction (Willman and Morris 1995).

How were unions to mount a strategic response to this set of circumstances? Two questions arise. First, can unions, either individually or collectively, mount a strategic response? Second, if yes, how do they do so? We look at each question in turn.

Reviewing the literature on membership decline, Mason and Bain distinguished those 'structural determinist' authors for whom unions were the passive beneficiaries or victims of exogenous factors from 'union interventionists' – those who felt unions could do something about events (1993: 333). For the former, inflation, unemployment and real wage growth together with employment composition effects defined the capability of unions in a combination of trend and cycle effects. For the latter, a mix of endogenous factors sustained a more optimistic view about membership prospects (1993: 336)[3]. The difference may be a unit of analysis effect. The former group was concerned primarily with aggregate unionism, the latter with specific unions. A parallel may be drawn with the analysis of firms in contracting industries; market size and market share are different.

The extreme determinist position seems implausible. Unions are likely to be able to make critical choices about ends and means which account for variations in performance (Boxall and Haynes 1997). Indeed, there is some evidence of such performance differences (Charlwood 2002). *How* they make strategy is a rather different question and it may be that models of strategy development appropriate for imperatively co-ordinated organizations do not help that much. As Boxall and Haynes (1997: 570) put it, within unions there is the conflict between the constitutional commitment (democracy) and the practical disposition (hierarchical control) imparting complexity to the process of strategy formulation and implementation.

The range of strategic options is potentially large, at least to judge by the range of activities unions undertake in different countries. Hyman (2001), for example, explores a geometry of union activities encompassing economistic labour market activity, anti-capitalist mobilization of class interest and agent of social integration; UK unions are located somewhere between the first two. Faced with the failure of a current strategy, unions individually or collectively might opt to alter purpose as well as process. Hyman also notes that, within this decision space, UK unions did not boldly go. Faced with marked decline, they tried six options; these were, the development of individual services, the promotion of employment rights not conditional on union membership, partnership with employers, active social campaigning on non-traditional but work related issues, raised organizational efforts and increased communication with members (2001: 108–10). This is a fairly conventional agenda, which does not substantially relocate UK unions within the Hyman spectrum. Surely the question is: why such a conservative set?

Leadership failure is an obvious candidate but is probably simply an attribution error. This picture of strategic conservatism within a field would be familiar to institutional sociologists who might predict convergence of strategy and structure under various external isomorphic pressures (DiMaggio and Powell 1983). The business strategy literature that focuses on resources and capabilities would imply that it is extremely difficult for an organization or set thereof fundamentally to alter purpose in the face of external shock (Grant 2001). The literature on strategic decision-making would further suggest that such options might not even occur to strategy makers (Audia *et al.* 2000). We can illustrate the issues by a brief excursion into counterfactuals.

What *might* unions have done? We can illustrate this by examining the strategic options faced by UK unions experiencing membership decline over the last two decades. We set aside for the moment the problems of strategy implementation within ostensibly democratic organizations.

One option of a hard headed variety might have been to treat membership contraction as simply a revenue problem. On this model, a combination of severe cost cutting and subscription price hikes might have at least bought breathing space; unions might have chosen to farm a contracted core membership. The peculiar nature of unions as intermediary organizations makes the first difficult. The most radical way to restructure a union's cost base is to give the workload back to the membership by reducing administrative support (i.e. union officials) and enhancing participation rates. However, this depends largely on the employer's willingness to support employee participation and is difficult to do where recruitment of employers is also taking place (see Chapter 8). Price hikes around a contracted membership – returning to a modified form of 'craft' or professional union – only increase revenue where they do not prompt exit and depend on delivery of membership benefits. We know that the union wage premium in the UK has been shrinking to zero and thus the financial benefits for many union members may have been diminishing (Blanchflower and Bryson 2003). In fact, it appears that union subscriptions as a percentage of real earnings have been stable and low for some time and thus real revenue increases do depend on the rate of increase of real earnings (Willman *et al.* 1993).

A second strategic approach is to change the marketing proposition. If, the argument goes, collective bargaining representation is a shrinking market, unions should seek to diversify into other services within their current markets. As Hyman (2001) noted, some tried it. Bassett and Cave (1993) have explored many of the difficulties involved in developing suites of insurance products for members to compete with those provided by the for-profit insurance sector. These involve lack of finance and lack of expertise. There is some empirical evidence that it does not significantly aid recruitment (Sapper 1991). A second option is to seek new membership markets for existing products. It remains the case that trade union members are predominantly older whites in full-time employment in large establishments implying that diversification of product away from this particular demographic base has not been successful (Brook 2002; see also Perrons, this volume). Developing products for the employer market essentially involves provision of high quality voice at levels of cost and risk lower than that which would be incurred should the employer provide it herself (Willman *et al.* 2003). However, although the cost of union voice (proxied by the wage premium) and the risk associated with it (proxied by the strike rate) have both fallen, employers overwhelmingly choose non-union voice in the private sector (see Chapter 8).

A third strategic option for unions involved changing the regulatory structure of the 'representation industry' by lobbying government. This has traditionally been a central feature of union strategy in the UK and unions were perhaps unfortunate in the general attitude of the governmental audience for these efforts in office for much of the contraction period since 1979. Currently, the recognition provisions of the ERA and the European Works Council Directive may reintroduce demand for union voice on the part of employers and employees. Generically, what unions seek to do in influencing the regulatory regime for employment is to increase the switching costs away from union representation for both employers and employees, usually by seeking to acquire a monopoly provision of a core area of expertise (for example, health and safety representation).

These three options are not considered in greater detail here; the list itself is obvious rather than exhaustive. However, their presentation does allow several points to be made about union responses to prolonged membership decline. These three broad approaches – change the price, change the product, change the rules – all involve a need for co-ordinated action. There are clear first-mover disadvantages in strategic options one and two such that strong co-ordination of union action over prices and membership services would be necessary to sustain the approach. There is no history of the TUC being involved in such detailed and intrusive involvement, moreover, the systems of management requiring co-ordination are highly variable (Undy *et al.* 1996). However, there is clear historical precedent for pursuit of strategy three, which leaves union action relatively unco-ordinated; indeed it has perhaps been the *raison d'être* of the TUC. Given the emergence of large unions not reliant on the TUC for services other than lobbying co-ordination, it remains the most likely form of co-ordination. In Frege and Kelly's terms (2003) the repertoires of contention remain constrained by historical preferences.

In short, the events generating the contraction that has negatively impacted trade unions in the UK since 1979 were likely to reinforce historical biases towards exerting influences over government and other field-defining agencies, rather than encourage patterns of internal reform. As we shall see, there has been change, but it is of a reactive nature and in some ways makes the problem worse. We look in more detail at endogenous factors in the next section.

Organizational issues

Three issues will be considered. First, given the growth of large unions, we examine whether scale is an issue. Second, given the growth of conglomerates, we examine their structure. Third, we look at resource allocation issues. All are related.

Scale

The largest unions are becoming larger but the 'tail' of small unions shows no sign of rapidly disappearing. This raises serious questions about whether the largest unions are pursuing scale economies when they seek to grow and, if they do, whether they are successful. In fact, there is evidence to show that scale economies do not emerge and that their pursuit is not likely. We can look at this in two ways. An economy of scale emerges when the unit cost of a product or service declines with size. The basic measure in unions is cost per member and, almost independent of the measure chosen, this does not happen in UK unions. Specifically, the administrative cost of union services does not appear to decline with union size (Willman *et al.* 1993). A second way to look at it is to examine whether unions that merge subsequently achieve efficiency gains. Aston (1987) and Willman *et al.* (1993) found evidence of post-merger efficiency gains elusive in the post-war period, even in those instances where *ex ante* financial issues had been important in merger discussions. One reason for this appears to be that the creation and maintenance of federal structures in large unions is a comparative advantage for unions seeking merger (Undy *et al.* 1981); absorbed unions negotiate to keep officials and governance sustaining some measures of internal autonomy and, since there is often competition for absorption, they can strike a deal.

Working in favour of the absence of scale economies is a trend peculiar to collective action organizations; centralization of functions often brings costs onto the balance sheet, specifically where services provided by members to members (a first order collective action issue) are subsequently provided by union employees (a second order collective action issue). A key organizational design issue for trade unions is to secure a supply of membership participation by ensuring the development of internal mechanisms balancing the supply of participative opportunities with members' demand for them. Under-supply raises costs or lowers service levels; over-supply demands 'willingness to act' from those who have only 'willingness to pay' (Flood *et al.* 1996, 2000; Offe and Wiesenthal 1980). The folk theorem would suggest that any equilibrium between supply and demand in an absorbed union should be sustained and, through the maintenance of operational autonomy, unions appear to attempt to do so.

This is an important paradox for many collective action organizations. Pursuit of scale encourages centralization of resource provision that in turn moves activities from the volunteer to the employee and thus raises rather than reduces cost. Decentralization encourages participation but keeps other forms of overhead to sustain participation and sets up control issues. The emerging structure has certain properties.

Conglomeration

The structure which emerges in many large unions is what Streeck and Visser (1997) have termed 'conglomerate unions'. In fact, these involve a modified 'M' form structure in which the union centre uses fairly tight financial controls to manage a system of tax and cross-subsidy across a range of bargaining units with different cost and risk properties (Willman 2001; Willman and Morris 1995). The strategy this structure delivers is probably best considered in terms of flexibility and risk management rather than economies of scale (Donaldson 1998). A conglomerate union with a portfolio of bargaining units across which resources can be transferred can do the following:

1 First, as noted, it can act as safe haven for smaller unions seeking absorption but wishing to retain autonomy.
2 Second, it can use surplus resources from well-established bargaining units to pursue objectives such as recruitment.
3 Third, it can survive the loss of bargaining units in declining industries.
4 Fourth, it can vary the cost and risk of voice provision across a range of employers.
5 Fifth, it can vary the costs of membership and the market for participation across different, perhaps heterogeneous, membership groups.

Mobilizing these organizational capabilities is not straightforward, for several reasons.

In many countries the growth of diversified unions has occurred in the context of bargaining decentralization from industry to firm or establishment level (Katz 1993; Soskice 1990; Visser 1990). One consequence, as Jarley *et al.* (1997) have noted for the USA, is that representative and administrative functions are uncoupled and respond to different environmental pressures. Representative structures tend to cluster around the bargaining unit which is itself the main focus of participative opportunities (Flood *et al.* 1996, 2000). Increasingly, the role of the centre is administrative; specifically, portfolio management involving cross-subsidy of activities and centralized service provision, in which limited activity set there may indeed be scale economies (Willman *et al.* 1993). In fact, the degree of financial centralization may be extreme in the UK compared to the USA, since in the latter case locals tend to retain their own funds whereas in the UK few do (Willman and Morris 1995). However, the potential exists in both cases for certain groups within the union to generate high levels of operational autonomy.

The emerging structure approximates the 'M' form structure evident in diversified firms. Viable bargaining units develop substantial autonomy, but may coexist within the union with units highly dependent on the formal union. Its ingredients have been well documented. The relationship between unit and union has been characterized by Hemingway (1978: 172–3) as a bargaining process dependent upon the 'balance and efficacy of resources' available to both sides. The contingencies which constitute these resources and affect the level of bargaining unit independence have been well documented by Boraston *et al.* (1975: 153–88); those endogenous to the unit include size, organizing experience and unity, while exogenous ones are management facilities and union policy.

More generally, the reasoning here is similar to that of Kochan and Katz (1988: 123–31). They argue that union goals, bargaining structure and organizational structure are fairly tightly coupled. Decentralization of control over bargaining structure is likely to be efficient, in the sense of reducing transaction costs, where members have diverse interests (Fiorito *et al.* 1991). Co-operative employers will encourage decentralization, Fiorito *et al.* argue, because they share efficiency gains with employees and support local activism (1991: 123).

Resource allocation

The role of the centre in this modified 'M' form structure is of interest. In the classic formulation (Williamson 1975), the centre operates an internal capital market with lower informational asymmetries than those in the external market; reallocation of surpluses takes place in the pursuit of profitability. In this union conglomerate model, the allocative role of the centre tends towards the inverse of this, where viable units of the union extend cross-subsidy to inviable areas. There is a pure insurance aspect to this where parts of the union may subsidize each other during specific periods, for example, action during pay disputes. However, there may be long-term or even permanent subsidies to weaker areas – notably in pursuit of growth – and it is the latter form of subsidy which isolates the institutional interests of the union from the interests of existing members and co-operating employers.

There are few obvious benefits of portfolio diversification for existing members. Evidence from the USA implies that membership acquisition outside existing collective agreements has little effect on members' bargaining power (Voos 1984). There are unlikely to be wage benefits for existing members from cross-sectoral recruitment. I have argued elsewhere that, since bargaining unit surpluses tend to emerge from employer subsidy, there is in effect a tax involved on co-operating employers where long-term cross-subsidies support diversified growth (Willman 2001).

The growth of conglomerate unions, well documented for the UK, Germany and the Netherlands (Streeck and Visser 1997; Undy *et al.* 1981), in fact follows from the essentially institutional interest of reducing portfolio risk. The issue for the leadership is to devise governance structures that reconcile divergent membership interests *and* sustain employer co-operation while preserving leadership discretion.

We can elaborate the organizational politics of growth with the help of Figure 5.1. It illustrates growth mechanisms available under four different organizing conditions, in ways similar to those used elsewhere (Kelly and Heery 1994; Willman 1989). Arguably, only type B benefits existing members and co-operating employers by increasing the quality of voice and union density under current agreements. Type A recruitment benefits will depend on merger terms. Types C and D will, it is argued, be empirically less likely, not least because the higher costs cannot be justified internally in terms of benefits to existing stakeholders. To see success in types C and D recruitment, as much of the 'union revitalization' literature does, as indicative of union resurgence is thus perhaps to focus on the victories which are endemically pyrrhic.

In summary, organizational developments within large conglomerate unions reflect membership decline but also condition the responses unions can make to it. Although one can clearly see the pressures that have led to decline as primarily exogenous, the ability to respond is conditioned by endogenous factors emerging from the economics and politics of union organization. And there are powerful endogenous pressures for strategic inertia. Emergence from a pattern of 'market share' unionism where resources are allocated towards activities in already unionized sectors in an attempt to

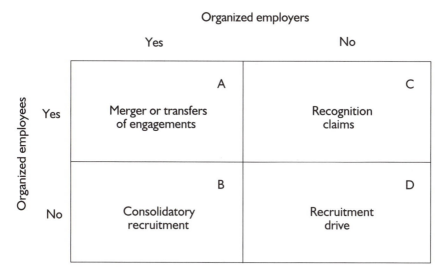

Figure 5.1 Union growth mechanisms

consolidate or recover membership positions is organizationally difficult because it requires resources to be diverted from existing stakeholders with no immediate prospect of net benefit. From this perspective, union revitalization – defined in terms of penetration of new territories – requires either far-sighted democratic intent or a greater degree of imperative co-ordination.

Effectiveness

The second aspect of strategic decision-making we need to consider is the set of decisions which might lead to differential effectiveness. The generic problems of effectiveness research are no easier when the focus is on union organizations. In fact, the problems may be compounded where the necessary conditions for the evaluation of effectiveness include the specification of a goal-set for ostensibly democratic organizations because this specification involves the possibly competing goals of different coalitions (Fiorito *et al.* 1993: 112–15).

In fact, it is a problem for much previous work on union effectiveness (or simply effects) that the possibility of competing objectives does not often take centre stage. The Ross–Dunlop debate – essentially an argument about the role of wage–employment trade-offs in union bargaining behaviour – assumed on both sides that it was possible to view unions as pursuing a single maximand (Mitchell 1972). Even more clearly, other economic work has treated union goals as coterminous with union leader goals (Clark and Oswald 1993). Most institutional scholars would put greater emphasis on the view of the union as a coalition of potentially divergent interests in pursuit of inconsistent or even mutually exclusive goals but they would, in consequence, shy away from specification of any models of effectiveness.

A second problem confronts a chapter such as this concerned primarily with administrative rationality. Administrative rationality is primarily about the implementation rather than the formulation of union goals. The latter falls more naturally within the examination of governance or representative structures. Effectiveness depends on the interaction of representative and administrative rationalities (Fiorito *et al.* 1993). A general specification of the conditions of effectiveness must therefore make some assumptions about generic representative goals. The approach here is to begin with the Webbs' definition of a union as a continuous association, involving employees, seeking improvements to terms and conditions of employment. This definition is taken to imply at a minimum the necessity to reconcile the institutional objective of continuity with members' objective of improvement while simultaneously encompassing objectives securing the position as bargaining counterparty with the employer. The reconciliation of these three interests is central to the union's survival; effectiveness can be analysed by devising performance measures in each objective domain and assessing the potential for conflict. This is attempted in Figure 5.2.

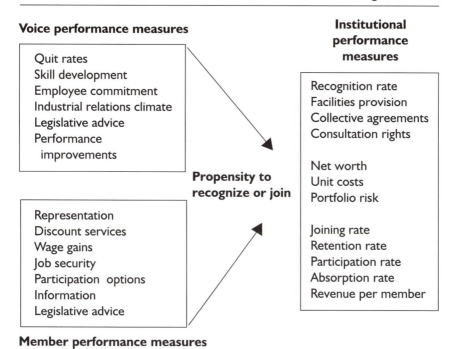

Voice performance measures

Quit rates
Skill development
Employee commitment
Industrial relations climate
Legislative advice
Performance
 improvements

**Propensity to
recognize or join**

**Institutional
performance
measures**

Recognition rate
Facilities provision
Collective agreements
Consultation rights

Net worth
Unit costs
Portfolio risk

Joining rate
Retention rate
Participation rate
Absorption rate
Revenue per member

Representation
Discount services
Wage gains
Job security
Participation options
Information
Legislative advice

Member performance measures

Figure 5.2 Performance indicators

Some of these measures may be compatible. For example, skill development and job security in the employer and member domains respectively, and participation options and participation rates in the member and institutional domains may be reconciled. However, in other cases, particularly in the area of wage gains, there may be direct conflicts of interest. Unions that generate employee voice and engage in collective bargaining are often involved in both wealth creation and rent extraction and as such are perhaps best regarded as agents both for employer and member (Aidt and Sena 2002; Faith and Reid 1987). Where wage gains are difficult to secure, the union will seek to offer members other forms of service for retention purposes and where they are extracted, compensatory voice mechanisms will be provided to maintain employer co-operation.

Figure 5.2 may then be seen as an attempt to devise performance measures for trade unions. The underlying approach is similar to the 'balanced score-card' approach used elsewhere in understanding strategy and performance linkages (for example, Becker *et al.* 2001). Overall union effectiveness is not secured by maximizing on any single set of performance measures – for example, membership satisfaction – but by understanding the linkages between the different performance measures and their implications for organizational performance.

Effectiveness in a conglomerate union involves flexing rent and voice activities across a bargaining unit portfolio at any point in time and managing switches between the activities over time; a wage dispute and a partnership agreement may be pursued in different places at the same time. Diversification across firms and sectors increases the likelihood that rent and voice opportunities will not be highly correlated; bargaining approaches to different employers must not be allowed to contaminate each other. This flexing is unavailable to single firm (or perhaps even single industry) unions and provides part of the comparative advantage of conglomerate forms. Exploiting this advantage involves substantial operational autonomy at bargaining unit level but considerable strategic decision space at the centre.

Conclusions: revitalization?

It is perhaps worth summarizing the environmental conditions. First, as Chapter 8 shows, the majority of employers want voice but the voice weapon of choice is non-union, even though many non-union employers say they are neutral on unions. Second, many employees want representation where they do not have it but they want consultation as well as union representation; on union membership, many non-members have not been asked to join (Gospel and Willman 2003). So there is demand for voice in both key markets, but there are serious questions about the union role in voice provision. However, third, the union wage premium has disappeared. Fourth, density under collective agreement has collapsed. So, there are questions about whether unions can deliver both voice to the employer and wage benefits to the employee where they have every opportunity to do so. The voice market is buoyant but unions are not.

Frege and Kelly (2003) suggest six agenda items for union revitalization. Four are conventional; they are organizing, organizational restructuring, the search for partnership and political action. To different degrees, UK unions are trying all of these, but their success is moot. The last two – building coalitions with other anti-capitalist protest groups and forming international links – are more radical but less frequent. It is possible to be more specific, at least in the UK case. The current set of circumstances can be interpreted in very different ways. Employer indifference and a representation gap may be evidence of latent demand. Lack of union availability may indicate a marketing problem. No wage premium and low density under collective agreement may indicate lack of product. The current state of union organization and the evidence of employer and employee preferences hint very strongly that if the original wounds were not self-inflicted the current bleeding is. This conclusion, though reached by a different route, is similar to that of Hyman (2001); perhaps traditional market-based unionism can no longer survive. If the traditional game is up, what is to be done?

Unions operate in solution markets (Bryson and Gomez 2003); that is, employers want voice and employees want representation but unions are not the only way to get either and to the extent that there are perceived superior responses to each set of demands, unions suffer. Flanders, some time ago (1970: 88), noted that unions dealt with market relations (i.e. pay) and managerial relations (i.e. the exercise of authority in employment relations). The former is problematic; employers currently want union influence over pay so little that members can get no pay benefit from union membership. However, arguably, the latter is of continued importance. What would be a 'management relations' product that would appeal in both solution markets? The answer is more likely to fall into the set of joint issues about managerial authority than that of direct challenges to it. It also needs to be generic, i.e. appealing to employers and members across a range of firms in an environment where many employers regard 'human resource management' as a potential source of competitive advantage. It might be an offering that would be available to all unions, but if the political problems involved in developing it prove considerable, it might offer first-mover advantages. It needs to offer membership benefits.

As Hyman (2001: 19) puts it, 'to exert effective influence on the market, trade unions must address the state'. Unions can generate and receive political rent. Political rent is defined here as that set of costs that fall on an employer as a consequence of government decisions about employers' employment responsibilities. It is conceptualized in other ways by different disciplines. It need not be appropriated by unions, but appropriation is a union option and one which is independent of the union role in political rent generation. In practical terms, it means that unions are part of the employer solution to an employment related problem; for UK unions, location within the solution set is key. The source of rent may be entirely exogenous, lying in a requirement for employers originating external to trade union activity. Or it may be partly endogenous, in that it is something for which unions have acted as a pressure group on government. The latter circumstance has been the stuff of trade union activity in the UK at least since 1900. However, unions may also benefit from the former, for example legislation on discrimination at work for which unions, in the UK at least, did not lobby.

The product that might generate a bridge between the desire for voice and the involvement of unions in firms involves the exploitation of political rent. An example might be the EC Information and Consultation Directive. It is a universal employer obligation above a low employment size threshold. It requires permanent representative structures. There are costs for non-compliance. Unions have long experience of involvement in consultation processes. Active embrace of the process of implementation might offer unions a broader role in the governance of employment relations than reliance on more traditional methods.

Notes

1   All data are from Certification Office Reports.
2   Waddington (2003a: 222) gives figures indicating that approximately 30 per cent of the reduction in union numbers between 1979 and 2000 came from dissolution, the remainder from mergers or absorption.
3   With one exception – see Willman 1989.

Chapter 6

Public service unionism in a restructured public sector
Challenges and prospects

Stephen Bach and Rebecca Kolins Givan

The future of trade unionism in Britain is bound up with the fortunes and prospects for public service trade unions. Of the ten largest trade unions, four recruit almost exclusively in the public services and most of the remainder have a significant public service presence (Certification Officer 2002). Public service trade unions fared much better than their private sector counterparts during the neo-liberal assault of the 1980s and 1990s. Aggregate trade union density for all public sector employees is significantly higher than in the private sector, being 59 and 19 per cent respectively (Brook 2002: 348). More recently, substantial increases in public expenditure and employment during the Labour government's second term of office, have enabled some public service unions to increase membership levels.

These bald statistics, however, fail to capture the widely differing trajectories in membership patterns between individual trade unions (see Table 6.1). Membership in the main professional unions (especially teachers, doctors and nurses) has increased dramatically in the last ten years, while the more general unions in the public services have faced a slight decline in membership. Public sector trade unions that organized in the nationalized industries and public utilities covering gas, water, electricity, steel, coal and many parts of the transport sector faced large membership losses arising from privatization and technological change (Pendleton 1997). In comparison to union members in privatized industries that confronted unrelenting managerial pressure to maximize shareholder value, public service members, despite market-style reforms, remained sheltered from the direct impact of product-market pressures arising from privatization.

Public service reforms have intensified since 1997 with the election of a Labour government. Some aspects of Labour's modernization agenda have been welcomed by the public service trade unions, especially substantial increases in public expenditure. Nonetheless there has been widespread union antipathy towards the government's support for an extended role for the private sector in the provision of public services and uncertainty about how much the rhetoric of social partnership reflects a genuine concern to involve trade unions in public service modernization (Bach 2002: 326).

Table 6.1 Public service trade union membership trends, 1992–2002

		1992	2002	Change (%)
Association of Teachers and Lecturers	Male	46,442	52,854	+14
(ATL)	Female	106,353	149,731	+41
	Total	152,795	202,585	+33
British Medical Association (BMA)	Male	61, 884	71,387	+15
	Female	26,223	42,324	+61
	Total	88,107	113,711	+29
GMB	Male	496,471	425,753	−14
	Female	302,630	278,217	−8
	Total	799,101	703,970	−12
National Association of Head Teachers	Male	19,258	17,263	−10
(NAHT)	Female	18,828	23,082	+23
	Total	38,086	40,345	+6
National Association of Schoolmasters	Male	94,309	92,193	−2
Union of Women Teachers (NASUWT)	Female	96,328	173,026	+80
	Total	190,637	265,219	+39
National Union of Teachers (NUT)	Male	54,466	79,268	+46
	Female	159,190	252,642	+59
	Total	213,656	331,910	+55
Professional Association of Teachers	Male	7,118	4,623	−35
(PAT)	Female	34,146	29,540	−13
	Total	41,264	34,163	−17
Royal College of Nursing (RCN)	Male	22,194	29,533	+33
	Female	270,999	314,659	+16
	Total	293,193	344,192	+17
Secondary Heads Association (SHA)	Male	5,610	6,742	+20
	Female	2,417	3,919	+62
	Total	8,027	10,661	+33
UNISON[a]	Male	542,684	364,487	−33
	Female	944,300	924,513	−2
	Total	1,486,984	1,289,000	−13

Note
a The 1992 figure for UNISON is the total membership for National and Local Government
Officers Association (NALGO), National Union of Public Employees (NUPE) and Confederation
of Health Service Employees (COHSE) at the end of 1992. The apparently large decline in
UNISON membership after the merger is probably partly explained by reporting and record-
keeping problems associated with the merger (see also Waddington and Kerr 2000: 260).

This chapter considers the policy responses of public service trade unions
to public service modernization. This altered policy context has led to fierce
internal debate within public service unions related to: who they represent
in terms of membership constituencies; what interests are assigned priority
between diverse constituencies, as reflected in campaigns undertaken in
relation to government policy; and how these interests are represented and
articulated. The starting point for this chapter is a consideration of the state
of public service unionism and the degree to which a distinctively public
service trade union response can be discerned in response to the government

modernization agenda. It is argued that public service trade unions are challenging government policies more directly as they move beyond a narrow economic remit. These developments stem from the distinctive traditions of public service unionism, but in a context in which the relationship between the Labour government and the union movement is fracturing as both wings of the Labour movement develop a more distant and arm's-length relationship.

The chapter focuses on the core public services – especially health and education – which employ more than two million people (McGregor 2001) and include a variety of occupational groups and rival trade unions. As trade unions continue to search for strategies to arrest decline, doubts continue to surface about the viability and applicability of the organizing model for a variety of occupational groups and workplaces (Waddington 2003b: 350). In this context, the responses of public service trade unions are highly relevant to analysis of union revitalization because they have framed their demands in terms of public policy and influencing public agendas, relying less on bargaining power at the workplace (see Johnston 1994).

The research commenced in October 2002 and this chapter reports its first findings, drawing on three data sources. First, it includes an analysis of the form and state of public service trade unionism, incorporating an analysis of the 1998 WERS. Second, it draws on interviews with 18 general secretaries and senior public service trade union officials at national level from the education, health and social services sector; and, third, it includes observation and more informal interviews with union activists and union officials at national union conferences in the health and education sectors during spring 2003.

Public service trade unionism

Public service trade unions have been influenced by the wider debates about union revitalization and the concern to shift the debate from a preoccupation with contextual factors that precipitated union decline, towards the response of unions in reversing this position (see Frege and Kelly 2003). What has been largely absent from debate about union revitalization has been consideration of the historically specific characteristics of public service trade unionism and the context in which they operate. This is curious because there is long-standing recognition of the unique characteristics of state employment which highlight its essentially political rather than market character, the dominant role of professional and associate-professional staff in shaping public service provision, and the gendered character of the workforce (e.g. Morris 2000). These membership characteristics have been an important influence in shaping the identity and agendas of public service trade unions. Public services are by their nature in the public eye. The especially high political profile of public services in the UK stems from the uniquely centralized system of financing and political control in comparison to other OECD (Organization for Economic Co-operation and Development) countries (see Atkinson and Van den Noord 2001). This high political profile has been reinforced by the Labour government's emphasis on the reform of public services that has formed the centre-piece of the government's second term in office (Bach 2002). A central proposition of this chapter is that public service trade unions have assigned a higher priority than private sector unions to influencing government policy and policy implementation in an attempt to capitalize on the political sensitivity of public service delivery for the Labour government. These tactics have become more prominent not only in response to member concerns, but also because of the perception amongst many union leaders that they have only a limited ability to influence government policy (Undy 2002; Waddington 2003b).

A second characteristic of many public service unions is the degree to which their membership is dominated by professionals and associate-professionals. Many public service trade unions grew out of professional associations that privileged professional concerns about status, service quality and influencing state policy rather than a narrower focus on terms and conditions of employment. Nurses, teachers and social workers have often been characterized as semi-professionals (Etzioni 1969) because their training is shorter, their status and expertise is less legitimized and they have less autonomy from supervision of their work than the classic professions of medicine and law. It can therefore be argued that these semi-professions and their representative trade unions remain acutely sensitive to government policies that challenge their claims to professional status. Moreover, public service trade unions continue to seek legitimation and authority for their policies by reference to claims of professional expertise.

A third characteristic of public services unions relates to the gender composition of public service trade unions in which education, health and social services employ far more women than men (see Table 6.1; see also Perrons, this volume). While women make up only 42 per cent of the private sector workforce, they comprise 61 per cent of the public sector workforce (Cully et al. 1999: Table 3.1). There has been a long-standing acknowledgement of women's lack of engagement with unions. Public service trade unions have been in the forefront of addressing gender imbalance in union organization and practice and these concerns have been reflected in organizations such as UNISON that have been prominent in pursuing gender democracy (McBride 2001).

These characteristics have ensured that public service trade unions have articulated broader concerns about the quality of service provision as well as the conditions under which they work. Joyce et al.'s account of social work trade unionism in the 1970s highlights the attempts by social workers in London to prioritize the plight of homeless families and to engage in alliances with squatters in an attempt to alter council housing policy (Joyce et al. 1988: 75). This tradition was eroded during the 1980s and 1990s, in a period of union retreat, as their members became more concerned to maintain their terms and conditions of employment arising from policies of privatization. There are signs of a re-engagement by unions with these broader concerns. The emphasis on the public service ethos has signalled a principled framework for action that describes the values that motivate those who work for the public services (Public Administration Select Committee 2002) and who choose to work in the public sector 'to make a difference' (Audit Commission 2002). Public service trade unions have therefore adopted a more *campaigning* or social movement trade unionism that relates to the wider concerns of members.

WERS and the public sector

The Workplace Employee Relations Survey series has been used as the authoritative data on the state of employment relations in Britain[1] and therefore could be expected to provide important information about union presence and the preparedness of unions to address the challenges raised by public sector restructuring. Carried out in 1980, 1984, 1990 and 1998, and interviewing both employees and management, the WERS data set provides a broad-based description of public sector workplaces in Britain today, but there are gaps in the data that limit its utility in analysing public sector employment relations. An important consideration is that the WERS data set does not attempt to engage in the complexities surrounding the changes in ownership and control within the public sector and focuses on a simple private versus public sector dichotomy (Cully *et al.* 1999: 19). In particular, the data do not allow for the analysis of public services provided wholly or partially by private firms and the type of employment practices used within these firms. The WERS data set therefore provides only limited information about the form of public service unionism and needs to be complemented by qualitative data sources that can illuminate the character of public service unionism in relation to professionalism, campaigns and workplace activity.

The WERS data demonstrate the relative strength of trade unions in public sector workplaces, and illustrate key changes since 1990. Of the 2,191 workplaces surveyed in 1998, 677 of them were described as being in the public sector (Department of Trade and Industry 1999). This figure should be sufficient to create an accurate picture of public sector workplaces. However, worker representatives were interviewed in fewer than 50 per cent of these workplaces, already creating a rather small sample of only 298 establishments for which both management and employee representative responses are available. The WERS employee survey covered 9,896 employees identified as working in the public sector.

The data confirm that unions have a stronger institutional presence (on a range of different measures) in the public sector than in the private sector (see Table 6.2).

Table 6.2 Key comparisons of public and private sector union presence and activity, by percentage of workplaces, 1998

	Public sector	Private services	Private manufacturing
Union presence	97	42	55
Union recognition	87	23	29
Union rep in workplace	74	58	93
Joint consultative committee present	32	18	24

Sources: Cully *et al.* (1999); Millward *et al.* (2000).

There has been a much less sharp decline in public sector unionism than in the private sector but there are some indications of the fragility of public sector workplace organization. Union presence has changed very little, with unions present in 97 per cent of public sector workplaces (compared with 99 per cent in 1980). Union density has declined significantly. In the public sector, mean workplace union density has declined from 86 per cent in 1980 to 64 per cent in 1998, in workplaces where a union is recognized. This represents a steep decline, although public sector union density remains much higher than in manufacturing (55 per cent) or private services (42 per cent) (Millward *et al.* 2000: Table 5.2).[2] Nonetheless, even workplaces with a recognized union often had no workplace union representative. In contrast to the almost universal presence of trade unions, only 74 per cent of unionized public sector workplaces had an on-site union representative compared to 81 per cent in 1980 (Millward *et al.* 2000: 153).

Collective bargaining coverage has been declining across public and private sectors. Table 6.3 shows that public sector bargaining coverage has declined by about one-third since 1984, compared to about 40 per cent in the same time period for the private sector. These figures need to be interpreted with care because they could misleadingly be construed as indicating that large swathes of the public sector are no longer subject to collective regulation of pay and conditions. The dramatic decline between 1984 and 1998 is due to the establishment of pay review bodies for nurses and teachers. While trade unions and employers do not engage in collective bargaining on pay for these occupational groups, they exert an important influence on review body recommendations by lobbying and the submission of written evidence; a form of 'arm's-length bargaining' (see Bach and Winchester 1994; Burchill

Table 6.3 Collective bargaining coverage (%)

	1984	1990	1998
Private sector	52	41	31
Public sector	95	78	63

Source: Department of Trade and Industry (1999).

2000). Even amongst those groups covered by pay review bodies, agreements to introduce radical changes in pay and working conditions have been negotiated between trade unions and employers. During 2003 agreements on the reform of the NHS pay system, revisions to the general medical practitioner (GP) contract and teacher workloads, indicate that collective regulation of pay and working conditions remains a central feature of public service employment relations.

The majority (55 per cent) of public sector worker representatives interviewed stated that their management was generally 'in favour of trade union membership' (Department of Trade and Industry 1999). This positive depiction of workplace relationships is also reflected in the views of managers. Only 1 per cent of managers described the relationship between management and employees in their workplace as 'poor' or 'very poor' (Department of Trade and Industry 1999). This figure may seem low, considering the relative prominence of public sector disputes in recent years, but may represent a more positive feeling towards employees in general than towards unions. In contrast, 23 per cent of worker representatives and 19 per cent of general employees felt that the relationship was 'poor' or 'very poor', reflecting a much less optimistic view (Department of Trade and Industry 1999).

One of the most striking differences between public and private sector workplaces is the degree of trade union recognition. In the public sector 87 per cent of workplaces have one or more recognized unions, compared to only 25 per cent in the private sector (Millward *et al.* 2000: 96). Joint consultative committees, comprising management and employee representatives (predominantly but not exclusively union representatives), are much more common in the public sector. Almost one-third (32 per cent) of public sector workplaces had some form of joint consultative committee (increasing to 82 per cent when considering committees at any level of the organization), while in the private sector, only one in five workplaces (20 per cent) had this arena for consultation (see Table 6.2 and Cully *et al.* 1999: 99).

An important distinguishing feature of public sector workplaces relates to the preponderance of multi-unionism. While 75 per cent of private sector workplaces that have any single union presence have only a single union, 69 per cent of public sector workplaces have multiple unions present. This disparity is also reflected in the number of recognized unions in a workplace. Of workplaces with at least one recognized union, only 26 per cent of private sector workplaces recognize more than one union, compared with 68 per cent of public sector workplaces. This prevalence of multi-unionism in the public sector highlights the scope for inter-union competition and points to the complexity of the human resources function in the public sector. The presence of multiple unions in a workplace does not necessarily indicate competition. While in teaching the NASUWT and NUT are in direct competition to recruit qualified teachers, many of the NHS unions only recruit within a single profession, such as the RCN (nurses), the BMA (doctors) and the Chartered Society of Physiotherapy.

In summary, the WERS data illuminate some of the distinctive features of the public sector context and the implications for union revitalization. First, because union recognition is almost universal, public service trade unions are less preoccupied with gaining recognition than in other sectors, and this may also mean that membership levels hold up better, reducing the pressure to engage in organizing activity. As Wills (2002: 26) notes, it is trade unions that have faced the most severe crisis of membership and recognition that have been most committed to developing workplace organizing campaigns. Nonetheless the decline in the presence of on-site workplace union representatives indicates the fragility of union organization. Second, the degree of multi-unionism is very marked, and although it partly reflects the diverse workforce in some services e.g. health, it confirms the scope for inter-union competition in many public services and points to the importance of overcoming these divisions by mergers or other forms of union co-operation.

Many of the complexities of public service unionism remain under-developed in the WERS data. As public service workplaces change, with workers on many different sets of terms and conditions, and under different employers in any single workplace, the basic categories of 'public' and 'private' become less useful. The data presented below highlight three key elements of union responses to a restructured public sector: a focus on professional unionism, the extent to which unions take on broader political campaigns and the varying forms of workplace unionism.

Public sector modernization

In the last two decades there have been radical changes in the organization and management of public services that have altered traditional forms of employment relations (Bach and Winchester 2003). Public service trade unions have been confronted with a series of challenges arising from the increased use of market-type incentives and associated managerial reforms. These reforms have put pressure on managers and employees to alter employment practices. These new polices have evolved from compulsory competitive tendering that impacted on particular components of the public service workforce to a more encompassing policy of 'Best Value' and 'Comprehensive Performance Assessment' that has encouraged local authorities to benchmark all public services against private sector comparators in terms of cost and service quality. Within the health sector the Labour government has signalled its commitment to a more mixed economy of welfare in which services are publicly funded but not necessarily publicly provided. Most attention has focused on the Private Finance Initiative (PFI) in which private sector firms bid for contracts to finance, design, build and operate public service facilities such as new hospitals and schools-related infrastructure. Legislation to establish Foundation Trusts, which enables NHS Trusts to become public benefit companies, has also provoked strong opposition from public service trade unions.

These policies have raised challenges for public service trade unions in terms of who they represent and the appropriate response in terms of how the interests of members and potential members are addressed. A key question for public service trade unions is the degree to which they follow their members into the private sector or whether they should campaign against forms of public–private partnership to limit these developments or at least prevent the worst consequences of these reforms. Although these approaches may not necessarily be mutually exclusive, it may be difficult to persuade union and employer constituencies of the benefit of a trade union presence in a context in which the union has adopted a high-profile stance against the policy of public–private partnerships. Unions as membership organizations have to be sensitive to the views of existing members that act as a barrier to radical shifts in policy. In addition the development of a more plural system of welfare provision may erode the shared values associated with a public service ethos and require unions to balance the differing needs of a range of member constituencies. Trade unions have therefore argued strongly that new staff within PFI schemes should have the same pay and conditions as the protected employees to avoid the creation of a 'two-tier' workforce (UNISON 2000).

A second defining feature of these changes has been a strengthening of the authority and status of senior managers and the devolution of managerial responsibilities to more autonomous organizational units in which local managers have been granted greater discretion to shape local personnel practice. At the same time, however, central government accrued unprecedented levels of control over the funding and management of nominally independent service providers. The Labour government has largely continued the reforms they inherited from previous Conservative administrations. It has reinforced central control by revamping systems of performance management with more explicit service targets, whilst emphasizing the key role of senior managers in shaping workplace developments, for example, within the proposed Foundation Trusts.

For public service trade unions that have traditionally been organized on a centralized basis and orientated to national level bargaining, involving relatively few senior officials, the shift in negotiating and consultation towards the workplace level has exposed the fragility of workplace union organization and the difficulties in maintaining effective workplace organization in the face of continual organizational restructuring (Fairbrother 2002: 78). These reforms have therefore led some trade unions to confront questions about how they are organized and to what extent they can continue to pursue a form of union structure that is dependent on a cadre of full-time officers in conjunction with variable degrees of local union activity.

In addition to questions of how member interests are organized, the modernization agenda at enterprise level differs substantially in terms of the managerial objectives being pursued and what this means in terms of interest representation. This is not a new question in the sense it has been suggested that 'professional' unions may pursue a wider agenda than that which is focused simply on wages and conditions of employment (Burchill 1995; Kessler and Heron 2001). The managerial agenda at workplace level differs markedly from set-piece negotiations about pay and conditions that dominate national negotiations. Instead managers have sought to raise levels of performance that embody a variety of flexible work practices including changes in work organization, alterations in the composition of the workforce and tighter management of attendance, that local activists are often ill-equipped to tackle (for example, see Bach forthcoming). This broader human resource management and performance agenda may also provide opportunities for trade unions to engage with wider membership constituencies and focus on issues that are more related to professional development and training and to concerns about the quality of working life (Audit Commission 2002).

Union responses to public service restructuring

The modernization agenda therefore raises major challenges for public service unions but how far are these challenges reflected in union policies and practices? Using Hyman's (1997) typology as a framework, the major challenges for public service unions are examined in terms of the who, what and how of interest representation. Although there is clearly an inter-relationship between whom a union represents, which issues it prioritizes and how the union functions, these categories provide a useful lens to disentangle some of the current foremost concerns of the public service unions. In particular, the responses to public sector restructuring have been constrained by existing union characteristics and have in turn forced a re-evaluation of union priorities, in terms of membership, activity and organization. Union responses to the government's modernization agenda illuminate how public sector restructuring has led to reforms within the unions.

Whose interests are represented?

The restructuring of the public services has blurred the traditional boundaries of state employment, altering the division between the public and private sectors and therefore affecting traditional union jurisdictions. Unions that have traditionally represented public service employees must decide whether to follow their members into the private sector when work is privatized or outsourced. Unions were relatively successful in retaining the membership of workers in the privatized utilities in the 1980s, in contrast with other privatized industries. Union density in these utilities companies remains at 68 per cent, much closer to the average union density in the public sector (57 per cent) than the private sector (26 per cent) (Millward *et al.* 2000: 87,

Table 4.2). However, even once a union has retained recognition in a privatized company, it must still recruit new employees in order to maintain a high level of membership. While unions were relatively successful in this endeavour as the utilities were privatized in the 1980s, the complexities of contracting-out and the Private Finance Initiative, especially in local government, health and education, have made this task much more complex.

The blurring of occupational boundaries that comprises a core component of public service modernization, has forced trade unions to consider which occupational groups they represent. An important element in understanding the response to these questions arises from the division between the professional unions, who represent workers with scarce skills and considerable job security, and general unions, that represent a more diverse membership whose members have limited individual labour market power. The assumption that these groups have different goals, with the former focusing on professional issues and the latter on economic issues, has been contested, but nonetheless these tensions remain important in illuminating union practice in the public services (Burchill 1995; Kessler and Heron 2001). What then determines whether a union opens its membership?

For the general unions that historically have recruited horizontally across a number of industries amongst the less skilled, the decision to open up to new industries and occupational groups has been less contentious. The increased emphasis on public service recruitment in unions such as the GMB has stemmed from the decline of their membership base in manufacturing since the 1980s. The emergence of UNISON in 1993 was a response to membership losses amongst the partner unions arising from compulsory competitive tendering (Terry 1996). These general unions have sought to deepen and broaden their membership base by actively recruiting professionals and semi-professionals, such as nurses in UNISON and local government managers in the GMB. The challenge for these unions has been to persuade these membership constituencies that they will retain their occupational identities and not be swallowed up in an amorphous organization that is oblivious to their occupational concerns. Consequently, these members are provided with specialized professional advice and publications, along with the more general union services and differentiated fee structures. Of crucial importance has been the question of union governance, with the provision of relatively autonomous structures, for example, in relation to the British Association of Occupational Therapists within UNISON and the Managerial and Professional Officers (MPO) within the GMB. The dilemma for these unions is that the measures required to persuade these smaller unions to join them may set in train sectionalist pressures that militate against organizational unity (see Chapter 5).

Many of the professional unions have struggled with decisions about whether to open up membership, or to retain the narrow focus that has usually been built around one dominant occupational group. For these unions their influence has been premised on their *craft* exclusivity in labour market terms. They have tried to prevent dilution and substitution of their members, to reinforce their claim to be the authoritative voice of teachers (NUT) or nurses (RCN), for example, in order to maintain a central role in shaping public policy towards teaching and nursing.

Decisions about whether to broaden a union's constituency are therefore influenced by three main factors: first, the membership profile of the union; second, the type of union governance, affecting the influence that current members can exert over the union leadership in shaping union policy; and third, the degree of competition from other unions that recruit members from amongst the same occupational groups. Where professional identities are strong, and the union has always traded on its identity as a professional organization, there is usually great resistance to any broadening of membership. Within the health sector, the Royal College of Nursing (RCN) has opened its membership slightly, by allowing the most qualified health care assistants (HCAs, who are not registered nurses) to join. This has been a contentious process because the RCN distinguishes itself from UNISON, the other main union option for nurses, by emphasizing its professional nature. Tangible signs of this identity include non-affiliation to the TUC and a reluctance to take industrial action, despite the lifting of the formal ban on industrial action in the mid-1990s. Although the RCN is a certified union, it is perceived by many of its members as a professional association and is dominated by a national leadership that is relatively insulated from membership pressure. For example, the General Secretary is appointed not elected. The debate over opening RCN membership to health care assistants (HCAs) revealed fears about the dilution of the organization's professional focus. The decision in autumn 2000 to admit level 3 HCAs into associate membership reflected two factors: the growth of these occupational groups and concerns that they would be recruited by UNISON; and a greater acceptance by RCN members that health care assistants have become integral to the health care ward team. The decision has been implemented cautiously with restrictions placed on the representative and leadership roles that HCAs can fulfil (RCN 2001). Nonetheless the significance of this decision should not be underestimated because it set a precedent for the RCN in terms of recruiting beyond its traditional boundaries and this broader membership base was reinforced by the 2003 RCN congress that voted to extend RCN membership to nursery nurses.

Within education, the degree to which the teacher unions have been willing to open up their membership has been variable. Some teacher unions have allowed classroom assistants to become members (especially the Association of Teachers and Lecturers). ATL is widely perceived as the most moderate of the three main teaching unions, reflecting its historical roots in the independent and grammar school sectors, and has a more diverse membership amongst teachers, lecturers and support staff, enabling it to accommodate teaching assistants more easily within its membership. The National Union of Teachers (NUT) has always sought to reinforce the uncertain professional status of teachers which reflected the relatively small number of graduates, especially amongst primary school teachers (see Ironside and Seifert 1995: 75), and the absence of self-regulation in comparison to nurses. The NUT has been the most resistant to incorporating any non-teachers into membership. This reflects its dominant membership base within primary schools in which concerns about dilution, arising from the increased use of classroom assistants, have been most strongly expressed. This can be contrasted with the NASUWT position whose membership strength is amongst secondary school teachers that have more specialized and less substitutable skills and that feel less threatened by the growth of classroom assistants. The NUT has been concerned that the incorporation of classroom assistants would dilute its strong professional identity and create conflicts of interest within the union. An additional influence has been the long-standing history of factional opposition to the union leadership (see Hyman 1983: 50–1). The NUT has therefore remained narrowly focused on a single occupational group. It is too early to judge whether this will hinder future membership growth or prove a key source of competitive advantage by safeguarding the interests of its core teacher membership.

The Secondary Heads Association (SHA) and the National Association of Head Teachers (NAHT) have extended their membership to the 'leadership spine' in schools, allowing deputy heads and assistant heads into membership. As in other cases, these organizations considered whether opening up membership would result in the admission of groups with interests closely aligned to those of existing members, rather than non-complementary groups with conflicting interests. An important influence in viewing the leadership spine as essentially complementary has been the evolution of school management and public policy pronouncements that emphasize a team-based approach to school leadership. This is not to say that these decisions have not been hotly debated. Both unions, however, are aware that they are in competition for members (although SHA only represents those in secondary schools, the NAHT whilst predominantly primary school based has some secondary heads in membership). If one union were to open its membership and the other did not follow suit, the broader union would have a perceived advantage, and might achieve greater membership growth. Competition, rather than notions of professional identity, drove these changes. As in many other cases, unions that compete for similar membership groups have been very attuned to the actions of their rivals.

On the question of gender, public service union responses have varied widely. UNISON, whose membership is approximately 70 per cent female, set out to promote gender democracy from its foundation. UNISON has taken on many issues of particular significance to their female members: campaigning against the prevalence of very low pay work, filing legal claims for equal pay and campaigning against term-time only employment (in schools) and unfair treatment for part-time workers. The GMB and UNISON have both developed campaigns against domestic violence (with a focus on the workplace). Other unions have had a more ambivalent response to the particular concerns of female members. The Royal College of Nursing, which is over 90 per cent female, has sometimes had difficulty recruiting proportionate numbers of female stewards and full-time officers.

A broader membership constituency may alter the character of the union, raising important questions about whether a more open membership implies a dilution of the professional priorities of the organization. The union officers interviewed were virtually unanimous in rejecting the assumption that a potential conflict of interest exists between the priorities of a professional organization and a trade union. To varying degrees the unions representing main-grade teachers[3] articulated the same argument that in circumstances when the union has felt compelled to threaten industrial action this has been to safeguard the interests of members *and* pupils because industrial action has been sanctioned, for example, to ensure a disruptive pupil was removed from a particular school. Amongst both health and education unions there was a similar emphasis on the inter-connection between professional and more traditional economic concerns of unions. In practice, however, tensions remain because it is difficult to provide a full range of services as both a union and a professional organization. The dominant identity of the union, whether primarily orientated to professional concerns or geared towards more traditional, solidaristic broad-based union values, continues to shape union priorities as well as the allocation of resources and union governance.

What interests are represented?

Hyman argues that the kinds of interests that unions represent can be divided into a number of categories (1997: 517–18). These include collective bargaining over pay and conditions; the role of the state in defining the social wage including the broader political, economic and labour market context; and finally, a broader agenda not linked directly to the union member's status as an employee, but to wider community interests and institutions. These categories move from the narrowest and most traditional areas of union activity, to the broadest and arguably newest area of union activity, the community. The internal research of several unions, as well as work by the Audit Commission (2002), raises questions about whether pay levels are the highest priority of workers in the public services. This has encouraged trade unions to examine their bargaining priorities, a shift of emphasis that has been facilitated by the trend towards longer-term pay deals in the context of low inflation. Trade unions have therefore assigned a higher profile to representation and campaigning. The nature of a particular union's membership (the 'who' discussed above) also determines the kinds of issues available for campaigns. For example, a union with a narrow professional focus is unlikely to have either the resources or the inclination to work on broad community issues. A union with relatively well-paid members (such as doctors or headteachers) is unlikely to view issues of low pay and neighbourhood economic development as a high priority.

Key issues on the union campaigning agenda are shaped by the Labour government's modernization agenda, for example opposition to Foundation Trusts or National Curriculum Tests (usually known as SATs). A related question is the form in which trade unions will engage with the government's agenda. On some issues, while unions represent their own members, the TUC has played a central role in facilitating negotiations with government and attempting to bring about consensus among the affiliated unions (e.g. the recent workload agreement in education). In addition to inter-union competition the stance towards the Labour government has been influenced by the differences in union governance structures that have made some unions (e.g. the NUT) more open to pressure from union activists. Other unions have favoured maintaining a more positive relationship and tried to shape government policy by private lobbying, although this can be an uncomfortable position for union leaders given membership concerns about the direction of Labour government policy on issues such as PFI. Most unions have picked their public battles carefully in order to maintain some influence with government, whilst considering the impact of their stance on attracting new members. The recent decision by UNISON to support the piloting of fundamental pay restructuring in the NHS, the *Agenda for Change* proposals, despite major reservations amongst sections of its health membership, illustrated these contradictory pressures at work.

Unions that choose openly to reject government policy risk being excluded from the policy-making process. Some, such as the British Medical Association, have a monopoly on a prestigious profession and are able to maintain links with government even after major disputes, such as the rejection by members of a nationally negotiated contract. However, the Labour government has demonstrated its willingness to 'name and shame' unions that are not supportive of its modernization agenda, for example, the BMA in relation to the consultants' contract, and the NUT, following its unwillingness to sign the workload agreement for schools. As Charles Clarke (2003), the Secretary of State for Education, commented in relation to the other teacher unions that had signed the agreement:

> This is the sort of trade unionism that I want to do business with. Grown-up, forward-looking progressive trade unionism. Trade unionism that is focussed on the big issues and how we solve them. Trade unionism that delivers results. I value this new relationship. I value our partnership.

I have no time for the sort of militant opportunism that some people still cling to. There are no minority vetoes and old style vested interests will not stop us from delivering change for the better. I think that the old time religion has had its day.

(Clarke 2003)

On the so-called bread and butter issues of collective bargaining over pay and conditions, the unions still play a key role not least in ensuring that national agreements are implemented effectively at local level. Many public service workers are covered by pay review bodies and in these cases trade unions have been able to submit evidence that has ensured a high public profile for their concerns about recruitment and retention difficulties and high workloads. The constitution of each review body differs, but the pay review body system has not precluded substantial bargaining over conditions and longer-term questions of work reorganization and pay reform.

Hyman's third category, welfare and political economy, describes a strong element of the work of the larger public service unions. Union responses to public sector restructuring have varied considerably. Perhaps the key issue is the mixed economy of the public services, incorporating various forms of private sector financing and service provision. In general, public service unions have been against programmes such as the Private Finance Initiative (PFI) and the pervasive use of private contractors. However, some unions have been very active in campaigning on these issues, while others have remained silent.

The private provision of public services has been the key target of UNISON's high profile Positively Public campaign. This campaign has attacked the 'creeping privatization' of public services in all areas, including health, local government and education. It has worked on two levels, both helping local UNISON branches to fight contracting out and informing the general public (via newspaper and cinema advertisements) about the growing role of the private sector. The GMB has also used a public campaign (featuring full page advertisements in national newspapers), particularly targeting private companies now providing public services, such as Amec and Jarvis. Both UNISON and the GMB represent many of the workers whose employment is directly affected by the transfer of services to the private sector. Other unions have been much less proactive on these issues.

Many of the professional unions are affected less directly by the transfer of services like cleaning and maintenance to private companies. For example, teachers and nurses are not subject to changes in their terms and conditions of employment under PFI. However, their working environment may change considerably. The RCN has recently turned its attention to PFI, realizing that the initiative has serious implications for its members. New hospitals built under PFI have had significant design problems which have made it difficult for nurses to perform their duties (Lister 2003). The teaching unions have not invested a great deal in research or campaigning on PFI. While several have passed conference resolutions expressing opposition to PFI they have not prioritized this issue, because their members are not facing transfer of employment, and because they are confronting other, more pressing concerns.

The cautious approach by some unions to issues of private service provision also reflects the complexity of these issues. Although numerous problems with PFI hospitals and schools have been highlighted, it is very difficult to demonstrate that these problems stem solely from the PFI procurement process, rather than from more long-standing problems of poor hospital design and project management or budgetary pressures imposed on ancillary services, all of which can also be problematic under traditionally procured public services. It has therefore often been simpler for some unions to attack PFI from an ideological perspective, arguing that public services should not be operated for profit.

Hyman's final category describes what has come to be known as community unionism (Johnston 1994; Wills 2002). The unions which have been most active in the community have been more general unions, representing large numbers of relatively low-skilled and low paid workers, including the GMB and UNISON. The most prominent example of community unionism is Telco, The East London Communities Organization (Wills 2001). Although Telco has achieved broad publicity, it is currently the only fully-fledged campaign of its kind in the UK. However, for many of the smaller, more professional public service unions, such wide-ranging campaigning is neither desirable nor viable, as it serves neither current nor potential members directly and requires financial support.

How are interests represented?

The existing membership and the types of issues addressed by a union are intricately connected with its organization and structure. The major public service unions fall into two main categories – those with a strong workplace presence and those with a minimal workplace presence. To some degree the type of organization is determined by choice, but it is largely influenced by the type of membership and by financial considerations. The structure of the union has a considerable effect on which issues it can address, and how it might address them. The debate over organizing versus servicing is not applicable to the major public service unions (for an overview see Heery 2002). The unions do not view the functions of organizing new members and servicing current members as distinct. If unions expect to both recruit and retain members, they must simultaneously organize and service. Literature on organizing generally comes from the United States, where unions have suffered a massive decline in coverage, as well as density (Bronfenbrenner and Juravich 1998). The organizing emphasis was on building up membership and achieving recognition in unorganized workplaces (so-called greenfield sites). For unions in the UK public services, there are very few greenfield sites. Coverage is high, 63 per cent according to WERS and possibly even higher, depending on the precise definition of union coverage (Burchill 2000: 155; Cully *et al.* 1999: 242). While in-fill recruitment is a priority, in order to cut down on the number of non-union members in organized workplaces, major organizing initiatives are not a concern.

The role of unions in the workplace varies considerably across the public services and has been influenced by the shift from a highly centralized system of pay determination towards one in which employers have been granted greater local flexibility within an overall national framework to shape pay and working conditions. The highly centralized unions have been forced to reconsider their organizational structures. At present three distinctive approaches can be identified. First, the large, general unions may have several thousand members in a single workplace, covering a variety of occupational groups and strive to have representatives present in every workplace. In practice many workplaces do not have representatives and much of the work-load falls to full-time officers (see TUC 2002a).

Second, the large professional unions, such as the RCN, NUT and NASUWT, have a more mixed model. They use workplace representatives, and aim to have them in all workplaces, but much of the casework still falls to full-time officers and headquarters staff. A member with a question or a problem would ordinarily seek advice from a workplace shop steward, who would then decide whether to refer the matter on to a full-time officer or deal with it him/herself. The complaint might move to the regional or national level, but only if it is sufficiently complex that the local branch cannot resolve the problem. In practice there are not workplace representatives for every union in every workplace. As in most of the public services, the increasing demands on employees' time mean that it is difficult to recruit an adequate number of workplace representatives.[4] The degree and structure of workplace union presence largely depend on both the size of the union and its degree of professionalism. The RCN is an example of a union with many members in the same physical workplace, but a limited workplace presence. Instead, its focus is on professional services available from the centre.

The third type of workplace presence is typified by the head teachers' unions. Since these unions represent highly dispersed employees with no more than a handful of members in each workplace, with a smaller overall membership, the role of the workplace representative is de-emphasized (or non-existent). Consequently the heads' unions (SHA and the NAHT) have similar structures that are very different from those of the main teachers' unions (the NUT and NASUWT). The SHA and the NAHT rely on a network of part-time field staff, often retired heads, to perform most of their casework, handling individual grievances and concerns. Members generally access a field worker by contacting the union's head office. The head office then delegates the issue to the appropriate part-time staff member. These unions therefore have a high degree of central control and coordination. This model allows a union to resolve the twin difficulties of a relatively low resource base and a dispersed membership. However, the unions that adopt this model tend to have a lower profile in the workplace, and rely on their professional identity for continued recruitment. While this model seems appropriate for the head teachers' unions, it is also utilized by the smaller teaching unions, ATL and PAT. With this low profile in schools, these unions are unlikely to significantly increase their membership, although they may be able to adequately service existing members. The British Medical Association, although its membership is both concentrated (in hospitals) and dispersed (in local practices), generally uses a more centralized model to offer members professional service and support. However, the majority of negotiations and major decisions are performed by lay members, reflecting a belief that doctors should negotiate on behalf of doctors, a stance that may be reviewed in the light of recent negotiations over the consultant contract. In contrast to the smaller teaching unions, the BMA has a very large resource base (in part because of its property holdings) and is therefore able to operate parallel structures to provide both lay representation and extensive high quality professional services. Both the union membership (who) and the structure of the union (how) play a part in determining the issues that the union addresses and the policy stances it takes.

Conclusions

This chapter has examined public service union responses to restructuring and the degree to which they have been shaped by the distinctive political context of public service employment and the occupational and gender identities of their membership. The balance in terms of the type of membership (professional or less skilled), the particular focus (narrow or broad), and the organizational structure (centralized or decentralized) all play a part in determining viable union responses to these political and economic changes. Despite the wide-ranging changes in the organization and management of public services, our own evidence and the WERS data indicate that public service unions have responded in distinctive ways to the challenge of union revitalization arising from the particular context in which they operate. These responses have broader implications for union practice.

First, within all the public service unions and irrespective of their primary orientation, there has been a broadening of the union agenda. This incorporates a workplace component in terms of addressing membership concerns about their own professional development and aspects of the working environment such as stress, bullying and violence. There is also a national component as unions engage more actively in trying to shape and influence national Labour government policy through campaigning and related activity. This latter development is underpinned by far-reaching changes in the relationship between the Labour Party and the public service unions as a more distant relationship between the two parts of the Labour movement has developed (Undy 2002; Waddington 2003b). The emergence of the so-called 'awkward squad' of left-wing union General Secretaries that were elected on an explicitly anti 'New Labour' platform exemplifies this shift in trade union orientation and has placed further strains on government–union relations.

There is sufficient common ground amongst the diverse strands of union opinion on issues such as Foundation hospitals to enable UNISON, GMB and the TGWU to campaign against the government's proposals. It remains to be seen whether these very public campaigns against government policy reflect member frustration at union weakness at the workplace, alongside an implicit recognition that private lobbying has failed, or signify the emergence of a new period of mobilization amongst union members. For UK trade unions that have traditionally relied on workplace organization and the involvement of lay activists, the public service unions provide pointers in terms of distinctive forms of organization, representation and campaigning.

This contrasts with the dominant model for union revitalization that focuses on building workplace organization, despite uneven results associated with the organizing model (see Kelly and Badigannavar, Moore and Perrons, this volume). As discussed earlier, the degree to which an organizing model or models is appropriate for a public service context requires further investigation and analysis. Within our own research union officers frequently attested to the difficulties of building vibrant workplace organization within public service organizations that are subject to continuous reorganization and in which union members are confronted with severe work pressures. By developing a broader based agenda, grounded in some of the professional concerns of members, e.g. UNISON's 'duty of care handbook' (UNISON 2003), possibilities exist to develop an agenda that is viewed as more relevant to member concerns.

Finally, this chapter has highlighted the need for researchers to be more engaged with issues of union governance. The responses of individual public service unions to the modernization agenda have been influenced by inter-union competition, changing membership constituencies, and the permeability of union structures to lay activist influence. The multi-union environment of the public services continues to be associated with union rivalry, as has been only too visible in the recent past. Nonetheless, as the boundaries of the public services continue to evolve and unions merge and/or open up their membership to wider constituencies, an increasingly important issue is the degree of intra-organizational conflict within individual trade unions and how these processes are accommodated within public service unions.

Notes

1   The authors acknowledge the Department of Trade and Industry, the Economic and Social Research Council, the Advisory, Conciliation and Arbitration Service and the Policy Studies Institute as the originators of the 1990 Workplace Industrial Relations Survey and the 1998 Workplace Employee Relations Survey data, and the Data Archive at the University of Essex as the distributor of the data. None of these organizations bears any responsibility for the authors' analysis and interpretations of the data.

2   These density statistics cover only those workplaces with a recognized union. Overall union density in the public sector stood at 57 per cent in 1998, and has subsequently risen slightly (Millward *et al.* 2000: 94).

3   An important exception to this consensus is the non-TUC affiliated PAT. The General Secretary explained that it is a cardinal rule of the PAT that members do not take industrial action because, she argued, it would harm the interests of children that the organization is there to serve, rather than impacting on the managers whose behaviour the industrial action is aiming to alter.

4   The TUC is now heavily promoting workplace learning representatives, who now have statutory rights in the UK. Early evidence shows that some union members who are not interested in becoming stewards are attracted to the role and responsibilities of the learning rep. While the presence of a learning rep in the workplace clearly increases union visibility, it does not fulfil the same function as having a steward in a workplace.

Chapter 7

Labour–management partnership in the UK public sector

Vidu Badigannavar and John Kelly

Introduction

> There has been a sea-change in our employee relations ... many unions
> are changing too. They are looking to form partnerships with employers
> to foster productivity and competitiveness. They are willing to engage
> with us because many of them have seen the sterility of old confronta-
> tional ways ...
>
> (Geoff Armstrong, Director General of the Chartered Institute of
> Personnel and Development (CIPD), cited in TUC 1998: 12)

These remarks seem to indicate that unions who adopt a traditional adversarial
approach to industrial relations are not representing the best interests of
their members. Advocates of social partnership claim that it would provide
mutual benefits to the parties of such agreements: for workers, there would
be greater employment security, involvement in workplace decisions and
better working conditions. For trade unions, there would be greater influence
over business decisions and for the employer there would be higher productivity (Guest and Peccei 1998; IPA 1997). These different outcomes are
supposed to be linked through the partnership agreement in which the union
exchanges acceptance of labour flexibilities for improvements in employment
security, training, pay and working conditions as well as greater influence
over workplace decisions. Thus in the context of declining union power,
partnership has been defended by some advocates as a means of regaining
power (Ackers and Payne 1998; Deery *et al.* 1999). One would expect that,
by virtue of partnership, if unions can deliver better terms and conditions for
workers, that would make it relatively easier for them to attract new members
and organize existing ones. Better union organization is in turn likely to
increase union power resources and to augment both direct worker influence
over workplace decisions and indirect influence over policy decisions. The
higher union profile and better workplace influence and employment conditions enjoyed by workers under partnership arrangements are likely to

improve their perceptions of union effectiveness as compared to workers in non-partnership organizations, especially where unions continue to have an adversarial approach to industrial relations.

Although there is growing interest amongst academics and practitioners in labour–management partnership, there is little unanimity about its precise meaning and implications (Bacon and Storey 2000; Cohen-Rosenthal and Burton 1987; Guest and Peccei 2001; Hudson *et al.* 2001; Kelly 2004; Oxenbridge and Brown 2002; Stuart and Martinez Lucio 2004). According to the Trades Union Congress for instance, partnership embraces six principles: focus on the quality of working life, employer commitment to employment security, transparency in the management of the enterprise, recognition of legitimate differences of interests, shared commitment to the success of the enterprise and mutual gains. Likewise the British Involvement and Participation Association (IPA), employer bodies such as the CBI and CIPD and the Department of Trade and Industry (DTI), have their own interpretations of partnership, which overlap to an extent. For the purposes of this chapter we have used the TUC's six principles of partnership as our analytical framework.

Many of the well-known partnership agreements have been signed in private sector organizations, such as Blue Circle Cement or Hyder. In recent years however there has been growing interest in labour–management partnership within the public sector and it is this development which provides the focus of the current chapter. The broader context of public sector partnership is the reform of public services which has become a major subject of political debate in Britain and is central to Labour's domestic policy agenda. In a recent publication Alan Milburn, then Health Secretary, stated:

> Public service reform is the key battleground for this decade ... with the investments going in, the challenge now is to prove that collective public service provision can deliver for the individual. If we fail to do so it will reinforce the Right's argument that public service provision can never deliver – no matter what the level of investment, no matter how much we try to reform ...
>
> (Milburn 2003)

Much of the new investment, however, particularly in hospital construction, is being provided by the private sector through the Private Finance Initiative (PFI) and through Public Private Partnerships (PPP) as part of Labour's approach to privatization (see Bach and Givan, this volume). Another key element in Labour's approach is the decentralization of management control and collective bargaining to the level of the individual NHS Trust. Union leaders such as Dave Prentis of UNISON have expressed their concern about the implications of decentralized bargaining in NHS Trusts for members' pay and conditions and for union organization and influence (Prentis 2003;

and see also Bach and Winchester 2003). The government however, has urged unions to engage in partnership with management to improve the working lives of their members and deliver better quality public services. For instance, in September 1998, the Minister of State for Health launched the 'Working Together' initiative, the first human resource management framework covering the NHS as a whole. This framework emphasizes social partnership conceptualized as: staff involvement in decision-making, good staff management practices and a positive industrial relations climate. The latter is understood as union engagement as partners with management in implementing major reforms in the health services, especially around different forms of flexibility (Department of Health 1999, 2000).

Partnership has also made an appearance in the Civil Service, evident for example in the agreement signed with unions in the Cabinet Office in March 2000. Within the legal system, the Magisterial Courts Committees (MCCs) underwent major restructuring in the late 1990s with some 100 Committees across England merged into 42, resulting in major changes in staffing levels, job evaluations, gradings and terms and conditions. There could be further mergers within this sector by 2005 when the MCCs may well be merged with other branches of the Civil Service. Historically, the negotiations over pay and conditions in this sector have occurred at the national level. However, in the wake of major restructuring, the unions found these negotiations increasingly inadequate in scope to represent the interests of their membership. The Association of Magisterial Officers (AMO), which is the largest union representing workers in this sector, embarked on an organizing and recruitment drive at local level. Using the Employment Relations Act (1999) it pursued recognition for consultation and negotiation over restructuring with local MCCs and in 1999 signed its first partnership agreement with the MCC in the West Midlands.

Given that partnership has the strong support of the Labour government as part of its reform of the public sector (Undy 1999), the purpose of this chapter is to examine the outcomes of partnership in public sector organizations. In particular we concentrate on the outcomes for unions and employees and through comparing matched partnership and non-partnership organizations we aim to try and establish precisely what difference partnership makes.

Methods: settings, procedures and questions

The outcomes of social partnership were studied using a quasi-experimental matched-pairs design. Data was collected from two matched pairs of NHS Trusts and two matched pairs of Magisterial Courts Committees. The organizations were selected using a purposive sampling method because of the superior quality of the match they provided. For instance, both the NHS Trusts are ambulance Trusts, both have the same Chief Executive Officer and some members of the executive council, both have the same union recognized for collective bargaining (UNISON), and both are based in the same geographical location: Yorkshire. The only major difference is that one of the NHS Trusts has a partnership arrangement with UNISON while the other has a traditional collective bargaining arrangement. Likewise, the two MCCs provide the same service, employ similar numbers of workers (about 600 each), have the same union recognized for collective bargaining (AMO), and are based in large conurbations (one in the West Midlands, the other in Manchester). Here again the only major difference is that the MCC in the West Midlands has a partnership agreement with AMO while the Manchester MCC has a traditional bargaining arrangement. It is worth noting that the two NHS Trusts were recommended by the Department of Health as a good match for this study and the two MCCs were recommended by officers of AMO. The partnership agreements in both the NHS and MCC organizations were signed in 1999.

Data were collected using anonymous employee questionnaires in all four organizations. This involved a survey of all 3,200 workers employed in the two NHS Trusts and 1,200 workers in the two MCCs. We received 790 usable completed questionnaires from the two NHS Trusts giving us a response rate of 25 per cent. We received 401 completed questionnaires from the partnership NHS Trust and 389 from the non-partnership Trust. A total of 292 completed questionnaires were returned from the two MCCs giving us a response rate of 24 per cent. The response rate in the MCCs was, however, skewed in favour of the non-partnership MCC with 210 completed questionnaires as compared to 82 from the partnership MCC. In all four NHS and MCC organizations, the respondents were representative of the overall workforce on the demographic indicators of gender, occupation, trade union membership status, and employment tenure. We also conducted 13 interviews with union representatives and managers in the case study organizations to supplement our analysis of the survey data.

In designing the questionnaire, we operationalized the TUC's six principles of partnership into specific human resource management (HRM) practices and their outcomes, an approach similar to that adopted by Guest and Peccei (1998). This has inevitably resulted in some overlap of employee relations outcomes but that seems unavoidable given the vagueness of some of the principles involved. We used the TUC's six principles to analyse our data because the two partnership organizations adopted these principles to formulate their recognition agreements particularly so in the case of the partnership MCC where the recognition agreement specifically uses the TUC's six principles. For instance, the MCC agreement states that, 'the partnership will operate at all levels of the organization'. Employees are expected to have an influence over workplace decision-making that would result in an 'efficient, equitable, timely, high quality and visibly fair system of summary justice'. The partnership agreement also states that the union and management 'are committed to working in partnership with mutual trust and respect ...

for partnership to succeed each partner will respect legitimate differences [of interest]'. On employment security, the agreement states,

> The partners are committed to working together to maximize security of employment. The parties will attempt to avoid the need for redundancies by ongoing sharing of information and by advance joint discussion and planning ... every avenue will be used to avoid compulsory redundancies ... redundancy terms will be the best affordable, as defined by negotiation and agreement between the partners.

In the partnership NHS Trust, the union has signed a new procedural agreement (in addition to the existing recognition agreement) which provides for consultation and negotiation arrangements over a range of issues such as pay and conditions, Trust-wide policies and procedures, workforce and business planning and 'strategic human resource issues'. Here too the union recognition agreement states that the union and management side will work together to maintain a high quality of professional service and meet the targets set for the NHS Trust. It further states that the unions and the Trust 'will work to promote financial success of the Trust, recognizing that this is the best means of ensuring security of employment for all employees'. Another objective of the agreement is 'to promote mutual trust and cooperation between the Trust, employees and the unions'. Thus overall, the principles defined in the union–management agreements in the two partnership organizations closely match the TUC's six partnership principles.

Focus on the quality of working life

'Partnership should broaden the scope of employment and organizational issues tackled by unions and employers. It should lead to improvements to terms and conditions and more opportunities for employees to participate in decisions about their work.'

This principle could be operationalized into the HRM practices of direct worker involvement and influence on workplace level decisions and representational worker influence on a range of issues.

Commitment to employment security

'Many employers embrace partnership as a way of increasing flexibility in the workplace. Good partnerships complement flexibility with action to improve employment security in the workplace.'

This principle is quite straightforward and can be interpreted as provision of employment security and of HRM practices such as access to generic training to enhance employability.[1]

Transparency

'With successful partnerships, managers share information with unions about the business at an early stage, and conduct meaningful consultations with unions and staff.'

This can be operationalized as employees and their representatives having access to adequate information on key issues that affect terms and conditions of employment. Adequate information means sufficient to enable workers and their representatives to contribute meaningfully towards decisions on those issues.

Recognizing legitimate interests

'Genuine partnerships recognize that unions and employers will have differences in interests and views. There should be arrangements to resolve those differences in an atmosphere of trust.'

One would expect that if provisions for employment security and information sharing are in place they would generate a high level of trust amongst employees and their representatives towards management (Cully *et al.* 1999: 178), and a more positive perception of the overall climate of employee–management relations.

Commitment to success of the enterprise

'Effective partnerships are ones where unions and employers have a shared understanding of the organization's business strategy and a joint commitment to its success.'

This could be operationalized as employee support for organizational change initiatives and employee identification with the values of the organization.

Win–win or mutual gains

'The hallmark of an effective partnership is whether it delivers concrete improvements to business performance, terms and conditions, and employee involvement. Partnership is about mutual gains for unions and employers.'

We could operationalize this principle in terms of two outcomes for employees: first, their influence on workplace level decisions and the influence of workplace representatives on collective issues such as wages and conditions; and second, pay outcomes. From management's perspective we could explore the extent to which the organization has been able to implement various forms of flexibility to improve productivity.

Results

Direct worker influence on workplace decisions

How much involvement and influence do workers in partnership organizations have over workplace level decisions and how does it compare with workers from matched non-partnership organizations?

Table 7.1 shows there are few differences in perceived influence between the partnership and non-partnership NHS Trusts, apart from the issue of working hours. More employees in the non-partnership trust believed they exerted influence over this issue. Workers from the two NHS Trusts were then asked to give a scaled response ranging from 'strongly agree' to 'strongly disagree' to the following statement: 'Management values and encourages my suggestions for improvements in work-related matters.' Twenty-eight per cent of respondents from the partnership NHS Trust either 'strongly agreed' or 'agreed' with this statement and the corresponding figure for the non-partnership NHS Trust was 25 per cent. In other words there was no significant difference in the level of involvement of workers through suggestions for improvements in the two Trusts. Although there is a great emphasis on staff involvement in the delivery of services in the NHS (Department of Health 2000), the data revealed an acute sense of frustration amongst workers in the partnership Trust. This was evident for instance in the following employee comment:

> Union reps look after themselves first and everyone else can go to hell in my experience. Management feed you nothing but bullshit … They do not like you to think for yourself and often tell you 'you are not here to think'.

Data in Table 7.2 show a rather contrasting picture of worker involvement in the MCCs as compared to the NHS Trusts. Workers in the partnership

Table 7.1 Comparing direct worker involvement and influence in partnership ($N = 401$) and non-partnership ($N = 389$) NHS Trusts (%)

	Partnership		Non-partnership	
	Lot/Some	*Little/None*	*Lot/Some*	*Little/None*
Deciding how to do your job and organize work	59	41	60	40
Setting working hours	28	72	37	63[a]
Setting overtime	39	61	40	60
Setting time off	45	55	48	52
Deciding your pace of work	51	49	53	47

Note
a $p < 0.05$

MCC had significantly more influence over deciding how to do their job and regulate working time as compared to their counterparts from the non-partnership MCC. They were also more inclined to believe they could exert influence through the organization's suggestion scheme. In response to a statement 'Management encourages and values my suggestions for improvements on work-related matters', 61 per cent of employees in the partnership MCC strongly agreed or agreed whilst the corresponding figure for the non-partnership MCC was 46 per cent ($p<0.05$).

What could explain the differential impact of partnership on direct worker influence in the NHS and the MCC organizations? It could be argued for instance that direct worker influence over workplace decisions is likely to be higher in an organization where the union is better organized. Tables 7.3 and 7.4 present data on the outcomes of union activity in the two matched pairs of organizations.

Table 7.2 Comparing direct worker involvement and influence in partnership ($N = 82$) and non-partnership ($N = 210$) magistrates' courts (%)

	Partnership		Non-partnership	
	Lot/Some	Little/None	Lot/Some	Little/None
Deciding how to do your job and organize work	89	11	78	22[a]
Setting working hours incl. breaks	61	39	44	56[b]
Setting overtime	27	73	20	80
Setting time off	64	36	56	44
Setting pace of work	78	22	72	28

Notes
a $p<0.01$; b $p<0.05$

Table 7.3 Union outcomes in the two NHS Trusts (% of employees)

	Partnership		Non-partnership	
	Agree	Disagree	Agree	Disagree
The union rep encourages and facilitates my involvement in decisions affecting employees at this workplace	47	53	37	63[a]
The union has effectively voiced key concerns of employees at this workplace	62	38	50	50[a]
The union has made me better informed about the concerns of colleagues at this workplace	50	50	38	62[a]
The union has made me better aware of the key issues affecting employees in other workplaces/working on other shifts	42	58	31	69[a]

Note
a $p<0.05$

Table 7.4 Union outcomes in the two MCCs (% of employees)

	Partnership		Non-partnership	
	Agree	Disagree	Agree	Disagree
The union rep encourages and facilitates my involvement in decisions affecting employees at this workplace	55	45	70	30[a]
The union has effectively voiced key concerns of employees at this workplace	62	38	83	17[b]
The union has made me better informed about the concerns of colleagues at this workplace	46	54	77	23[b]
The union has made me more aware of the key issues affecting employees in other workplaces/working on other shifts	44	56	76	24[b]

Notes
a $p < 0.05$; b $p < 0.01$

The data from Table 7.3 suggest that workers in the partnership NHS Trust rated their union as more effective in encouraging worker participation in decision making, voicing key concerns of workers at their workplace, and sharing information within and between workplaces as compared to their counterparts in the non-partnership Trust. Despite these facts, 74 per cent of workers in the partnership NHS Trust reported they were dissatisfied with the overall influence they had on workplace decisions compared to just 31 per cent in the non-partnership Trust ($p < 0.05$). On the other hand, data from Table 7.4 suggest that the union is significantly better organized in the *non-partnership* MCC as compared to the partnership MCC. Despite these findings, fewer non-partnership MCC employees were satisfied with the level of influence they had on workplace decisions – 47 per cent as compared to 57 per cent under partnership. It may be that the link between worker influence and workplace union organization is complex and affected by a number of intervening variables. The extent of worker influence may depend, for example, on whether direct worker participation is a priority for the unions and management within the partnership framework. Another explanation could be the uncontrolled effect of prior union density in the partnership organizations, particularly in the partnership NHS Trust. The union there had achieved 95 per cent density prior to the signing of the partnership agreement but over the four subsequent years this declined to about 70 per cent, primarily due to outsourcing and redundancies. Higher union density prior to partnership may have been associated with better union organization which continued to some extent in the post-partnership period despite membership loss. However, pre-partnership union density doesn't seem to provide a credible explanation for outcomes in the MCCs. The partnership

MCC was never as well organized as the non-partnership MCC and yet a larger proportion of workers was satisfied with the overall influence they had over workplace decisions as compared to their non-partnership counterparts.

Representative participation

We examined the effectiveness of representative participation in partnership and non-partnership organizations by analysing the perceptions of workers on a range of issues.

It is commonly argued that partnership entails mutual gains for unions and management which, from the union's point of view, could be construed as more influence on terms and conditions. With regards to employment security, it is argued that partnership arrangements cannot guarantee job security, but unions would have significantly greater influence over the management of redundancies, e.g. ensuring redundancies are voluntary and negotiating a better redundancy package. Employee data reported in Table 7.5 suggest that there is no significant difference in perceived union effectiveness between the two NHS Trusts on pay increases, protection against unfair treatment, promoting employment security or managing redundancy. Only on one measure – sharing information about employer and workplace – does the partnership union fare better than its non-partnership rival.

Table 7.5 Perceived effectiveness of union representation amongst workers in two NHS Trusts (% of employees)

	Partnership (N = 401)		Non-partnership (N = 389)	
	Effective	*Ineffective*	*Effective*	*Ineffective*
Winning fair pay increases	58	42	61	39
Protecting workers against unfair treatment	80	20	77	23
Promoting employment security	73	27	70	30
Promoting retraining and redeployment wherever possible in cases of redundancies	66	34	60	40
Ensuring any redundancies are voluntary	71	29	72	28
Negotiating a fair redundancy package	68	32	70	30
Sharing information about employer and workplace	66	34	54	46[a]
Promoting equal opportunities	81	19	75	25
Working with management to improve quality and productivity	60	40	56	44

Note
a $p < 0.05$

There was a similar picture in the MCCs (see Table 7.6). Only on three items – information sharing, employment security and unfair treatment – was there a significant difference between the two MCCs and in these cases it was the non-partnership organization that fared better. Thus on the whole, partnership arrangements do not seem to deliver a better quality of representative participation to workers on key employment issues, as compared to traditional collective bargaining arrangements.

Provision of employment security

Eighty-five per cent of workers in partnership and non-partnership NHS Trusts reported their sense of employment security to be either 'high' or 'moderate' while only 15 per cent of workers in both NHS Trusts reported their sense of employment security to be 'low'. Overall employment security in the NHS is quite high with acute staff shortages faced by many Trusts across the UK. In Spring 2003 the Health Minister estimated another 80,000 medical and non-medical staff would be needed to meet the government's target on waiting lists by 2008 (Carvel *et al.* 2002). Although employment security was higher in the non-partnership MCC – 58 per cent compared to 49 per cent reported their employment security to be 'high' – the difference was not significant. This is not surprising as both MCCs had been subjected to mergers and restructuring over the three years prior to our survey as part of a national restructuring programme which is expected to continue until 2005.

Table 7.6 Perceived effectiveness of union representation amongst workers in two MCCs (% of employees)

	Partnership (N = 82)		Non-partnership (N = 210)	
	Effective	*Ineffective*	*Effective*	*Ineffective*
Winning fair pay increases	65	35	72	28
Protecting workers against unfair treatment	65	35	78	22[a]
Promoting employment security	44	56	59	41[a]
Promoting retraining and redeployment wherever possible in cases of redundancies	56	44	53	47
Ensuring redundancies if any are voluntary	50	50	57	43
Negotiating a fair redundancy package	64	36	63	37
Sharing information about employer and workplace	60	40	76	24[b]
Promoting equal opportunities	53	47	61	39
Working with management to improve quality and productivity	39	61	44	56

Notes
a $p < 0.05$; b $p < 0.01$

It is sometimes argued that partnership may not promote employment security in current employment but can enhance the overall employability of workers through the provision of generic training as against job specific training. Generic training is likely to help workers secure alternative employment either within the same organization or outside if they were to lose their current jobs. We found no significant difference in access to generic training for workers in the partnership and non-partnership NHS Trusts. Thirty-one per cent of workers in the partnership Trust reported having access to generic training as against 28 per cent of workers in the non-partnership Trust. In the MCCs, however, the difference was significant and striking. Sixty-three per cent of workers in the partnership MCC reported having access to generic training, almost twice the level of 37 per cent found in the non-partnership MCC ($p < 0.001$). This finding probably reflects the fact that AMO negotiates training budgets and priorities in the partnership MCC while training is not even on the bargaining agenda for UNISON at the partnership NHS Trust.

Information sharing and consultation

There is agreement amongst both advocates and critics of partnership arrangements that 'transparency' or information sharing either directly with workers or through their representatives is an important element of a meaningful partnership. Transparency on the part of management is likely to elicit higher levels of trust and commitment amongst workers towards their organization. But information sharing by itself is unlikely to be of much relevance if it is not linked with employee participation in decision-making (hence the category 'information sharing and consultation'). What is being shared and for what purposes should matter a great deal in terms of winning employee trust and commitment. It could be argued that employees would value information on issues that were salient and which then allowed them to exert some influence.

Workers were asked to give a scaled response ranging from 'strongly agree' to 'strongly disagree' to the statement, 'I get adequate information from my employer on key employment issues that would enable me to contribute meaningfully towards decisions on those issues'. There was no significant difference in the access to information enjoyed by workers in the partnership and non-partnership NHS Trusts, with 25 per cent of workers from the partnership Trust and an almost similar proportion – 24 per cent – from the non-partnership Trust agreeing with this statement. In the Magisterial Courts Committees, however, the picture was quite different. Sixty-eight per cent of workers from the partnership MCC reported having access to adequate information while only 40 per cent of workers from the non-partnership MCC reported having the same level of access to information on employment issues, a statistically significant difference ($p < 0.001$). During interviews with union officials it was reported that there was a structural difference in the communication mechanisms in the partnership and non-partnership MCCs. The former contained a Joint Consultation Committee (JCC) which preceded union recognition and which had always been used by management as its main consultation and communication channel. Its elected membership included non-union employee representatives. Post-union recognition, management retained the JCC in order to give representation to the 30 per cent of non-union employees in the MCC and the union very reluctantly agreed to this arrangement. Thus, it may be that the management's use of dual structures of communication (through the JCC and through the union) results in the dissemination of more information on key employment issues to workers in the partnership MCC. No such non-union forum exists in the non-partnership MCC.

Employee–management trust

The TUC has emphasized that partnership arrangements should be characterized by higher levels of employee trust in management. Forty per cent of employees in both partnership and non-partnership NHS Trusts agreed with the statement, 'I trust my employer to fulfil its obligations to me' (60 per cent of workers in both NHS Trusts disagreed). Fifty-five per cent of employees in the partnership MCC agreed with this statement while the corresponding figure for the non-partnership organization was 48 per cent. Thus on the whole there was no significant difference between the level of employee trust in management between the two matched pairs of NHS and MCC organizations in our study.

Organizational commitment

We also explored the levels of worker commitment towards their organization to see if workers under partnership arrangements were more committed to their organizations as compared to those without partnership. The TUC and the IPA argue that partnership arrangements foster commitment amongst workers towards their organization and one could argue that as a consequence these committed workers are more likely to be flexible in their attitudes and work practices. Thirty-six per cent of workers in the partnership NHS Trust reported that they would like to work for their organization even if they had better options elsewhere while the corresponding figure for the non-partnership Trust was very similar at 40 per cent. In the Magisterial Courts Committees too, only 33 per cent of workers in the partnership MCC were willing to work for their organization even if they had better options elsewhere as compared to 40 per cent in the non-partnership MCC. Thus in both the NHS Trusts as well as the MCCs levels of continuance commitment showed virtually no difference as a result of partnership.

Employee–management relations climate and mutual gains

Recognition of legitimate interests of the stakeholders is likely to occur in, and be aided by, a positive perception of the overall employee–management relations climate in the organization. In the NHS, only 23 per cent of workers in the partnership Trust rated their workplace employee–management relationships as 'excellent' or 'good' (77 per cent rated them as 'only fair' or 'poor'). The figures for the non-partnership NHS Trust were almost identical at 26 and 74 per cent respectively. In the MCCs however, a slightly smaller proportion of workers from the partnership organization – 33 per cent – rated their employee–management relationships to be 'excellent' or 'good' as compared to 41 per cent of workers in the non-partnership MCC but the difference was not significant. These findings are contrary to expectations about the positive impact of partnership on the climate of employment relations.

The data on mutual gains were interesting and showed significantly higher proportions of employees in partnership organizations reporting concerns about a variety of workplace issues. Sixty-three per cent of workers in the partnership NHS Trust reported working time to be a problem in their organization as compared to 43 per cent of workers in the non-partnership Trust ($p < 0.01$). A significantly larger proportion of employees in the partnership Trust (36 per cent), as compared to the non-partnership Trust (27 per cent), also reported that over the last two years their working hours had steadily increased ($p < 0.05$). Likewise, a significantly larger proportion of employees in the partnership MCC (76 per cent), as compared to workers in the non-partnership MCC (63 per cent), reported pay to be a key issue of concern for them ($p < 0.05$). The union density level in the partnership NHS Trust declined from 95 per cent in 1998 to about 70 per cent in 2002 while density in the non-partnership Trust increased from about 60 per cent to 93 per cent over the same period. The number of shop stewards at the partnership NHS Trust (25) has remained about the same over the past three years while the union at the non-partnership Trust has improved its shop steward structure from 20 workplace reps in 1999 to its current figure of 42.

Partnership and industrial relations

Interviews with the CEO and some senior managers in the partnership NHS Trust revealed that their main purpose in entering into a partnership arrangement with the union was to harmonize pay within the Trust, restructure jobs and outsource functions such as security, portering and cleaning. The Trust also wanted to hire workers on fixed-term contracts, particularly those who wanted to pursue a 'second career' after having been made redundant in their earlier jobs or having taken early retirement. These initiatives would have helped the Trust significantly to reduce its labour costs which are quite substantial in the ambulance service. It was reported that there was some history of militancy on the part of the largest union (UNISON), which the CEO referred to as 'a residue of the late 80s'. The partnership arrangement was aimed at helping the management to 'rein in the union' and speed up restructuring. The CEO was quite proud of his 'partnership achievements' of having made the union more and more irrelevant to workers in his Trust by marginalizing its influence and operating an 'open door policy' at senior and line management level to address workers' grievances. There was also some evidence to suggest that the management chose to deal with 'management-friendly' union officials at branch and workplace levels and refused to deal with 'old style' union reps whom the CEO said 'just look out for enemies'. There were pressures on the partnership NHS Trust from the Department of Health to meet performance targets and maintain strict financial controls, and organizational reforms were considered to be an important element in addressing these issues. A compliant union would have certainly helped management to speed up these changes and achieve their financial and performance targets. Interviews with managers suggested that the partnership agreement had indeed helped them to reduce their expenditures if not to achieve performance targets. A quotation from an employee in the partnership NHS Trust is quite revealing:

> As the only trade union representative that management deals with is in the management's pocket, has his own office at the headquarters, has negotiated AWAY terms and conditions, does not believe in consultation with or ballots of his members (arguing that he is in office and they are his decisions to make), does not believe in industrial action, and has already negotiated his own agreements prior to staff side meetings, I would say union intervention in this case has kept us on ever decreasing wages on increasingly worse terms and conditions of service.

Recent developments shed further light on the dynamics of partnership in the NHS Trust. In February 2003, the independent audit body of the Department of Health – the Commission for Health Improvement (CHI) – discovered that senior managers at the partnership Trust had fiddled with performance data in order to meet their clinical targets, such as emergency calls attended within a stipulated time (CHI News Release February 2003). CHI's own assessment of the Trust's performance for 2001–2 revealed that the processes and practices in place to monitor and report performance accurately were poor. Interviews with union officials also revealed that the CEO knew about these problems but chose to remain silent. CHI also found the partnership Trust seriously lacking in its staff involvement practices and gave it a rating of 1/3 (where 1 means 'below average' and 3 'above average'). The CHI report also revealed that at the time of its investigations, workers at the Trust were protesting about pay, poor working practices and shift working and the unions were considering a ballot of their members on industrial action. The partnership NHS Trust's own staff surveys, reviewed by CHI, revealed that 71 per cent of staff were dissatisfied with pay, a finding similar to our employee survey in the Trust (www.chi.nhs.uk). As a result of these developments the HR and Finance Directors have resigned and the CEO has gone on a long sick leave (Letter from the Trust, 13 June 2003 and interviews with union representatives and workers). Interestingly, the non-partnership Trust received a rating of 2 (average performance) in meeting staff involvement targets. These independent assessments by CHI support our own findings from the two NHS Trusts.

In the partnership MCC, the union was in dispute with management in October and November 2002 over pay reforms. The management announced job regradings as a result of which a substantial proportion of employees in the organization would have suffered a pay cut over the next three years. The union balloted its members for industrial action and organized a half-day strike over this issue. Although the industrial action helped the union to renegotiate the pay arrangement, it has not resulted in substantial wage gains. Instead of a pay cut, the workers' salaries will now be frozen for the next three years until those on the lower pay points catch up. Once that has happened employees will then receive a reduced increment for a fixed period of time. Thus management in the partnership MCC has achieved cost savings. A review of union records also revealed that contracts over working time, leave and holidays, and redundancy pay were significantly better in the non-partnership MCC as compared to the partnership MCC. The union official attributed these outcomes to better union organization and density in the non-partnership MCC. The current union density in the partnership MCC is about 70 per cent while in the non-partnership MCC it is over 90 per cent. It was also reported that the union found it difficult to mobilize and recruit workers in the partnership MCC. In part this was because employees had access to an alternative structure called the Joint Consultation Committee which preceded the partnership agreement and which includes both union and non-union employee representatives. Although management agreed with the union that it would not use the JCC for negotiations over terms and conditions, the Committee does appear to provide workers with more information than would otherwise be the case. The union had some representatives elected onto the JCC 'simply to keep an eye on it' although the AMO's full-time union official reported that the JCC reps don't really see themselves as a part of the union or as representing the 'union collective'. They seldom meet prior to JCC meetings either with non-union JCC reps or with other union reps to formulate their agenda or discuss strategies. The management's strategy of holding onto the JCC and thus providing an alternative forum of employee representation may have paid off in encouraging more free-riding on the union. In our survey, 69 per cent of non-union employees in the partnership MCC reported that they don't want to join the union because they get all the benefits anyway but only 41 per cent gave this reason in the non-partnership MCC ($p < 0.05$).

Discussion and conclusions

The strengths of this research lie in its use of a matched-pairs design and a large set of employee data, features lacking in most previous empirical work on union–management partnership. However, we also recognize the limitations of the study. There are problems of generalizing from just two matched pairs of organizations in one part of the public sector. The data is cross-sectional although it may be possible to return at a later date and do some form of follow-up study. It would have been worthwhile assembling 'hard' data on performance outcomes. However, given that the Department of Health has found the partnership NHS Trust guilty of misreporting its performance outcomes, any such comparisons for the two NHS Trusts would hardly be credible. We are in the process of collecting 'hard' performance data from the two MCC organizations. Another issue is the ambiguity of the concept of labour–management partnership itself although we have tried to address it by operationalizing the concept into HRM practices and outcomes using the TUC's six principles. Future research could benefit by developing a more robust definition of partnership.[2]

We examined the outcomes of partnership arrangements for workers, unions and employers by comparing matched pairs of partnership and non-partnership organizations in the health sector and the Civil Service. Rather than recapitulate the detailed evidence we want to emphasize three general points to emerge from the research. First, taking the findings as a whole, what is striking is the small number of employee outcome variables on which the partnership organizations were superior to their non-partnership rivals. In the MCCs, access to training and information and direct job influence were better; in the NHS Trust, union activity and information dissemination were superior. Otherwise the weight of evidence showed either no differences associated with partnership or showed superior outcomes in the non-partnership organizations. Second, even within the confines of the public sector there were significant differences in partnership outcomes between the health service and the Civil Service. What was striking about the NHS data was the frequency with which we found no significant differences in employee outcomes between the two Trusts.[3] By contrast the MCC data often revealed superior outcomes in the non-partnership organization. This was true for union activity, incidence of workplace problems and trade union membership density. Third, in explaining this pattern of findings we need to go beyond the presence or absence of partnership agreements to the interests, organization and power of the key actors, unions and management. The widespread absence of partnership effects in the NHS Trust could be explained by the existence of a clear managerial policy of restructuring and reform in which management's preferred role for the union was that of a subordinate partner. Given such an employer dominant partnership arrangement it is perhaps not surprising that we found so few effects across such a wide range of employee outcomes (see Kelly 2004). In the MCC by contrast the local union in the partnership organization had never been as well organized or achieved such high density as its non-partnership rival. Some of the favourable employee outcomes in the non-partnership organization may therefore have reflected pre-existing differences in union effectiveness.

What implications do our findings have for partnership arrangements in general and in the fast growing private service sector in particular? According to some researchers, partnership is more likely to be meaningful in mature industry sectors, with established unions, high union density and buoyant product markets (e.g. Heery 2002; Kelly 2004). The NHS for instance satisfies all these criteria. The health service has been in existence for more than fifty years, has high union density (62 per cent in autumn 2001: Brook 2002: 348) and, unlike manufacturing, there is growth in employment. Between 1999 and 2001 alone 63,000 new jobs were created in the NHS (Hardwidge 2002: 40). Likewise, in local government, which includes Magisterial Courts Committees, 91,000 new jobs were created between 1999 and 2001 (ibid.: 40), and union density in this sector was 61 per cent in 2001 (Brook 2002: 348). Thus the NHS and MCCs should provide an ideal environment for partnership to prosper. However, our findings do not indicate any substantial gains for workers and unions through partnership arrangements in these two sectors.

If we were to examine the prospects of partnership in the private service sector, particularly retail, which is one of the fastest growing sectors of the economy, the situation would not look very promising. Union density in the wholesale and retail sector was just 12 per cent in autumn 2001 (Brook 2002: 348). Moreover only 13 per cent of retail sector employees surveyed in the British Worker Representation and Participation Survey (BWRPS) reported that their employer was in favour of trade unions compared to 64 per cent in the public administration and Civil Service and 55 per cent in the health sector. According to Gall (2001) the finance sector contains the highest concentration of partnership agreements in Britain. However in 2001, union density in the sector was just 27 per cent (Brook 2002: 348) and just one in four finance sector employees surveyed in the BWRPS reported that their management was in favour of unions (calculated from data in Diamond and Freeman 2001). With poor union organization and unwillingness on the part of most employers in these sectors to accept unions, it is unlikely that partnership arrangements would deliver substantial gains to workers and unions. For instance, the management of ASDA doesn't bargain with GMB over pay and conditions although the company has signed a partnership agreement with the union (Taylor and Ramsay 1998). In HSBC bank, for instance, the management has signed a partnership agreement (which in fact is a re-recognition after the union was derecognized in 1996) with UNIFI. However, the agreement clearly states that the bank would only 'consider' issues raised by the union and not negotiate or even consult on them (HSBC bank and UNIFI recognition agreement 2001: 2). In a recent evaluation of partnership projects funded by the DTI it was found that many of the reported 'bottom line improvements' by managers in partnership organizations were achieved in the context of difficult changes for employees including job losses and other forms of flexibility. Moreover, the authors found no evidence of the emergence of formal employment security agreements or any significant improvements in pay and conditions reflecting improved company performance (Terry and Smith 2003: 75). In fact the report states: 'the possibility that partnership may be seen as operating "one-way" was identified as a possible source of instability' (ibid.: xii).

On the whole, our findings lend little support to the 'mutual gains' assertions of partnership advocates that unions who engage in partnership with employers are likely to enjoy higher influence on workplace and policy issues resulting in better outcomes for workers or that partnership would deliver better 'voice' for workers.

Notes

1   We appreciate that there is a fundamental difference between employment security and employability. It is sometimes argued that partnership may not improve employment security but by providing access to better generic training, it may increase worker employability. This would enable them to secure alternative employment either within or outside their organizations if they were to lose their current jobs. It is precisely for this reason that we measured both variables.

2   It could be argued that partnership is simply a lay theory of industrial relations or a political phenomenon rather than a social scientific concept and hence does not warrant a robust definition. These claims are not mutually exclusive. Our view is that even a political phenomenon such as 'partnership' requires a proper definition in order to measure and draw meaningful inferences about its outcomes.

3   One straightforward explanation for the absence of significant differences in employee relations outcomes between the two NHS Trusts could be that both had the same CEO. On the other hand, both the senior and local management personnel of the two Trusts were completely different. Thus even if we were to assume that by virtue of having the same CEO, the two NHS Trusts would operate the same personnel policies (which in fact is not the case), there are likely to be differences in the way the policies are implemented.

Chapter 8

The end of the affair?
The decline in employers' propensity to unionize

*Alex Bryson, Rafael Gomez and
Paul Willman*

Introduction

This chapter examines the influence of employer decision-making and behaviour on union organization. A simple adversarial view of the employment relationship may lead us to expect that this influence would be predominantly negative; as the opponents of trade unions, employers might be expected to engage in a variety of preventative activities ranging from the aggressive – for example victimization of activists – to what Kochan (1980) termed 'substitution' – namely the provision of a work environment removing the perceived need for representation. However, until recently, UK employers' decision to recognize unions was purely voluntary (see Moore, this volume). In addition, employers provide time and facilities for trade union representatives and check-off mechanisms for trade union subscriptions which, whether conceded by bargaining pressure or not, support union activity. Employers also take other decisions on matters such as where to locate, how to deploy labour, and how much labour to deploy which, while not perhaps directly about industrial relations matters, will influence the contours of union organization. In this chapter, we focus primarily on employer decisions about trade union matters although, as we shall show, unionization is affected by compositional change among employers.

Our central contention is that employer decision-making and behaviour is crucial in determining the nature of union organization and activity. In particular we address the following three questions. First, what influences employers' choice of voice regime? Second, to what extent is the decline of union voice since the early 1980s the result of employer choices, and to what extent is it the involuntary 'fall-out' from compositional change among employers? And, finally, how can organized labour increase the probability of employers choosing union voice as opposed to non-union voice or no voice at all?

We begin in the first section by establishing the logic for this position, then go on in the second section to establish what the basis for employer choice of union might be. The third section, which is empirical, describes the pattern of employer choice; the most significant trend is the decline in union voice. The fourth section looks at the balance between compositional and choice effects in explaining this decline. The fifth section looks at the prospects for unions exerting influence over employer choice. The final section concludes by assessing the implications of employer behaviour for the future of union organization.

Determinants of union presence

The probability of union organization within an establishment may be defined in terms of the values of and relationships between the following three variables:

(a) Employee propensity to join a union
(b) Union propensity to organize a workplace
(c) Employer propensity to deal with a union.

Union organization may be generated by several combinations of employer, union and employee action. It might be the case that employees become active around a grievance or set of grievances and seek out a union to join. It may be that a union focuses organizing activity on a workplace. It may be that an employer pre-emptively recognizes a union which then recruits. These are the simplest cases and the three proximate influences on organization probably operate in complex and varied combinations in practice.

The possible combinations of (a)–(c) at any point in time are presented in dichotomized form in Figure 8.1. Their characteristics are as follows:

1   $E+, U+, M+$: there is consensus between all parties about the desirability of union organization.
2   $E+, U+, M-$: the employer sees the need for union organization and the union is willing to be recognized but there are low membership levels, perhaps because the establishment is a greenfield site.
3   $E+, U-, M+$: the employer wishes to have union organization and the membership levels are high but the union does not regard the proposed bargaining unit as financially viable.
4   $E+, U-, M-$: only the employer is enthusiastic. A typical case might be where the employer proposes a redundancy and wishes to have a union co-operate to ensure its legality. However, the union does not wish to be drawn in and employees do not see the union as offering job security or other benefits.
5   $E-, U+, M+$: the union has high membership levels and is pursuing recognition from a recalcitrant employer, for example by using the recognition provisions of the ERA.

Employer propensity to accept unionization [E]	Union propensity to organize workplace [U]	Employee propensity to join union [M]	Likely voice regime outcome
High [+]	High [+]	High [+]	Union voice
		Low [−]	Union voice
	Low [−]	High [+]	Union voice
		Low [−]	Non-union voice[a]
Low [−]	High [+]	High [+]	Union voice[a]
		Low [−]	Non-union voice
	Low [−]	High [+]	Non-union voice
		Low [−]	Non-union voice

Figure 8.1 Likelihood of union or non-union voice based on cross-classification of employer, union and worker preferences

Note
a Unstable voice regime outcome

6    $E-$, $U-$, $M+$: there are high membership levels but the employer and union are unenthusiastic. It may be that the union regards the probability of continued employer recalcitrance as high and the proposed bargaining unit as unviable on those grounds (Willman 2001).

This is a static view, and dynamics are dealt with below. All combinations are logically possible; arguably, none is empirically unlikely although it is difficult to estimate relative frequencies.

The pattern thus broadly dichotomizes on employer preference except in the two sets highlighted:

1    $E-$, $U+$, $M+$: where the recalcitrant employer is pressured for union organization by both union and employees.
2    $E+$, $U-$, $M-$: where the employer would like to recognize a union but can find neither a willing union nor employees who will join.

Employer preferences may be overridden in both cases. In the first, pressure, often supported by statute, overcomes employer opposition. In the second, apathy leads to a choice of non-union voice or, where the benefits of voice are outweighed by the costs of its provision (Millward *et al.* 2000), no voice at all. No voice may occur where there is a combination of high labour turnover and abundant labour supply, as in some call centres.

In summary, employer preference for a particular voice regime is likely to be a prime factor in its emergence. Employer preferences may change, but we will argue below that there are costs in switching voice regimes once chosen, resulting in 'persistence' or 'stickiness'. Why, then, would the employer want a union organization?

Theory

Freeman and Medoff (1984) identified voice as one outcome of trade union activity beneficial for the firm. Although innovative in the study of employment regimes, the formulation is essentially that of Hirschman (1970), introduced in the analysis of consumer organizations. In both formulations, the benefits of voice are contingent. For Hirschman, consumers may collectively voice concerns, for example when product quality declines, if the costs of collective action are less than the costs of replacing the product with a substitute. In this case, voice will benefit the firm through the improvement of product quality. For Freeman and Medoff (1984), voice is one of two faces of union activity (the other being monopoly wage bargaining), and the beneficial effect of voice depends on its returns exceeding the costs of the monopoly wage activities of unions. These benefits include reduction in employee turnover and skill loss, information about production or service delivery improvements and feedback on employee attitudes and motivation.

Two questions arise. First, when would employers want voice? Second, if an employer wants voice, what would lead to the choice of a union-based voice mechanism? Although Freeman and Medoff identify voice with union activity, there are non-union routes to achieving the same firm benefits. We look at each question in turn.

Why do firms want voice?

The reasons why firms might remain voice-free primarily concern exit and governance costs but there are also considerations relating to wage costs. Returning to Hirschman's original formulation, consumers who experience some fall in product or service quality will act collectively to form consumer groups where their exit costs – i.e. their costs in switching to another product – exceed the costs of collective action. Producers (firms) will encourage such groupings to reverse quality falls where they in turn experience losses through consumer exit greater than the costs of consumer voice. These considerations generate two uncontested cases: where exit costs are greater than voice costs for both parties, voice mechanisms will emerge and where the reverse is true, they will not. Where the relationships between exit and voice costs differ for the two parties, outcomes are indeterminate. Where the firm wants voice, but the consumer does not, the firm may lower the costs of collective action for the consumer. Where the consumer wants voice but the firm does not, voice is least likely to emerge. We would argue parallel considerations obtain where the relationship is between employer and employee.

Any voice mechanism generates costs of provision. These may, following Williamson (1991), be considered as transaction governance costs which will tend to rise with the specificity of the assets engaged in the transaction. In the employment relationship, high asset specificity tends to come from specific on-the-job training and other firm-specific investments that bind firms and employees together. Other things being equal, parties with high exit costs will endure higher governance costs. However, governance costs may not vary simply with exit costs. There may be forms of transaction where the governance costs are too high to permit voice. A firm may choose to have no voice mechanisms, even where asset specificity is high, if governance costs exceed exit costs. This might emerge where small firms are engaged in complicated transactions.

Another set of considerations applies primarily to the employment relationship. In Freeman and Medoff's model, the benefits of union voice can more than outweigh the wage costs arising from unions' wage bargaining. This might appear to make unionized voice less attractive than non-union voice unless the latter involves higher wages paid to keep unions out (Flood and Toner 1997). There may, in addition, be temporal variations, with voice mechanisms emerging to deal with major internal or external shocks but disappearing when such shocks have passed. So, for example, lay-offs or major process reorganization might justify expenditure on temporary voice, but the collective organization so created may disappear in time.

In summary, then, we reason as follows. First, voice emerges under specific conditions which, while widespread, are not universal. Second, voice is most likely where net benefits emerge for both parties and least likely where net costs emerge for both; where there are differences, employer choice is primary. Third, there are likely to be scale effects, with voice a more affordable benefit when spread over a large number of transactions. Fourth, there is likely to be volatility, with firms opting for temporary voice measures in difficult conditions.

Why would firms want union voice?

The second step in this analysis involves the employer decision about what one might term the voice regime, i.e. once a firm has decided it needs voice, it makes a choice about voice mechanisms. This is parallel to the make or buy decision analysed by institutional economists. A particular dimension of this decision is the use of the union as agent or supplier of voice regimes. We argue that there are circumstances in which the employer may, on grounds of cost or risk, seek to sub-contract aspects of the management of labour to a union and, further, that this helps explain the continued recognition of trade unions in many firms. We also explore the implications of this 'agency' model of unions for the future structure and conduct of trade union activity. There is in fact a dual form of agency here. The union may act both as the agent for members in representations to the employer and as the firm's agent in securing voice.

Transaction cost economics suggest that in exchanges characterized by asset specificity, frequency of interaction and uncertainty, choices about transaction governance structures are required and, in particular, the choice whether to make or buy, or, more accurately, own or contract. All else equal, the more idiosyncratic the investments, the greater the frequency of inter-action (and duration of exchange) and the greater the uncertainty facing the 'purchasing' party, hierarchy rather than market will be preferred (Williamson 1975, 1985, 1991). The vertical integration decision by the firm is paradig-matic. This choice of governance mechanism is made by parties operating under bounded rationality, faced with the possibility of seller opportunism,[1] and operating on a risk neutral basis.

The decision tree on which we focus is shown in Figure 8.2. The firm may seek employee voice or not. Where voice is not chosen, it may be assumed either that the employer is not concerned by employee exit, or that the costs of voice exceed those of exit. Where voice is chosen, we conceptualize the employer options within the transaction costs framework as follows:

(a) Buy (i.e. union)
This is closest to the Freeman and Medoff view of voice where the employer sub-contracts to one or more unions the responsibility for the generation of voice. This involves, in Williamson's terms, a long-term relational contract in which the employer's direct costs in the production of voice are low but the risks of supplier opportunism are high. So, the employer uses a union for voice provision but risks the attempt to extract monopoly wage gains.

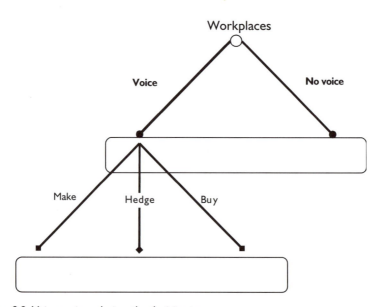

Figure 8.2 Voice regime choice: the decision tree

(b) Make (i.e. non-union)
This is akin to the 'sophisticated HRM' approach and involves employers choosing directly to provide a set of employee voice mechanisms excluding third party intervention. Direct costs are correspondingly higher and, while there is a risk that the approach may not generate the voice required – for example, because the voice lacks legitimacy in employees' eyes – there are no risks of union opportunism.

(c) Hybrid (i.e. dual channel)
Following Williamson (1991), we include a mixed option in which union and non-union voice mechanisms co-exist. This may be seen as a form of employer hedging, attempting to control both cost and risk. For simplicity, we treat this as a single option in what follows, acknowledging that a range of hybrids is possible across firms.[2]

A key assumption here is that each regime has the potential to deliver voice of the same quality. If, for example, 'employer produced' voice suffered from a systematic legitimacy problem in the eyes of employees, then one would need to introduce the idea of a cost/quality trade-off in employer decision-making. For simplicity, we avoid this complication here. We assume instead that costs C_i^j and risk θ^j vary by choice of regime j indexing the three possible forms of voice U, N, and D, which represent union, non-union and dual channel voice regimes respectively.

The key cost items are as in Figure 8.3, which depicts hypothetical firm A in three possible states. In reverse order, in case 3, the firm experiences C_i^U, having entered a long-term relational voice contract with a reliable union ($\theta^u \approx 1$). If the union becomes less able to elicit voice and/or becomes more militant, the firm may seek to move to case 1, with costs C_i^N, providing that HRM itself is a reliable alternative ($\theta^N \approx 1$); this could occur through de-recognition. Where union and non-union prospects are equally risky ($\theta^u = \theta^N \approx 0.5$) the firm may seek to 'hedge' and adopt a dual channel of union and non-union voice with costs C_i^D, as in case two. The figure also outlines the variable elements of any C_i^j. They are market wage and administrative costs, α, and we assume the former to be regime-independent and the latter regime-dependent. For both C_i^U and C_i^D, there is the possibility of a wage mark up, δ, variations in which might generate regime switching behaviour. Note that the 'pure' administrative cost of voice is highest in the make case and lowest in the 'pure' buy case. Hedging, the highest cost option, is also assumed in this illustrative example to be the lowest risk option ($\theta^u + \theta^N = 1$).

So, the answer to our original question is that employers will buy union voice where on grounds of cost, quality and risk, it is worth it. Recall that we have omitted here employee influences for the moment, although it is worth noting that there is evidence from both the UK and USA that employees are

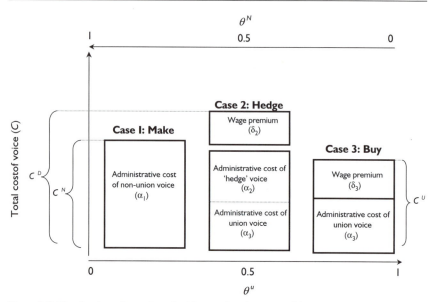

Figure 8.3 The firm's make or buy decision under three possible cases

influenced in their voice preferences by the probability that the chosen mechanism will meet with employer approval (Diamond and Freeman 2001; Freeman and Rogers 1999). In the next section, we look at the frequency with which employers make or buy different forms of voice.

What has happened to voice regimes?

In this section, we use WERS data to describe the distribution of voice regimes at two points in time, 1984 and 1998. It is striking that although the forms of voice regime chosen by employers have changed markedly across the period, the balance between those wanting a voice regime and those choosing 'no voice' workplaces has remained stable (i.e. 16 per cent and 18 per cent respectively). This fact is depicted in Figure 8.4 which is a reprise of Figure 8.2 with the respective unconditional probabilities inserted.

The characteristics of 'no voice' workplaces appear to be as follows. First, the probability of having no voice rises as workplace size falls. Second, foreign ownership increases the probability of 'no voice'. Third, single, independent and more recently established workplaces have a higher probability of 'no voice' (see Willman *et al.* 2004). The high tide of workplace-level union recognition in Britain was the 1950s (Millward *et al.* 2000: 101–2). Data available since 1984 show a steep decline in union-only voice arrangements, and a less marked decline in 'dual-channel' voice involving union and non-union channels in combination. These two changes were offset by a steep increase in voice arrangements that did not involve unions.

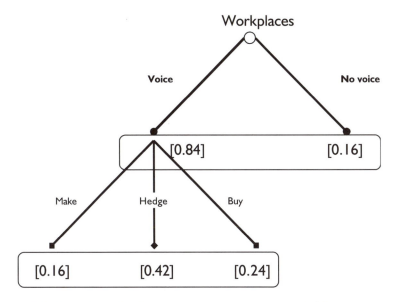

Figure 8.4a Unconditional probabilities of voice regime choice in 1984
Note: it was not possible to determine the precise nature of voice in 2% of cases

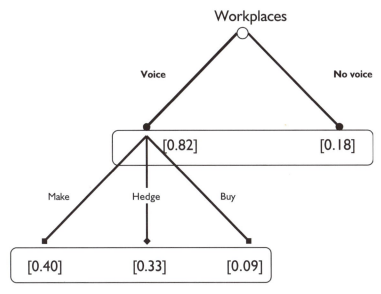

Figure 8.4b Unconditional probabilities of voice regime choice in 1998
Sources: WERS 1984 and 1998

In fact, the majority of unionized workplaces have had combined union and non-union voice since the early 1980s (see Table 8.1). Dual channel voice predominated in 1984 even among those workplaces set up in the 1950s, suggesting that it may have been the dominant regime for some time. However, the adoption of non-union voice by unionized workplaces became increasingly common in the 1980s and 1990s so that, by 1998, four-fifths were dual channel.

Something has made union organization, particularly union-only voice, much less attractive to employers in Britain over this period. On the surface, an interesting paradox emerges. In Britain (and the United States), there is evidence that the union wage premium has fallen (Blanchflower and Bryson 2003; Hildreth 1999). Referring back to Figure 8.3, this should mean that union-based forms of voice should fall in cost, all other things being equal, relative to non-union voice. In addition, over the last two decades, the number of days lost through strikes has fallen massively (Monger 2003). Strike frequency and duration may be considered as proxies for the risk involved in union voice regimes and on this measure, the risk of union voice relative to non-union has also fallen. Yet increasingly, non-union voice has been chosen by employers. The question is, why?

One possibility is that non-union HRM has become cheaper and more reliable than buying union voice, perhaps because the capability (in the shape of a new cohort of human resource managers) is more readily available than in the past (Millward *et al.* 2000: 52–6). But another is that unions no longer provide the quality of voice employers require. The latter proposition is supported by the fact that, where union voice is selected, it is overwhelmingly as part of a dual channel arrangement. If one adds to this proposition the more concrete fact that the decline in the union wage premium might discourage potential members, the decline in preference for trade union voice

Table 8.1 Union and non-union voice arrangements in unionized workplaces, 1984–98

| | Column percentages | | |
	1984	1990	1998
Union only	35	26	21
Union and non-union	63	73	78
Voice, but nature not reported	2	1	1
Weighted base	1,327	1,053	845
Unweighted base	1,593	1,416	1,116

Source: Workplace Industrial Relations Surveys, 1984–98.

Base: all workplaces with 25 or more employees recognizing unions for pay bargaining. Union voice is defined as one or more recognized trade unions or a joint consultative committee meeting at least once a month with representatives chosen through union channels. Non-union voice defined as a joint consultative committee meeting at least once a month with representatives not chosen through union channels, regular meetings between senior management and the workforce, briefing groups, problem-solving groups or non-union employee representatives.

becomes more understandable. In fact, there has been a substantial decline in union density within the unionized sector which might lead to a lowering of the quality of union voice for both employers and employees.

Decline in workplace unionization, 1984–98: compositional change or employer choice?

This section considers the extent to which reduced employer usage of union voice is attributable to structural change among employers, and the extent to which it is the result of employer choice.

Since the early 1980s, there has been substantial change in the composition of workplaces in Britain. Table 8.2 shows this compositional change has contributed to a decline in the proportion of workplaces with union voice because traditional union strongholds, such as the public sector and workplaces belonging to larger organizations, have fallen as a percentage of the

Table 8.2 The decline in workplace unionization, 1984–98

	% establishments		Percentage point change	% unionized		Percentage point change
	1984	1998		1984	1998	
Sector						
Private Manu.	21	18	−3	55	29	−26
Private Services	43	54	+11	43	23	−20
Public	37	28	−9	97	86	−11
Size						
24–49	52	52	0	60	36	−24
50–99	25	25	0	64	38	−26
100–199	13	12	−1	76	55	−21
200–499	7	8	+1	80	63	−17
500–999	2	2	0	90	72	−18
1,000+	1	1	0	95	85	−10
Single	18	27	+9	34	19	−15
Multi-site	82	73	−9	72	50	−22
Foreign	5	9	+4	54	20	−34
Domestic	95	91	−4	66	44	−22
Set up pre-1980	94	47	−47	66	56	−10
Set up post-1980	6	53	+47	59	30	−29
% part-timers						
<10%	54	42	−12	65	34	−31
10–29%	18	18	0	61	50	−11
30%+	28	41	+13	69	46	−23
% non-manuals						
<10%	7	8	+1	79	48	−31
10–29%	27	23	−4	61	38	−23
30%+	66	69	+3	65	42	−23

Source: based on WIRS 1984–98, establishments with 25+ employees. Union voice is defined as the presence of union-only or dual channel voice as defined elsewhere in the chapter.

total. With the exception of changes in the size composition of workplaces (artificially truncated at the minimum threshold of 25 employees in the WERS series), compositional change has worked against unionization, with the least unionized raising their share of workplaces.

Take sector, for instance. The private service sector, traditionally the least unionized (as shown in columns 5 and 6 of Table 8.2), expanded at the expense of private manufacturing and public services, where unionization is much more common. But perhaps more striking is the decline in unionization rates for all types of workplace, ranging between a 10 percentage point decline among the largest workplaces and workplaces set up before 1980 through to a 34 percentage point decline among foreign-owned workplaces. Irrespective of the changing composition of workplaces, union voice would have declined anyway because every type of employer had a lower probability of choosing a union voice regime at the turn of the century than they did two decades earlier.

We can quantify the relative contributions of workplace compositional change and within-group propensities for union voice using multivariate analyses (see the Appendix for details). The analyses allow us to separate out the decline that would have occurred through within-group changes in unionization holding workplace composition fixed at 1984, and the decline that would have occurred through change in workplace composition if within-group unionization had remained as it was in 1984. Table 8.3 summarizes the findings. Between 1984 and 1998, workplace unionization rates fell 24.5 percentage points from 66.6 per cent to 42.1 per cent. Column 4 shows what the rate of unionization would have been if compositional change had occurred as it did, but holding within-group unionization constant. This procedure shows that unionization would have fallen 7.2 percentage points to 59.4 per cent by 1998. The remaining 17.3 percentage point decline of unionization between 1984 and 1998 can therefore be attributed to within-group change, that is, choices on the part of employers who, during this period, were free to choose whether they recognized unions for pay bargaining or not. Thus, 70.6 per cent of the decline in union voice is accounted for by employer choice, and only 29.4 per cent by compositional change.

Table 8.3 Contribution of change in composition and within-group change to workplace unionization, 1984–98

Year	Actual unionization rate (%)	Rate compared with 1984 (%)	Rate with compositional change only (%)	Impact of compositional change (%)	Impact of within-group change (%)
1984	66.6	–	66.6	–	–
1990	52.4	–14.2	62.7	–3.9	–10.3
1998	42.1	–24.5	59.4	–7.2	–17.3

Source: Workplace Industrial Relations Surveys, 1984–98, authors' calculations.

Running the same analysis for the private sector only, where workplace unionization fell from 48 per cent in 1984 to 25 per cent in 1998, we find only 5 percentage points of the decline is accounted for by compositional change, with the remaining 18 percentage points due to declining within-group propensities to unionize. We conclude that the decline in the use of union voice by employers, both in the economy as a whole, and in the private sector, is due largely to a lower propensity for employers to choose union voice, with under a third of the decline in the whole economy, and a fifth in the private sector, due to compositional change among employers.

What do unions have to do to persuade non-union employers to choose union voice?

In this section, we consider the influences on non-union employers' attitudes towards unionization at the end point in our data, namely 1998. The purpose is to give some insight into the way the costs and benefits of union voice are perceived by employers facing the choice of whether to engage with unions. Since union concern about engagement with employers is most acute in the private sector, emphasis is placed on analyses of that sector.

WERS 1998 asked managers whether they favoured union membership at their workplace. Perhaps not surprisingly, column 3 of Figure 8.5 shows

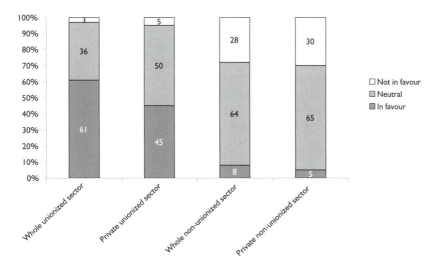

Figure 8.5 Management attitudes to union membership at their workplace in 1998
Source: WERS 1998, workplaces with 10+ employees.
Note
Managerial respondents were asked: 'How would you describe management's general attitude towards trade union membership among employees at this establishment? Is management ... in favour of trade union membership, not in favour of it, or neutral about it?'

support for union membership is low among employers in the non-unionized sector: only one-in-twelve favours membership, a figure which falls to one-in-twenty when analysis is confined to the private sector (column 4). (Columns 1 and 2 present the data for the whole unionized and private unionized sectors for comparison.) An employer may express a preference for unionization, yet not recognize a union, for one of three reasons. First, the perceived costs of unionization may outweigh the perceived benefits as we have noted above. Second, the decision to recognize may not be within the employer's gift, either because the decision must be taken by another manager in the workplace or, in establishments belonging to larger organizations, the decision is made beyond the workplace by people further up the managerial hierarchy. Third, to return to the determinants of union presence (see above), either the employees or the union do not wish to organize the workplace.

Although there is employer opposition to union membership in over one-quarter of non-unionized workplaces, around two-thirds of non-union employers declare themselves neutral on the issue, yet these same employers probably have no intention of adopting union voice. There are various reasons for this. They may have little or no experience of unions and so may not have fixed views on them. It is also possible that some employers are not prepared to divulge their true opposition (or support) for unions to the survey interviewer. A third possibility, which emerges from our model of voice choice, is that switching from one voice regime to another is not a costless exercise. Therefore even in the presence of a better alternative a manager may feel compelled to maintain the (non-union) status quo. In any event, it appears that the main obstacle to organizing the non-union sector is employer indifference to unions rather than explicit employer opposition to them.

So what can unions do to increase the percentage of non-union employers who are favourable towards unionization? The answer is presented in Figure 8.6: it identifies factors associated with changes in the probability of being 'in favour' of membership, holding other factors constant, as described in the footnotes to the figure. Management is more favourable towards membership where unions are thought to contribute positively to workplace performance[3] – in our terms, where the net benefits of unionization are high; and where union density is higher and thus, in our terms, more likely to deliver effective voice. In general, there is no association between the presence of non-union forms of voice, or HRM practices, and desire for union membership, suggesting that they are not simple substitutes for one another. There are two exceptions. First, there is lower support for unionization where employers use financial participation in the form of profit-related pay or cash bonuses. Second, other forms of employee representation (joint consultative committees and European Works Councils), rather than substituting for unionization, actually increase employer support for union membership. This may be because their experience of these other representative mechanisms has not been positive, or else relatively positive engagement

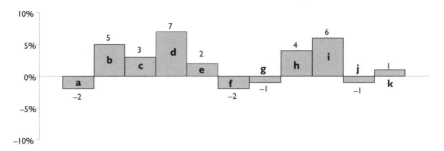

Figure 8.6 Management 'in favour' of membership in non-unionized private sector
Source: WERS 1998.
Notes
a: strongly agrees would rather consult direct with employees than with unions; b: agrees unions help find ways to improve workplace performance; c: 1–9% density (ref: 0%); d: 30%+ density (ref: 0%); e: workplace covered by formal strategic plan; f: profit-related pay; g: cash bonuses; h: functioning joint consultative committee; i: European Works Council in UK; j: newsletter; k: formal procedure for dealing with collective disputes.

Columns are marginal effects from ordered probit models for non-unionized (where no unions are recognized for pay bargaining) private sector workplaces (N = 789). The percentage differences are evaluated for a private sector non-unionized workplace with mean sample characteristics. Dependent variable is (1,3), where 1 = 'not in favour', 2 = 'neutral', 3 = 'in favour'. The marginal effects reported are the percentage change in the probability of being 'in favour' holding other factors constant at the mean for the sample. The mean probability of being in favour of membership under the model is 2 per cent. All effects reported in the figure are statistically significant at a 95 per cent confidence level or above, apart from European Works Council, newsletter, and formal procedure for dealing with collective disputes, all of which are significant at a 90 per cent confidence level.

Models also control for the following workplace variables: gender and tenure of respondent, presence of a specialist employee relations manager, employer's perception of industrial relations climate, establishment size, age, sector, region and whether single or multi-establishment organization, standard industrial code (SIC), percentage of workforce that is female, whether workplace produces goods for sale to consumers or other companies, foreign ownership, IiP (Investors in People) award, formal written policy on equal opportunities or managing diversity, grievance procedure, workplace score on an HRM index, regular meetings with senior management, team briefings, quality circles, performance-related pay, employee share options scheme, non-union representative voice, management chain, suggestion scheme or other consultation methods.

with non-union forms of employee representation has led to a desire for union involvement. Either way, it suggests non-union representation of employee interests can complement union involvement, rather than substitute for it. The formalization of personnel practices also plays a role. Formal strategic thinking on the part of the employer is associated with stronger support for union membership, as is the presence of a formal procedure for dispute resolution. In these cases, it may be that unionization is viewed by employers as a mechanism for the enforcement of good industrial relations.

If unions are to operate effectively for employers as an agent in the management of employees, employers must feel that they can 'do business' with them. Asked how much they agreed or disagreed with the statement 'We would rather consult directly with employees than with unions', 40 per cent of non-unionized private sector employers in WERS 'strongly agreed', and a further 47 per cent 'agreed'. Only 3 per cent 'strongly disagreed' or 'disagreed'.

What factors affect non-union employers' desire to consult with unions? The rarity of managers in non-unionized workplaces desiring consultation through a union means we combine employer neutrality with employer support for the union as a positive outcome for the union. The largest effect relates to the presence of a union representative on-site (see Figure 8.7). Where such a person is present, the probability that management is not averse to union consultation rises by 35 per cent. Thus, although the union has not been recognized by the employer, a union representative can substantially increase the employer's desire for consultation through a union. This, coupled with the fact that preparedness to consult through a union also rises significantly with union density, indicates that employer appraisals of whether the union could deliver effective voice, may feature prominently in their attitudes towards dealing with unions. Management's use of regular meetings with the workforce does substitute for consultation through the union, as does the use of two forms of financial participation – performance-related payments and cash bonuses.

Conclusions

It is against a backdrop of declining union recognition and a rise in non-union forms of workplace voice regime that this chapter addresses three issues fundamental to unions' future well-being. First, what influences employers' choice of voice regime? Second, to what extent is the decline of union voice since the early 1980s the result of employer choice, and to what extent is it the 'fall-out' from compositional change among employers? And, third, how can unions increase the probability of non-union employers choosing union voice?

Not surprisingly, only a very small percentage of non-unionized workplaces actively support unionization: in only one-in-twenty non-union private sector workplaces does management favour union membership, and a mere 3 per cent would rather consult with a union than directly with employees. These figures illustrate the scale of the task facing unions. However, the news is not all bad. In the first place, it is employer indifference, or neutrality, that is born of limited experience with unions and the potential costs of switching from one voice regime to another, rather than overt employer opposition, which characterizes most non-unionized employers' attitudes to unions. This fact is of substantial interest since there is *employee* evidence of an enthusiasm for forms of representation which will gain acceptance from employers and

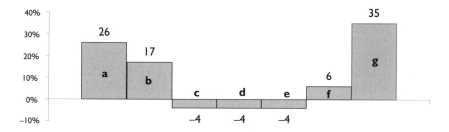

Figure 8.7 Probability that management is not averse to union consultation, non -
unionized workplaces in the private sector

Source: WERS 1998.

Notes

a: in favour of union membership (ref: neutral); b: 30%+ density (ref: 0%); c: performance-
related pay; d: cash bonuses; e: regular meetings between senior management and whole
workforce; f: formal written policy on equal opportunities or managing diversity; g: union
representative on-site.

Columns are marginal effects from logit model for non-unionized (where no unions
are recognized for pay bargaining) private sector workplaces (N=789). The percentage
differences are evaluated for a private sector non-unionized workplace with mean sample
characteristics. Dependent variable is (0,1), where 1 = 'strongly disagree/disagree' or
'neither agree nor disagree' with the statement 'we would rather consult directly with
employees than with unions'. The marginal effects reported are the percentage change in
the probability that management is not averse to union consultation holding other factors
constant at the mean for the sample. The mean probability of a positive outcome under
the model is 6 per cent. All effects reported in the figure are statistically significant at a 95
per cent confidence level or above, apart from union density and union representation at
the workplace, both of which are significant at a 90 per cent confidence level.

Models also control for the following workplace variables: gender and tenure of
respondent, presence of a specialist employee relations manager, employer's perception
of industrial relations climate, establishment size, age, sector, region, single or multi-
establishment organization, SIC, percentage of workforce that is female, production of
goods for sale to consumers or other companies, foreign ownership, award of IiP, employer
agrees unions can improve workplace performance, score on HRM index, formal strategic
plan, profit-related pay, employee share ownership scheme, functioning joint consultative
committee, European Works Council, non-union representatives, management chain,
suggestion scheme, newsletter, other consultation methods, team briefings, quality circles,
formal procedure for resolving collective disputes.

some notion of a 'representation gap', i.e. a desire for more voice mechanisms
by employees (Diamond and Freeman 2001; Gospel and Willman 2003).

Second, a small but nevertheless sizeable minority (14 per cent) of managers
in non-unionized workplaces agree that unions help improve workplace
performance.

So how can unions improve on this position and increase union organizing
capacity in the non-union sector? First, unions need to find ways to persuade
management that they can make a positive contribution to workplace
performance, since this increases the likelihood that non-unionized employers

will support union membership. Second, they should organize as many workers as possible since non-unionized employers are more supportive of the union where density is higher. Third, where they have established a union presence, unions should set up procedures and devote resources to ensure on-site union representation, since employers prefer to use unions as a consultation mechanism where an on-site representative is available. Fourth, unions must devise means of combating the negative effect that financial participation and, in some cases, direct forms of communication, have in reducing employer desire for unionization. Finally, unions should identify ways in which they can work alongside other forms of collective representation (works councils and joint consultative committees) to gain a foothold at the workplace, since non-unionized employers are more positive about unionization where other forms of collective representation are present.

The biggest obstacle to greater union influence in the unionized sector is employer indifference to unions, rather than explicit opposition, which remains quite rare. There are signs of employer disillusionment in what can be achieved through unions, since in only one-quarter of unionized workplaces do management state a preference for union consultation over direct consultation with employees. In the private sector, the figure is still lower (15 per cent). On the other hand, over four-in-ten believe unions find ways of improving workplace performance. The way for unions to improve employer support for membership is to increase these percentages, since unionized employers in the private sector are most supportive of union membership where unions help improve performance and where they are valued as a means for consulting employees. It is therefore not surprising to find unionized employers prefer strong unions to weak ones since stronger unions are better able to perform these tasks.

Appendix

Linear probability estimation of union voice

Linear probability models are a multivariate extension of the shift-share technique for assessing changing determinants of unionization. Let

$$Y_i = \beta X_i + \varepsilon_i$$

where Y_i is a 0/1 dummy variable denoting whether employer i is unionized, X_i is a vector of variables representing employer characteristics, β is a vector of coefficients and ε_i is an error term. The estimated predictions βX_i are interpreted as the probabilities that employer i is unionized. There are two drawbacks to the technique. First, the value of βX_i may be outside the range 0–1, so that it cannot be interpreted as a predicted probability. In fact, the linear probability model gives results close to the logit model which transforms the probability to avoid this problem. Running our models as logits confirms that results were indeed very similar. Following Green (1992) we chose to use the linear probability model because it is the closest multivariate analogue to the shift-share analysis. The second drawback is that the model is prone to heteroscedasticity (Kennedy 1998: 243). We employ the Huber–White robust variance estimator that produces consistent standard errors in the presence of heteroscedasticity.

There are two sets of estimates to identify the separate contributions of employer compositional change and within-group change. The first set of analyses models unionization in 1984, 1990 and 1998, generating a mean predicted rate of unionization based on employers' characteristics for each year. We call these our 'unrestricted predictions'. The second set of analyses are run for the base year 1984: these estimates are used to predict rates of unionization in 1990 and 1998, effectively holding within-group changes constant. (In essence, the model coefficients for 1984 are applied to the characteristics of the employers in later years.) The difference between predicted unionization rates under the unrestricted models versus the restricted models indicates the contribution of compositional change to falling unionization. The contribution of within-group change to declining unionization is simply the difference between the actual unionization rate for a year, relative to 1984, minus the amount of the change arising from workplace shares.

The models on which the analysis is based are presented in Table 8.4. Coefficients are for linear estimation, with t-statistics presented in parentheses.

Table 8.4 Linear estimation models for union voice

	(1) Pooled	(2) 1984	(3) 1990	(4) 1998
Sector (ref: private services)				
Public	0.484	0.496	0.441	0.543
	(24.20)[b]	(15.90)[b]	(11.98)[b]	(14.95)[b]
Private manu.	0.037	0.063	0.028	0.026
	(1.42)	(1.33)	(0.66)	(0.63)
Establishment size (ref: 25–49 employees)				
50–99	0.049	0.055	0.053	0.038
	(2.45)[a]	(1.58)	(1.49)	(1.17)
100–199	0.151	0.137	0.117	0.194
	(7.61)[b]	(4.31)[b]	(3.24)[b]	(5.78)[b]
200–499	0.230	0.131	0.255	0.299
	(11.36)[b]	(3.99)[b]	(6.87)[b]	(8.90)[b]
500–999	0.275	0.214	0.287	0.351
	(12.43)[b]	(6.91)[b]	(8.10)[b]	(7.67)[b]
1,000+	0.270	0.223	0.248	0.329
	(12.96)[b]	(7.62)[b]	(7.09)[b]	(7.60)[b]
Foreign	−0.098	0.007	−0.074	−0.146
	(3.02)[b]	(0.09)	(1.18)	(3.83)[b]
Single	−0.192	−0.183	−0.237	−0.146
	(7.74)[b]	(3.85)[b]	(5.82)[b]	(3.67)[b]
Proportion part-timers	−0.118	−0.157	−0.231	−0.012
	(2.92)[b]	(2.55)[a]	(3.57)[b]	(0.16)
Proportion non-manuals	−0.110	−0.151	−0.113	−0.074
	(4.47)[b]	(3.39)[b]	(2.57)[a]	(1.94)
Set up after 1980	−0.107	0.024	−0.155	−0.091
	(4.86)[b]	(0.37)	(4.48)[b]	(2.99)[b]
Survey date (ref: 1984)				
wirs1990	−0.074			
	(3.52)[b]			
wirs1998	−0.113			
	(4.88)[b]			
Constant	0.551	0.564	0.540	0.348
	(18.39)[b]	(11.83)[b]	(11.33)[b]	(7.08)[b]
Observations	5,575	1,879	1,886	1,810
R-squared	0.36	0.33	0.31	0.40

Notes
a = significant at a 95% confidence level; b = significant at a 99% confidence level or above.

Acknowledgements

We would like to thank John Kelly for his comments and the Regent Street Polytechnic Trust and the Leverhulme Trust for financial assistance. We acknowledge the Department of Trade and Industry, the Economic and Social Research Council, the Advisory, Conciliation and Arbitration Service and the Policy Studies Institute as the originators of the 1998 Workplace Employee Relations Survey data, and the Data Archive at the University of Essex as the distributor of the data. None of these organizations or individuals bears any responsibility for the authors' analysis and interpretations of the data.

Notes

1 Little changes when you assume bilateral opportunism (Willman 1982).
2 For example, firms may vary in the balance between union and non-union voice and in the number of unions used as suppliers.
3 According to WERS 1998, this is the employer perception in 14 per cent of non-unionized workplaces.

Chapter 9

Beyond New Unionism

Frances O'Grady and Paul Nowak

When the TUC's New Unionism Task Group was set up in 1996 it was given an ambitious remit and two years within which to fulfil it. Seven years on and the Task Group still exists – its remit just as ambitious, and only partly fulfilled. This chapter reviews the progress made by the Task Group, and more importantly the progress made by unions as a whole, toward meeting the challenge outlined by former TUC General Secretary John Monks in his address to TUC Congress in 1996:

> What must we do? First, as Joe Hill said – 'Organize'. The potential is there ... there are five million workers in Britain who are not in unions but who would like a union to act on their behalf – five million 'union wannabes'.
>
> We need to develop new services to meet new needs. We need to set aside old rivalries between unions and within unions. Above all, as the unions are doing in the States, as we saw this morning, we need to double the resources we commit to recruitment. Then double them again and again and get this issue higher on our priorities.
>
> (TUC 1996)

As well as reviewing progress against this challenge, this chapter also flags up some ideas for taking forward the organizing agenda in the UK. If it is taken as a given that the last few years have seen individual unions, and individual union organizers, take a more strategic and consistent approach to organizing, it is equally apparent that UK unions are a long way away from a movement wide approach to this issue. As new TUC General secretary, Brendan Barber, remarked at an event to mark the fifth anniversary of the TUC's Organizing Academy, 'Unions have to raise the game if we are going to move beyond our stable platform and really turn the tide in membership'.

This chapter will suggest ways of moving from individual commitment and initiatives, toward building a wider understanding that organizing for growth requires a collective commitment across the entire British trade union movement. Two factors are central to developing this collective commitment.

First there needs to be a 'one movement' approach to organizing for growth – one founded, not on sentimentality, but on the fact that real, sustained growth, requires unions and the TUC to work together rather than in competition. Comparatively speaking, UK unions are resource poor; and this lack of resources becomes painfully obvious when unions start squaring up to well-resourced multi-nationals who are more than willing to spend six-figure sums to keep unions out. In this context, resources spent squabbling over existing pockets of membership, or competing for potential members in declining sectors makes little or no sense at all. Working co-operatively – with other unions (domestically and internationally), with the TUC, and with other groups and organizations – will be a key challenge for unions in the coming years (see Willman, this volume).

The second key factor is the acceptance that unions need to build organizing into everything we do – and to be prepared to ask fundamental questions about our structures, the services we provide, the way we negotiate with employers and the relationship we have with our members. Too often organizing is still seen as something distinct or different from the day-to-day work of the union, a 'tack-on' or optional extra (see Chapter 3). Bargaining agendas are developed with no clear sense of what impact, positive or negative, these may have on the ability of the union to recruit and organize. Structures and rulebooks are retained not because they help the union grow, or make the union more relevant to members and potential members, but because, 'that's the way things have always been'. How many union structures are still geared to the way industries or companies were structured two or more decades ago?

In addition to outlining the need to build a wider understanding that organizing for growth requires a collective commitment across the entire British trade union movement, this chapter will also highlight how unions need to influence employers and government, in order to support membership growth.

Unions today

On the surface, unions in the UK are on the crest of a wave, albeit a small one. Over the last two years unions have signed over 800 new recognition agreements; membership, in freefall for most of the last two decades, has stabilized; and there is growing evidence that unions are beginning to rebuild their influence in the workplace and beyond. Certainly unions have cause for optimism in comparison to the dark days of the mid-1990s. When the New Unionism project was launched in 1996, TUC unions had approximately 6.7m members, down from 12.1m in 1979 and overall union density had fallen steadily over the same period (from 56 per cent to 39 per cent). In addition to steadying membership and new recognition deals, unions are more actively, politically engaged at a national, and increasingly important, at regional and local levels – formally expressed, for example, through the recently published Skills Strategy White Paper (DfES 2003) and comprehensive trade union representation on bodies ranging from Regional Development Agencies to Local Learning and Skills Councils. Of course, the relationship between government and unions remains tense in areas – but this should in no way overshadow the fact that unions have far more political access and influence than they did through most of the 1980s and 1990s.

The reasons for this nascent revival are well documented. A more positive political environment, better legislative framework, tighter labour market, increased public sector spending and employment – these external factors have all contributed to the progress that has been made over the last five years. But just as important as these external factors has been the increased focus on organizing and recruitment which has filtered throughout UK unions since the mid-1990s – an increased focus that we will return to later in this chapter. However, before we do – a caveat.

Whatever limited revival there has been still leaves absolutely no room for complacency. Despite successes in winning numerical growth in some areas, the fact remains that mid-way through the second term of a Labour government, union membership density is continuing to fall (down to below 30 per cent across the UK as a whole) and less than one in five private sector employees holds a union card. Even in areas of traditional strength – such as local government – union density is poor. The general decline of national collective bargaining frameworks and sectoral agreements over the last 20 years also means that, despite new recognition successes, only around 36 per cent of the UK's workforce is covered by collective agreements, and like density, this proportion is falling slowly but steadily over time.

In unorganized sectors there is clear evidence that unions are running out of 'easy hits' and beginning to encounter what Tony Burke, Chair of the TUC's New Unionism Task Group, has described as the 'permafrost', that layer of employers who take an 'over my dead body' approach to union recognition. In spring 2003, the Communication Workers Union (CWU) and Connect lost a recognition ballot at T-Mobile, thanks mainly to the intervention of Malibu based 'union-busters' The Burke Group, who boast of a '92 per cent union recognition ballot win rate' on their website. That an established European multi-national, which has a European Works Council and recognizes unions in Germany, would call in Californian union-avoidance consultants speaks volumes of how much effort and resources they, and potentially other employers, are prepared to put in to stay union-free. And of course neither recognition, nor rising membership, should be seen as ends in themselves. Turning recognition into real outcomes for members and potential members remains a challenge as Chapter 3 shows. These caveats apart, UK unions are undoubtedly more confident, more hopeful and better-positioned organizations than they were even a decade ago.

New Unionism

The creation of the New Unionism Task Group (NUTG) heralded the first occasion in the TUC's 135-year history that the organization was tasked with intervening directly in the way that unions recruited and organized members. In addition, the Task Group's creation and remit was an explicit acknowledgement that trade union decline, and efforts to reverse this decline, were not the preserve of one or another union, but of critical importance to the trade union movement in the UK as a whole.

The Task Group was set a number of key objectives. The first, and possibly most important (and certainly most difficult to measure) was to support unions in their efforts to develop an organizing culture – practically expressed through increased resources and investment going into recruitment and organization. Second, the Task Group was asked to look at ways that unions could develop their existing membership bases, while at the same time exploring the potential for growth in new and emerging sectors of the economy. Finally, the Task Group was set the challenge of sharpening the appeal of unions to traditionally under-represented groups of workers, including women, young workers, workers from black and ethnic-minority backgrounds and those at the fringes of the labour market for whom trade unionism appeared to have little or no relevance.

Measuring the success or otherwise of the Task Group was always going to be difficult. While it is clear that progress has been made against its key objectives, what is not so clear is to what extent the NUTG can claim credit, or blame, for this progress.

The shift toward organizing

The shift toward organizing evident in UK unions shows that rather than remaining content to manage decline, or to continue servicing their existing and dwindling membership bases, unions have begun to grasp the organizing nettle. This new approach – evidenced to an extent by stabilizing membership and significant organizing successes – is based at root on the premise that membership decline is neither inevitable nor irreversible. Unions *can* organize their way into growth.

Perhaps the most visible expression of increased and continued investment in organizing has been the New Unionism Task Group's development of the Organizing Academy. Since it opened its doors in 1998, the Academy has trained over 160 Academy Organizers – with just over half of those going through the programme being women, and some 55 per cent being aged under 30. The relative success of the Academy has been well documented (most importantly by Heery *et al.* 2000b), and will not be rehearsed again here. However, one key point to note is that some 21 unions, representing over 59 per cent of the TUC's total affiliated membership, have supported

Academy Organizers at some point during the last five years. These unions have ranged greatly in size and scope – including the ISTC, BALPA, Accord and UNISON – and so too has the way they have used the Organizing Academy and its Organizers. As the Academy has developed, so this 'flexibility' has increased, as has the scope of the programme itself. For example, 2003 saw the first Academy programme aimed at existing union staff and full-time officers – a major departure from the original 'vision' of the Academy. In addition, a small number of unions, including the shop workers' union USDAW, are developing internal 'Academies', deepening and widening the impact of the original initiative.

But of course the shift toward organizing is about more than just the Organizing Academy, and indeed about more than just employing specialist organizers – vital though these have both proved. Even a tenfold increase in the number of dedicated organizers would leave UK unions barely scratching the surface of the membership challenge. Nor should employing dedicated organizing staff be seen as a 'quick-fix' solution. Too often over the last five years unions have taken on Academy and/or specialist organizers on the assumption that this was all that was needed to turn around an organization which previously seemed to be in almost terminal decline. As Michael Crosby, co-director of Australian Council of Trade Unions' (ACTU) 'Organizing Works', noted in a critique of UK organizing strategies following a visit to the UK in late 2002:

> Organizing is about much more than putting resources into growth and getting a few new members. It is in fact a profound change in the way that every part of the union does its business... Real organizing – rather than just selling a bunch of union tickets to prospective members – takes time.

Unions committed to cultural change need to build organizing into every-thing the union does – and win support in the medium to long term for this shift from members and activists, as well as existing staff and officers.

There is some limited evidence that movement has been made in this area. A recent survey of union full-time officers found that 73 per cent reported that recruitment was one of the most important aspects of their job, with some 86 per cent reporting that encouraging lay reps and activists was also a key element of their work (Heery et al. 2002). These figures compare well with those reported by Kelly and Heery (1994) following their study of union FTOs between 1985–91, which found that less than 20 per cent of FTOs reported 'recruitment' as being one of their main three activities. Of course these figures do not strictly compare like with like – but they do suggest a trend towards an increased focus on recruitment and organization amongst union FTOs over the last ten years.

Another key group that unions need to engage in this change process are the 230,000 lay representatives and activists who are the face of the union in workplaces across the country. For many of these reps, overwhelmed by a multitude of competing pressures, organizing barely registers as a priority. In a recent survey of UNISON representatives, only 13 per cent of those surveyed identified recruitment as one of the three tasks which they spend most time on and only 11 per cent identified engaging members more effectively as a 'top three' priority. A recent TUC survey showed that the bulk of reps' time is not spent on building the union, but on resolving difficulties between individuals and management, with almost a third of reps (28 per cent) reporting spending more time doing this than any other union activity. This is not to demean the work that reps do in servicing and representing their members, because after all this is a vital part of their role. But its does flag up the need for unions to further drive home the importance of recruitment and organizing to lay reps and activists (TUC 2002a).

Partly as a response to the results of the reps' survey highlighted above, UNISON has been at the forefront of efforts to engage members and activists in the shift toward organizing – driving change from the bottom-up as well as the top-down. Around 48 per cent of UNISON's 1,200 branches have branch development and organization plans, and from 2004 all branches will be required to draw up a Branch Organizing and Recruitment plan. In addition nearly a third (30 per cent) of UNISON branches currently take part in the union's annual Organizing Awards, which celebrate local and regional organizing successes. Separately, these and other initiatives may appear trivial, but taken together they are vital in the development of a 'whole union' approach to organizing.

The TUC too is exploring ways of pushing organizing higher up the agenda of reps and activists. Organizing is now an important element of the work being carried out by the TUC's Education Service, both through the integration of *Winning the Organised Workplace* (WOW) materials into core stewards and representatives' programmes, and through the development of tailored provision for individual unions. WOW 2, launched in Autumn 2003, combines a bank of flexible, short session materials with an on-line organizing 'toolkit', and the materials are designed to be delivered both formally, through TUC Education Units, and informally, by organizers briefing groups of reps and activists using stand-alone 'lunchtime' sessions.

Ironically, the increasing use of full-time recruitment or organizing staff – which on the whole has been an extremely positive development – can at times accentuate the problems outlined above. Where full-time organizing staff are set prescriptive and defined membership targets, there can be a tendency for these staff and officers to focus more on returning back to the office with a briefcase full of membership forms than on encouraging reps and activists to take the responsibility, and credit, for this work for themselves. Other problems have stemmed from the way organizers have been used, or misused. 'Drive-by' organizing – identifying organizing targets on the basis of techniques not far removed from that of the pin in the map/business directory – often means good, capable organizers, are allocated to unwinnable campaigns, or campaigns or projects which have no strategic value to the union.

Over the last few years, unions have got better at laying the groundwork for, and putting in place, the infrastructure to support organizing. The GPMU's recently launched campaign to organize the book publishing sector in Oxford is a good example of this – focusing the union's resources on a sector identified as a strategic priority by the union because of its potential for membership growth and the longer-term prospects for employment. But this sort of example remains relatively isolated. While the TUC and unions have identified and mapped potential areas for growth, there is still some scope to develop a greater strategic analysis of which targets offer maximum leverage to expand union influence. A 'one movement' approach to this work may mean the TUC working more closely with unions to 'map' key sectors; identify strategically important companies and organizations; co-ordinate union efforts to recruit and organize in these areas; and mobilize the movement's resources to support organizing efforts. Likewise, there is more unions could do on the bargaining front to support efforts to recruit and organize. Making increased and more flexible facility time a key element of agreements, opening access to company IT systems for communicating directly with members and non-members, negotiating 'introductions' to non-unionized companies in supply chains or industrial clusters – these are just three examples of how unions could use their existing collective bargaining arrangements to boost recruitment and organization.

On balance it is fair to say that UK unions have not yet managed to effect the '*cultural change*' originally identified as a priority by the New Unionism Task Group. This doesn't mean that unions have been standing still – but it does mean that unions need to undertake a 'step-change' in their approach. Individual initiatives and successes are, of course, important but in the absence of a broader practical framework for changing the culture of the union, these successes and initiatives will only ever have a short-term impact. In any process of cultural change, leadership is vital, and this is especially the case within trade unions, where the bulk of the organization's human 'capital' gives its time and effort voluntarily. Unlike company Chief Executives, union General Secretaries cannot simply order change from on high. In recognition of this fact the TUC has developed a 'Senior Leaders Programme', launched in autumn 2003, designed to equip senior union officers at a regional and national level with the skills and knowledge they need to develop, lead and implement this process. Finally, thoroughgoing cultural change is a long-term process – one senior officer in a large UK union reckons the switch to organizing will take his union at least ten years. Annual Conferences and regular leadership elections can militate against long-term strategic planning.

This is not to argue that modern unions should dump internal democracy to facilitate organizational change – but it does raise questions about how unions set, and address, long-term strategic objectives (see Willman, this volume).

Breaking out

As well as supporting unions to make the switch toward organizing, the New Unionism Task Group was also asked to look at ways of 'broadening out' trade unionism in the UK – taking the trade union message out to traditionally non-unionized areas of the economy, and sharpening the appeal of unions to women, black workers and other under-represented groups.

A quick glance at the list of the 800-plus new agreements secured by unions since the introduction of statutory recognition, shows that little progress has been made against the first of these objectives. The overwhelming bulk of these new deals have been secured in areas of traditional strength – manufacturing, production and engineering, and to a lesser extent, parts of the former public sector. This suggested bias towards areas of traditional strength is reinforced by union density figures. Manufacturing – 27 per cent, utilities – 53 per cent, public administration – 59 per cent, compared to retail – 12 per cent, business services – 11 per cent and hotels and catering – 5 per cent. On the plus side these figures show that, perhaps sensibly, unions are concentrating resources into those areas where they are most likely to secure wins, and most likely to walk away with recognition deals after resource-intensive organizing campaigns. That said, of course, if unions in the UK are to grow as a whole, then diversifying the industrial base of our membership is absolutely crucial. With the exception of the public sector, union membership is still too heavily concentrated in those sectors and industries with poor or negative jobs growth. The narrowness of our industrial base also goes a long way to explaining our continued failure to recruit and organize younger workers – a point we will return to.

While the industrial profile of the majority of the new recognition deals signed by unions looks relatively traditional, it should not be taken as a blanket suggestion that unions have made little or no effort in these areas – or indeed have made no progress. There are enough new 'wins' in areas such as catering, new media and, more generally, the private service sector as a whole, to suggest that unions can make inroads into areas of traditional weakness. Successful recognition campaigns in Romeike Media Intelligence (GPMU August 2002), Telewest (CWU July 2003) and significantly the TGWU's recent national framework agreement with catering giant Compass Catering (covering some 90,000 workers), show that there are very few 'no-go' areas for unions prepared to invest in serious organizing campaigns.

Just as unions need to break into growing areas of the economy, so too is there a need for them to do more to recruit and organize previously under-represented groups. Again, there has been some limited progress against the

New Unionism Task Group's stated objective to, 'sharpen unions' appeal to "new" workers, including women, youth and those at the rough end of the labour market'. Union membership amongst part-time women workers, for example, has risen steadily over the past few years – in fact accounting for a significant proportion of new membership growth. Women now account for around 47 per cent of total union membership – and since the beginning of the 1990s the 'gender gap' in union density has been rapidly diminishing. Indeed, for the first time in union history women full-time workers are now more likely to belong to a union than male full-timers. This is partly explained by increasing numbers of women entering the labour market, and, in particular, the fact that women are more likely to work in the public sector than men, but it also reflects union efforts to recruit and organize women workers.

However, and predictably, we must enter a qualification when assessing these efforts. It is clear that, while real progress has been made, there has not been a commensurate increase in the proportion of women reps, stewards, full-time officers or executive officers. Likewise, union cultures and structures sometimes fall short of delivering either the values and/or practical arrangements that will facilitate the involvement of more women in the internal life of the union (see Perrons, this volume).

Whatever progress has been made in closing the gender gap in union density, it is clear that unions in the UK still struggle to attract young workers, those at the fringes of the labour market and workers from specific black and ethnic minority groups (TUC 2002a).

The reasons for this are many and various, but perhaps the most significant is simply that unions are poorly organized in those industries and sectors where these workers are likely to be employed. Add to this high staff turnover, increased job mobility, casual and temporary patterns of employment, low pay, job insecurity – all features of employment at the lower end of the private service sector in particular – and unions find themselves in unfamiliar, and unrewarding, territory.

But unfamiliar though this territory may be, there are significant areas where unions could make real inroads. For example, according to the National Group on Homeworking (NGH) there are around 1 million industrial homeworkers in the UK – assembling, packing or manufacturing a huge range of products at home. Unionization amongst this group is extremely low and few unions organize homeworkers in any systematic way. Indeed, no UK union has made any real, long-term, properly resourced attempt to organize this significant group of workers. On the surface the reasons for this lack of engagement are pretty obvious – geographic isolation, confused legal status and unco-operative employers are just three of the potential barriers to traditional collective organization that unions face. But this is just one side of the story. A recent report by NGH revealed that four out of ten homeworkers would actively welcome some sort of trade union involvement, with only

5 per cent of those surveyed feeling that unions have nothing to offer them (NGH 2002). Indeed, individual unions at a local level have had some success organizing in this area – and international experience, most notably that of the Textile, Cloting and Footwear Union of Australia (TCFUA), shows that unions can effectively organize and represent this group of, often, vulnerable and exploited workers. To all these factors can be added the fact that many unionized high-street retailers and supermarkets openly acknowledge that they have significant numbers of UK homeworkers in their supply chains.

There are difficulties and barriers, but this is a group of workers that wants a voice – that wants to be organized – but who to date have found unions either unresponsive or wanting. Why? Of course there are plenty of 'external' reasons why unions find organizing homeworkers, and indeed other atypical groups, difficult. But all too often it is our structures, our own ways of working, and our own cultures that actively diminish our ability to organize these workers. At their best, unions find ways of tailoring their structures and ways of working to the needs of their members and potential members.

Making unions fit 'atypical workers' rather than expecting them to slot nicely into our existing ways of working remains a key challenge. Sometimes this may mean amending rulebooks; sometimes it may even mean rewriting rulebooks altogether, but we would argue that a few sacred cows are a price worth paying to organize the unorganized.

One recent development which supports the need for unions to develop flexible structures and ways of working is the rise of the Union Learning Rep. When the New Unionism Task Group was set up, Union Learning Reps didn't exist. At the time of writing, there are now well over 7,000 ULRs across unionized workplaces in the UK, identifying their members' learning and training needs and providing information and advice about learning and training. By 2010, the government estimates that there will be in excess of 23,000 ULRs, directly providing advice and support to half-a-million union members. Of these 7,000-plus ULRs, some 20 per cent are brand-new reps – people who previously were not attracted to the traditional steward or safety rep's role. These new reps are more likely to be women, more likely to be black or from an ethnic minority, and more likely to be younger than our existing reps. Although they now have statutory rights similar to those enjoyed by health and safety reps, the first Union Learning Reps were the product of practical workplace initiatives, developed by the TUC and unions, rather than union rulebooks.

Beyond the workplace

Reaching out to under-represented groups may also mean thinking beyond the workplace. 'Community Unionism' is a much-abused term and one which means many things to many different people, but we would argue that there is real value in unions building genuine long-term alliances and working relationships with community and other groups. In the US context, the communities in question are often local geographic areas – but in the UK 'Community Unionism' could include the work unions are developing with, for example, groups of lesbian, gay, bisexual and transgender members. It may mean developing links with black and ethnic minority community organizations on issues such as tackling the far-right, or working with specific groups of migrant workers, or faith groups. Community Unionism is a not a replacement or substitute for developing strong, effective workplace organization – but it could be a valuable tool in reaching out to groups of workers which have failed to engage with our traditional structures.

Employers

So far this chapter has focused exclusively on the role of unions – and how what they do as organizations impacts upon their ability to organize the next generation of workers. Also important, however, are the attitudes and actions of employers. Roughly speaking, where managements are broadly favourable to trade unions, union membership is higher and vice versa. As a consequence, unions need to think about how they engage employers positively. At this point, it is important to define what we mean by 'positive engagement'. In the rush to secure new recognition agreements and members, unions could risk 'bidding-down' the terms of collective agreements, often in an effort to prevent a company or organization awarding recognition to a rival union. Winning recognition in these circumstances benefits nobody except the unscrupulous employer – and there is evidence to suggest that even this is not the case. Where unions are recognized, the majority of employers would prefer to deal with a meaningful organization that can claim to effectively represent the views of its membership, rather than an unrepresentative organization which exists purely on the say-so of the employer (see Chapter 8).

But engaging employers positively needn't mean 'selling out' or unions placing themselves in the pocket of the management. The overwhelming majority of employers enjoy a positive and constructive relationship with their recognized unions. In some cases this may be formally recognized through the development of a 'partnership' agreement. In other cases it will simply be reflected in the development of decent working relationships between union representatives and management. Union efforts to widen the scope of collective bargaining in recent years – raising issues around, for example, work/life balance, equal pay, lifelong learning and workforce development – provide a basis for further strengthening these positive relationships.

Accompanying union membership decline throughout the 1980s and 1990s was the similarly significant decline in the number and scope of industry or sector-wide employers' organizations and federations. Those that do remain, such as the Engineering Employers Federation, had a much reduced collective bargaining role. This trend is problematic for unions. Resources which could be allocated to organizing are diverted to support collective bargaining at a workplace or enterprise level; employers who recognize unions and negotiate decent terms and conditions face being undercut by non-union competitors; and sector or industry-wide initiatives around, for example, skills, can be difficult if not impossible to deliver.

Unions can begin to tackle this issue by organizing across labour markets or sectors – targeting all major employers of a particular kind of skilled worker, for example, or within a particular sector (Heery and Simms 2003). Unions can also begin to use their influence on bodies such as Sector Skills Councils or Regional Development Agencies to encourage employers to work together, alongside external bodies and agencies including trade unions, around specific issues such as skills or cluster development. A good example of this approach to 'organizing employers' is the GMB's role in the development of the Tyneside Maritime Group, which brings together employers in the ship repair, shipbuilding, and related industries in the north-east of England. The Group, which includes several non-union companies, is chaired by the regional secretary of the TUC and effectively acts as a regional employers' organization. As well as lobbying government on issues of common concern, the Group is also taking a joint approach to drawing down government funding and support, skills, health and safety and labour supply – all of which is undertaken with the active involvement of the local trade unions. This sort of initiative highlights how unions can begin to extend their influence beyond the level of the individual workplace or enterprise.

Government

The legislative framework within which unions operate has a significant, though not necessarily defining, impact on their ability to recruit and organize members. As we mentioned earlier in this chapter, new rights to statutory recognition have seen an unprecedented rise in the number of new recognition deals secured by UK unions.

Of course legislation alone is not enough – how unions use and exploit the opportunities presented by this legislation is also crucial. New legislation coming on-stream around rights to information and consultation presents unions with both challenges and opportunities. Will employers be able to use this legislation as a means of keeping their workplaces union-free? Or can unions use this new legislation to break into previously unorganized parts of the private sector? We believe that, on balance, this new legislation could become a crucial part of the organizer's toolkit, allowing unions to increase their influence in non-union workplaces, and to show workers the value of independent trade union representation. Union members and activists could play a leading role on embryonic in-house consultative bodies, effectively capturing them for the union.

While the government has undoubtedly delivered a more positive frame-work for union organizing than that which existed throughout the 1980s and 1990s, it is clear that significant legislative improvements to the current framework cannot be relied upon. In its recent submission to the government's review of the Employment Relations Act, the TUC identified a number of key points for government action. These included lifting the 40 per cent threshold on recognition ballots, extending the provision for statutory recognition to small businesses, tackling employers using 'unfair labour practices' to intimidate union activists or scupper recognition ballots, and strengthening the provisions around the right to individual representation. If there is likely to be little progress in these, limited, areas, it is perhaps wishful thinking to believe that government has the political commitment and will to radically reshape the structure of industrial relations in the UK. Genuine social partnership, based on government and employer recognition of the unquestioned role and value of trade unions, remains elusive, even in areas where unions have shown their undoubted value such as skills and workforce development. Recent disputes in the public sector, most notably in local government and the Fire Service, show that there is clear scope for government, unions and employers to build a genuine partnership, which addresses key questions such as public sector pay and the long-term future of public services. The recently established Public Services Forum suggests that government is beginning to edge toward this approach, but a stronger government lead in this direction would undoubtedly send a clear signal to private sector employers about the value of engaging constructively with unions.

Conclusions

Unions in the UK still have a long way to go to repair the extensive decline they underwent throughout most of the 1980s and 1990s – but we would argue that there are clear signs that unions are no longer content to simply manage decline. Increased investment in organizing and organizers have resulted in steadying membership and record numbers of new recognition deals. This doesn't mean that all in the union garden is rosy. We know there is still plenty of work for unions to do and plenty of hard decisions for union leaders to take. This chapter has stressed the need for unions to make a step change in the way that they organize; to increase the investment they make in organizing; to strategically focus their organizing efforts; and to do more to reach out to those workers for whom unions still have little appeal or relevance.

Alongside this we believe that the TUC needs to do more to support union efforts to recruit and organize the next generation of union members; to help prioritize key sectors and industries; and to lay aside traditional rivalries which stand in the way of a 'one movement' approach to organizing the unorganized. The way that we structure our unions, and indeed the wider movement, should be constantly reviewed to ensure that they facilitate, rather than hinder, growth. Finally, but by no means least, we need to ensure that our relationships with government, employers and other social partners deliver on behalf of our existing and potential members alike. Skills and lifelong learning represent just a fraction of the contribution that unions can make to the economic success, and social cohesion, of the UK. Government policy should reflect the scale of this unique potential contribution.

To conclude, we believe that confident, positive unions, focused on growth and operating within a supportive social and political framework, can and will deliver real benefits to their members in the workplace and beyond. More than this, strong unions can also give a voice to our wider communities, shaping and influencing the development of social policy. Rebuilding our membership is not an end in itself, but the means by which millions of working people and their families can get the respect and rewards they deserve.

Chapter 10

Conclusions

John Kelly and Paul Willman

Declining union membership and density have prompted a variety of responses from British trade unions. After the leadership change at the TUC in 1994, two strategies, organizing non-union members and securing partnership agreements with employers, became the dominant leitmotifs of the union movement. The American 'Organizing Model' was widely discussed and became influential in union circles although as Heery and others have pointed out the model underwent some modifications as it was imported into the UK context (Heery *et al.* 2000a). The British variant comprises three main components each relating to the major agents within the industrial relations system, unions, employers and the state, identified in Chapter 1. The union role is sometimes thought of as recruiting members and signing a recognition agreement. In fact there are four union objectives embedded within most organizing campaigns: recruiting non-union members, building a union organization based around a cadre of activists, securing a recognition agreement and establishing a bargaining relationship with the employer. For analytical purposes, it is vital to separate out these different objectives because although they are interconnected – building membership is normally a precondition for recognition, for example – the former does not necessarily lead to the latter, as we shall see. Unions supply personnel and financial resources in pursuit of these objectives. The role of the state has been to enact legal regulation of union recognition covering all four aspects of the organizing process. The relevant provisions of the ERA (1999) provide unions with limited access to establishments in order to recruit members; they protect activists against discipline or dismissal on grounds of union activity (or at least provide financial disincentives for employers to engage in such actions); they ensure that recognition will be granted where a majority of workers, comprising at least 40 per cent of the bargaining unit, votes in favour; and employers are then obliged to sign a recognition agreement covering several designated areas and to negotiate with the union. Finally the role of employers within the organizing model is to comply with the law, rather than embark on US-style counter-mobilization, and perhaps to enter a co-operative relationship with the union through a partnership agreement to try and achieve mutual gains.

In what ways would the Organizing Model help revive the trade union movement? Organizing is often thought of primarily in terms of union membership and it is true that in the liberal market economies of the UK and the US, membership is probably the most frequently used yardstick in judging the health of the union movement. In the UK, levels of union density and collective bargaining coverage are very similar and over a long time period the two series have risen and fallen together. However, in many other parts of Europe these two indicators of union health are only loosely associated. Bargaining coverage throughout most of northern and western Europe as of 2000 was approximately 80 per cent, but union density the same year varied enormously from a low of 8 per cent in France to a high of around 80 per cent in Sweden. Moreover some of the union movements with relatively low levels of density, as in France and Spain, were able to exercise a significant degree of political power, even when right-wing governments held office. These points suggest that in a comparative context at least, the extent of union revitalization needs to be captured by a number of dimensions. One recent framework suggests we can analyse union revitalization along four dimensions: union membership, economic (bargaining) power, political power and institutional flexibility (Behrens *et al.* 2004). In principle organizing seems most likely to have an impact on two of these dimensions, membership and bargaining power. As British union membership is closely correlated with bargaining coverage, new recognition agreements should bring more workers under the coverage of collective agreements, other things being equal.

Some evidence in this volume (and in the previous volume: Gospel and Wood 2003) suggests there has been an improvement in the trend of union membership since 1997 and that the future prospects for unions in Britain are therefore promising. However, we also have evidence that points to a number of problems which would need to be overcome if union revitalization is to be sustained. On the positive side, unions have demonstrated a capacity to use the recognition law to good effect. In particular they have proved capable of taking on some highly recalcitrant employers and securing recognition in some difficult cases that have been handled by the CAC (see Moore, this volume). The level of voluntary recognition has also risen. They have also shown a capacity to break out of the heartlands of trade unionism in manufacturing and public services, by successfully recruiting in the expanding private service sector of the economy amongst media and call-centre workers (Perrons *et al.*, this volume). Meanwhile unions in the public sector have consolidated their strong bargaining position and many of them have increased both membership and density (Bach and Givan, this volume). In several cases these membership gains have developed out of improved workplace organization, as in the Civil Service or the health service (Badigannavar and Kelly, this volume). Whilst some employers remain hostile to unions and have fought recognition through the legal process (Moore, this volume) it appears that most non-union employers are not so much hostile as indifferent to unions: they simply do not see what unions can offer their firm or its employees (Bryson *et al.*, this volume). The logic of this position is that if unions were able to recruit a high percentage of a workforce then they would be well placed to establish bargaining and consultative relations with the employer. All of this evidence augurs well for the future of unions in Britain, but we have also identified a series of problems connected with each of the three parties, unions, employers and the state. Unions have experienced problems in organizing because of worker attitudes, local union leadership, union resources and strategies. Employers have been able to compound union problems by a variety of methods, in particular the use of incentives to employees to remain non-union, the use of threats to raise the costs of unionization and the creation of non-union forms of employee voice. The state's role has been mixed, as we shall see.

First, workers who experience job dissatisfaction or have problems at the workplace may still prove very difficult to recruit. In one of our cases workers attributed their problems to the external environment and did not blame their employer. Not surprisingly many also believed there was little or nothing the union could do for them under these circumstances (Kelly and Badigannavar, this volume). Where the union successfully recruits members, its nascent workplace organization will typically be centred around a handful of activists as most union organizing has occurred in small and medium-sized establishments. Several of our cases demonstrate that such a small cadre of activists is highly vulnerable both to employee turnover and to employer intimidation. In a number of our cases the resignation of one or two key activists inflicted serious damage on union campaigns, reflected in loss of membership or ballot defeat. In other cases union campaigns were badly disrupted by the dismissal or redundancy of key activists. The mechanism by which activist loss damages the organizing campaign is not always clear: in several cases the union proved unable to replenish the activist group so it was no longer able to supply the same level of resources to organizing. Or it may be that the removal of union activists significantly raises the costs of unionization as perceived by employees, and discourages them from joining. Even where unions secured majority membership and protected their activist core, they still have to face the hurdle of signing a recognition agreement and establishing a meaningful bargaining relationship. In one of our cases an anti-union employer came to realize the union would easily win a ballot and switched tactics, opting for a minimal recognition agreement and protracted negotiations without ever reaching agreement. As the fruits of union recognition failed to materialize, the union steadily lost ground and soon found itself in the precarious position of having only a minority of the workforce in membership.

In addition to these problems, our research has also identified issues of union resources and union strategies. Our research on union structure has underlined the obstacles facing large multi-occupational, multi-industry unions in diverting resources from servicing existing members into the organization of new members in job territories remote from the union's core membership base. More detailed appraisal of the TUC New Unionism initiative has made the same point, that translating a policy commitment to organizing into a resource commitment is a process that passes through some very difficult structural barriers (O'Grady and Nowak, Willman, this volume). Even where resources have been committed to organizing, the issue of resource allocation is still present. We know from other research that many union organizers will try to identify and concentrate on workplaces with organizing potential (Heery *et al.* 2002). For example, there may be a recent history of employee discontent or there may be a small number of union members already present in the workplace. Unions will also try to map the workforce and its characteristics in order to identify the probable outcomes of any organizing campaigns. In other words unions will try to 'pick winners'. However, the logic of this systematic approach is that unions will anticipate victory in many of the campaigns they undertake, by quickly building up membership to the point where they can approach the employer for recognition with a reasonable prospect of success. This typical campaign is unlikely to be prolonged and will therefore not consume substantial union resources. But what happens if the union has miscalculated either the employee or the employer response? What happens if the employer decides to mount a prolonged counter-offensive? At some point the union may be faced with a strategic dilemma: should it continue to commit the scarce resource of its full-time staff to a prolonged campaign, often in a small or medium establishment with no more than a few hundred workers? Or should it cut its losses and abandon the campaign, moving on to more fruitful areas? One reason for employers to prolong campaigns is that by signalling a determination to fight they may induce the union to quit. In one of the cases reported in this volume (see Chapter 3) the dismissal of a key activist was the event which triggered the union's withdrawal from an increasingly difficult campaign against a determined US-owned adversary.

We found that union strategy became an important issue especially where the employer is determined to oppose the union and does so by deploying a wide range of tactics. Three in particular stand out as significant. In several cases employers offered pay rises to workers as an inducement to remain non-union and to vote against the union in a ballot. This type of measure is a calculated risk: the employer hopes it will demonstrate the beneficence of the firm but the union is likely to offer the attribution that such rewards are a reflection of union efficacy not a demonstration of union redundancy. Where the union's persuasive communications fail then the organizing drive is in difficulty, as the Amazon case demonstrated (see Kelly and Badigannavar, this volume). Second in the employers' arsenal are threats of closure and relocation and these can operate in two ways. They can raise the perceived costs of unionization and, insofar as the union lacks any credible strategy for keeping open a threatened plant, they may also demonstrate the weakness of the union. However, as Moore's research (this volume) demonstrates, threats of this kind are effective only under certain conditions and also carry risks. The most significant determinant of threat effectiveness, whether in bargaining or organizing, is perceived credibility. Where the employer's threat lacks credibility, then employees are unlikely to be deterred from supporting the union. But threats, like bribes, also carry risks. Insofar as successful unionization depends in part on some degree of antagonism to management, then low credibility threats may intensify anti-managerial sentiment amongst employees and thereby strengthen the organizing campaign rather than weaken it.

A third employer tactic is to create a non-union form of voice; indeed, as Bryson *et al.* show, this was almost the default position in the 1990s. Once again our research suggests the impact of such a measure is complex and mediated by a number of other variables, in particular the balance of power between the union and the employer and the characteristics of the union activists. In the Amazon case the union secured very little representation on an employer-created consultative body but its membership base was too fragile to enable an effective challenge from outside and union support began to dwindle as a result (Kelly and Badigannavar, this volume). Where a union does secure representation on such a body, the results vary according to membership strength and the character of the activists. A union with high membership density and activists committed to a strong bargaining relationship with the employer is unlikely to be weakened by a consultative forum despite the employer's intentions (Kelly and Badigannavar, this volume). By contrast a union with lower membership and fewer militant activists may well find that a consultative forum weakens the overall worker demand for union representation (Perrons, this volume). In effect strong unions may be unaffected by such tactics, but weak unions may become weaker still.

The passage of the ERA (1999) arguably signified the recovery of trade union political influence after many years of union exclusion from government policy-making under the Conservatives (1979–97). As research by Moore (this volume) and others has shown, the ERA was a very important factor in stimulating an increase in union organizing activity and encouraging a pragmatic accommodation to union recognition by many employers (see also Gall 2003b). However, it has also become clear that there are severe limits to the areas and degrees of influence which unions can exert over the Labour government. The DTI review of the union recognition provisions was regarded by the TUC and other union leaders as a valuable opportunity to engage the government in dialogue over improvements to the operation of the recognition law. The government, however, largely ignored many of the representations submitted by the TUC and proposed very few statutory amendments (Moore, this volume).

In areas beyond employment legislation unions have also found it difficult to influence the government. Many public sector unions have adopted policies of outright opposition to PFI but have so far failed to make much headway in persuading government to abandon, slow down or even review the planned role of PFI throughout the public sector. In some cases, as Bach and Givan (this volume) make clear, unions have been handicapped by competition amongst themselves which has hindered effective bargaining, as in the health sector. In other areas of the public sector, such as education, government ministers have exploited deep policy divisions between unions in order to secure a coalition of support behind contentious measures while isolating their most vocal opponents. If the modest impact of unions on government has not been helped by problems on the union side, it is only fair to note the structural difficulties confronting the unions (Hamann and Kelly 2003). The British parliamentary system centralizes power in the hands of a small prime-ministerially dominated cabinet. The first past the post electoral system has twice delivered huge parliamentary majorities to Labour over its opponents thus neutralizing the House of Commons as an effective channel of influence. The same non-proportional voting system also ensures that the electoral threat of a party to the left of Labour is minimal (by contrast with many other countries in Europe). The result is that many unions remain affiliated to the Labour Party despite growing disquiet over government policy. Even if the new generation of union leaders were to succeed in launching a more coordinated campaign inside the Labour Party around issues such as PFI for example, the changes in party structure, rules and funding over the past ten years have seriously eroded the potential for union influence.

Looking forward, we can identify a number of events which might disturb current trends. The radicalization of national trade union leaderships is one (Murray 2003). While this radicalization emerges from democratic choices made by existing union members, its role in assisting the broadening of the membership base remains to be seen. Leadership change has been particularly evident in predominantly public sector and industrial unions and may thus exert its greatest effect in the remaining bastions of union strength. A second event with very different possible implications is the translation of the European Directive on information and consultation. This has two likely consequences. First, the 'no voice' sector identified by Bryson *et al.* (this volume) is likely to shrink substantially under the impact of this statutory requirement: only the smallest firms will escape. Second, since the Directive requires representative structures, it will impact those workplaces where direct communication is the dominant voice mechanism. It is difficult not to see in this measure a major opportunity for trade unions to assist employer compliance in ways which might increase membership and perhaps bargaining coverage. However, the evidence on employer resistance to union organizing in Britain also suggests that the union opportunity will not be without problems.

Bibliography

Ackers, P. and Payne, J. (1998) 'British trade unions and social partnership: rhetoric, reality and strategy', *International Journal of Human Resource Management*, 9(3): 529–50.

Aidt, T.S. and Sena, V. (2002) 'Unions: rent extractors or creators?', Mimeo, Cambridge: Department of Applied Economics.

Amazon UK (2002) 'Company report', available online at http://fame.bvdep.com.

Aston, B. (1987) 'Trade union mergers in Britain, 1950–82', PhD thesis, London: London School of Economics.

Atkinson, P. and Van den Noord, P. (2001) 'Managing public expenditure: some policy issues and a framework for analysis', OECD Working Papers, Paris: OECD, available online at www.oecd.org/eco/eco.

Audia, G., Locke, E.A. and Smith K.G. (2000) 'The paradox of success: an archival and a laboratory study of strategic persistence following radical environmental change', *Academy of Management Journal*, 43: 837–53.

Audit Commission (2002) *Recruitment and Retention: A Public Service Workforce for the Twenty-first Century*, London: Audit Commission.

AUT (2002) 'UK academic staff casualisation 1994–95 to 2000', available online at www.aut.org.uk.

Bach, S. (2002) 'Public-sector employment relations reform under Labour: muddling through or modernization?', *British Journal of Industrial Relations*, 40(2): 319–39.

—— (2004) 'Employee participation and union voice in the NHS', *Human Resource Management Journal* (in press).

Bach, S. and Winchester, D. (1994) 'Opting out of pay devolution? The prospects for local pay bargaining in UK public services', *British Journal of Industrial Relations*, 32(2): 263–82.

—— (2003) 'Industrial relations in the public sector', in P. Edwards (ed.) *Industrial Relations* (2nd edition), Oxford: Blackwell.

Bacon, N. and Storey, J. (2000) 'New employee relations strategies in Britain: towards individualism or partnership?', *British Journal of Industrial Relations*, 38(3): 407–27.

Bassett, P. and Cave, A. (1993) *All for One: the future of the unions*, London: Fabian Pamphlet 599.

Baumol, W. (1967) 'Macroeconomics of unbalanced growth: the anatomy of the urban crisis', *American Economic Review*, 56: 415–26.

Beck, U. (2000) *The Brave New World of Work*, Cambridge: Polity Press.

Becker, B., Huselid, M. and Ulrich, D. (2001) *The HR Scorecard: Linking People, Strategy and Performance*, Boston, MA: HBS Press.

Behrens, M., Hamann, K. and Hurd, R.W. (2004) 'Conceptualizing labour movement revitalization', in C. Frege and J. Kelly (eds) *Labour Movement Revitalization in Comparative Perspective*, Oxford: Oxford University Press.

BHC (2002) *Housing. The Wellbeing of the City. Housing Strategy 2001–2006*, Brighton: Brighton and Hove Council.

Blanchflower, D. and Bryson, A. (2003) 'Changes over time in union relative wage effects in the UK and the US revisited', in J.T. Addison and C. Schnabel (eds) *International Handbook of Trade Unions*, Cheltenham: Edward Elgar.

Blyton, P. and Turnbull, P. (1998) *The Dynamics of Employee Relations* (2nd edition), London: Macmillan.

Boraston, I., Clegg, H. and Rimmer, M. (1975) *Workplace and Union*, London: Heinemann.

Boxall, P. and Haynes, P. (1997) 'Strategy and trade union effectiveness in a neo-liberal environment', *British Journal of Industrial Relations*, 35(4): 567–92.

Bronfenbrenner, K. and Juravich, T. (1998) 'It takes more than house calls: organizing to win with a comprehensive union-building strategy', in K. Bronfenbrenner, S. Friedman, R. Hurd, R. Oswald and R. Seeber (eds) *Organizing To Win: New Research on Union Strategies*, Ithaca, NY: ILR Press.

Bronfenbrenner, K., Friedman, S., Hurd, R., Oswald, R. and Seeber, R. (eds) (1998) *Organizing To Win: new research on union strategies*, Ithaca, NY: ILR Press.

Brook, K. (2002) 'Trade union membership: an analysis of data from the autumn 2001 LFS', *Labour Market Trends*, 110(7): 343–54.

Bryson, A. and Gomez, R. (2003) 'Buying into trade union membership', in H. Gospel and S. Wood (eds) *Representing Workers: Trade Union Recognition and Membership in Britain*, London: Routledge.

Buchanan, R. (1981) 'Union concentration and the largest unions', *British Journal of Industrial Relations*, 19(2): 232–7.

Burchill, F. (1995) 'Professional unions in the National Health Service: issues and membership trends', *Review of Employment Topics*, 3(1): 13–42.

—— (2000) 'The Pay Review Body system: a comment and a consequence', *Historical Studies in Industrial Relations*, 10(Autumn): 141–57.

Carvel, J., White, M. and Elliot, L. (2002) 'Wanted: 80,000 staff for NHS', *The Guardian*, 19 April.

Castells, M. (2001) *The Internet Galaxy. Reflections on the Internet, Business and Society*, Oxford: Oxford University Press.

Certification Officer (2002) *Annual Report of the Certification Officer 2001–02*, London: Certification Office.

Charlwood, A. (2002) 'Why do non-union employees want to unionise?', *British Journal of Industrial Relations*, 40(3): 463–91.

—— (2003) 'Willingness to unionise amongst non-union workers', in H. Gospel and S. Wood (eds) *Representing Workers: Trade Union Recognition and Membership in Britain*, London: Routledge.

Child, J., Loveridge, R. and Warner, M. (1973) 'Towards an organisational study of trade unions', *Sociology*, 71(1): 71–91.

Clark, A. and Oswald, A. (1993) 'Trade union utility functions: a survey of union leaders' views', *Industrial Relations*, 32(3): 391–406.

Clark, P.F. (2001) *Building More Effective Unions*, Ithaca, NY: ILR Press.

Clarke, C. (2003) 'Freeing teachers to teach is key to delivering tailor-made learning for every child', Press Release 8 July, London: Department for Education and Skills, available online at www.dfes.gov.uk/.

Clegg, H. (1976) *Trade Unionism Under Collective Bargaining*, Oxford: Blackwell.

Cohen, L. and Hurd, R.W. (1998) 'Fear, conflict and union organizing', in K. Bronfenbrenner, S. Friedman, R. Hurd, R. Oswald and R. Seeber (eds) *Organizing To Win: New Research on Union Strategies*, Ithaca, NY: ILR Press.

Cohen-Rosenthal, E. and Burton, C. (1987) *Mutual Gains: A Guide to Union–Management Cooperation*, New York: Praeger.

Commission for Health Improvement (2003) 'Report', available online at www.chi.nhs.uk/.

Cooke, W. (1983) 'Determinants of the outcomes of union certification elections', *Industrial and Labor Relations Review*, 36(3): 402–14.

Coyle, D. and Quah, D. (2002) *Getting the Measure of the New Economy*, London: The Work Foundation.

Cully, M., Woodland, S., O'Reilly, A. and Dix, G. (1999) *Britain at Work As Depicted by the 1998 Workplace Employee Relations Survey*, London: Routledge.

Daycare Trust (2001) *Who Will Care? Recruiting the Next Generation of the Childcare Workforce*, Policy Paper 4, London: Daycare Trust.

Deery, S., Ervin, P. and Iverson, R. (1999) 'Industrial relations climate, attendance behaviour and the role of trade unions', *British Journal of Industrial Relations*, 37(4): 533–58.

Department of Health (1999) *Report of the NHS Task Force on Staff Involvement*, London: Department of Health.

—— (2000) *Partnership in Action: The Action Plan to Implement the Recommendations of the NHS Task Force on Staff Involvement*, London: Department of Health.

Department of Trade and Industry (1998) *Fairness at Work*, London: HMSO, Cm. 3968.

—— (1999) 'Workplace employee relations survey, cross-section, 1998', Colchester: Essex University, The Data Archive, 22 December, SN 3955.

—— (2000) *Access to Workers during Recognition and Derecognition Ballots*, London: HMSO.

—— (2003a) *Review of the Employment Relations Act (1999)*, London: Department of Trade and Industry.

—— (2003b) 'Employment legislation, flexible working – the right to request: a basic summary (PL516 Rev 1)', London: DTI, available online at http://www.dti.gov.uk/er/individual/flexible.

—— (2003c) 'Flexible working. The business case – 50 success stories', London: DTI, available online at http://www.dti.gov.uk/work-lifebalance/publications.

—— (2003d) 'Work–life balance website', available online at http://www.dti.gov.uk/work-lifebalance/.

DfES (2003) *21st Century Skills: Realising our Potential*, London: Department for Education and Skills.

Diamond, W. and Freeman, R. (2003) 'Young workers and trade unions', in H. Gospel and S. Wood (eds) *Representing Workers: Trade Union Recognition and Membership in Britain*, London: Routledge.

DiMaggio, P.J. and Powell, W.W. (1983) 'The iron cage revisited: institutional iso-morphism and collective rationality in organisational fields', *American Sociological Review*, 48: 147–60.

Donaldson, L. (1998) *Performance Driven Organisational Change: The Organisational Portfolio*, Thousand Oaks, CA: Sage.

Doogan, K. (2001) 'Insecurity and long-term employment', *Work, Employment and Society*, 15(3): 419–41.

Dunn, S. and Metcalf, D. (1996) 'Trade union law since 1979', in I. Beardwell (ed.) *Contemporary Industrial Relations: A Critical Analysis*, Oxford: Oxford University Press.

Etzioni, A. (1969) *The Semi-professions and their Organisation*, New York: Free Press.

Ewing, K., Moore, S. and Wood, S. (2003) *Unfair Labour Practices: Trade Union Recognition and Employer Resistance*, London: Institute for Employment Rights.

Fairbrother, P. (2002) 'Unions in Britain: towards a new unionism', in P. Fairbrother and G. Griffin (eds) *Changing Prospects for Trade Unionism*, London: Continuum.

Faith, R.L. and Reid, J.D. (1987) 'An agency theory of trade unions', *Journal of Economic Behaviour and Organisation*, 8: 39–60.

Fantasia, R. (1988) *Cultures of Solidarity: Consciousness, Action and Contemporary American Workers*, Berkeley, CA: University of California Press.

Farber, H. and Western, B. (2002) 'Ronald Reagan and the politics of declining union organization', *British Journal of Industrial Relations*, 40(3): 385–401.

Fiorito, J., Gramm, C.L. and Hendricks, W.E. (1991) 'Union structural choices', in G. Strauss, D. Gallagher and J. Fiorito (eds) *The State of the Unions*, Madison, WI: Industrial Relations Research Association.

Fiorito, J., Jarley, P. and Delaney, J.T. (1993) 'National union effectiveness', *Research in the Sociology of Organisations*, 12: 117–37.

Flanders, A. (1970) *Management and Unions*, London: Faber.

Flood, P. and Toner, P. (1997) 'Large non-union companies: how do they avoid a catch 22?', *British Journal of Industrial Relations*, 35(2): 257–79.

Flood, P., Turner, T. and Willman, P. (1996) 'Union presence, union service and membership competition', *British Journal of Industrial Relations*, 34(3): 415–33.

—— (2000) 'A segmented model of union participation', *Industrial Relations*, 35(1): 108–14.

Folbre, N. and Nelson, J. (2000) 'For love or money – or both?', *Journal of Economic Perspectives*, 14(4): 123–40.

Freeman, R. and Medoff, J. (1984) *What Do Unions Do?*, New York: Basic Books.

Freeman, R. and Pelletier, J. (1990) 'The impact of industrial relations legislation on British union density', *British Journal of Industrial Relations*, 28(2):141–64.

Freeman, R. and Rogers, J. (1999) *What Workers Want*, Ithaca, NY: ILR Press.

Frege, C. and Kelly, J. (2003) 'Union revitalization strategies in comparative perspec-tive', *European Journal of Industrial Relations*, 9(1): 7–24.

Gall, G. (2001) 'From adversarialism to partnership? Trade unionism and industrial relations in the banking sector in the UK', *Employee Relations*, 33(4): 353–75.

—— (2003a) 'Introduction', in G. Gall (ed.) *Union Organizing: Campaigning for Trade Union Recognition*, London: Routledge.

—— (2003b) 'Employer opposition to union recognition', in G. Gall (ed.) *Union Organizing: campaigning for trade union recognition*, London: Routledge.

Gibson, O. (2003) 'Amazon posts first UK profit', *The Guardian*, 24 January.

Gill, R. (2002) 'Cool, creative and egalitarian? Exploring gender in project-based new media work in Europe', *Information, Communication and Society*, 5(1): 70–89.

Gomez, R. (2003) 'Unions, youth and the incumbency effect: what's the connection?', in D. Metcalf (ed.) *Future of Unions in Modern Britain, Mid-Term Report on Leverhulme Trust-Funded Research Programmes 2000–2002*, London: Centre for Economic Performance.

Gospel, H. and Willman, P. (2003) 'Dilemmas for workplace representation: negotiation, consultation and information', in H. Gospel and S. Wood (eds) *Representing Workers: Trade Union Recognition and Membership in Britain*, London: Routledge.

Gospel, H. and Wood, S. (eds) (2003) *Representing Workers: Trade Union Recognition and Membership in Britain*, London: Routledge.

Grant, R. (2001) *Contemporary Strategy Analysis: Concepts, Techniques, Applications*, Oxford: Blackwell.

Green, F. (1992) 'Recent trends in British trade union density: how much of a compositional effect?', *British Journal of Industrial Relations*, 30(3): 378–94.

—— (2003) 'The rise and decline of job insecurity', Paper presented at the Second ESRC Seminar on Work Life and Time in the New Economy, University of Manchester, February.

Greenhouse, S. (2000a) 'Unions pushing to organize thousands of Amazon.com workers', *New York Times*, 23 November.

—— (2000b) 'Amazon fights union activity', *New York Times*, 29 November.

Grogan, S., Stokes, F. and Nairne, B. (2001) *Setting the Scene: A Review of the Brighton and Hove Economy 2000–2001*, Brighton: Brighton and Hove Council.

Guest, D. and Peccei, R. (1998) *The Partnership Company*, London: Involvement and Participation Association.

—— (2001) 'Partnership at work: mutuality and the balance of advantage', *British Journal of Industrial Relations*, 39(2): 207–36.

Hamann, K. and Kelly, J. (2003) 'Domestic sources of differences in labour market policies', *British Journal of Industrial Relations*, 41(4): 639–63.

Hardwidge, C. (2002) 'Jobs in the public and private sectors', *Economic Trends*, 583, Office for National Statistics.

Heery, E. (2002) 'Partnership versus organizing: alternative futures for British trade unionism', *Industrial Relations Journal*, 33(1): 20–35.

Heery, E. and Simms, M. (2003) *Employer Responses to Union Organising*, London: Trades Union Congress, Organising the Future Series.

Heery, E., Simms, M., Simpson, D., Delbridge, R. and Salmon, J. (2000a) 'Organizing unionism comes to Britain', *Employee Relations*, 22(1): 38–53.

Heery, E., Simms, M., Delbridge, R., Salmon, J. and Simpson, D. (2000b) 'The TUC's Organising Academy: an assessment', *Industrial Relations Journal*, 31(5): 400–15.

—— (2002) *Survey of Full-Time Officers*, New Unionism Research Paper, Cardiff: Cardiff University.

—— (2003) 'Trade union recruitment policy in Britain: form and effects', in G. Gall (ed.) *Union Organizing: Campaigning for Trade Union Recognition*, London: Routledge.

Hemingway, J. (1978) *Conflict and Democracy: Studies in Trade Union Government*, Oxford: Clarendon Press.

Hildreth, A.K.G. (1999) 'What has happened to the union wage differential in Britain in the 1990s?', *Oxford Bulletin of Economics and Statistics*, 61(1): 5–31.

Hirschman, A. (1970) *Exit, Voice and Loyalty*, Cambridge, MA: Harvard University Press.

Hudson, M., Konzelman, S. and Wilkinson, F. (2001) 'Partnership in practice', Paper presented at the CMI Workshop on Corporate Governance and Human Resources, Judge Institute of Management Studies, University of Cambridge, June.

Hyman, R. (1983) 'Trade unions: structure, policies, and politics', in G.S. Bain (ed.) *Industrial Relations in Britain*, Oxford: Blackwell.

—— (1997) 'Trade unions and interest representation in the context of globalisation', *Transfer*, 3(3): 515–33.

—— (2001) *Understanding European Trade Unionism: Between Market, Class and Society*, London: Sage.

IER (2001) *Work–Life Balance 2000: baseline study of work–life balance in Great Britain*, Warwick: Institute of Employment Research.

IPA (1997) *Towards Industrial Partnership: new ways of working in British companies*, London: Involvement and Participation Association.

Ironside, M. and Seifert, R. (1995) *Industrial Relations in Schools*, London: Routledge.

Jarley, P., Fiorito, J. and Delaney, J.T. (1997) 'A structural contingency approach to bureaucracy and democracy in US national unions', *Academy of Management Journal*, 40: 831–61.

Javeline, D. (2003) 'The role of blame in collective action: evidence from Russia', *American Political Science Review*, 97(1): 107–21.

Johnston, P. (1994) *Success While Others Fail: Social Movement Unionism and the Public Workplace*, Ithaca, NY: ILR Press.

Joyce, P., Corrigan, P. and Haynes, M. (1988) *Striking Out: Trade Unionism in Social Work*, Basingstoke: Macmillan.

Katz, H. (1993) 'The decentralization of collective bargaining: a literature review and comparative analysis', *Industrial and Labor Relations Review*, 47(1): 3–22.

Kelly, J. (1996) 'Union militancy and social partnership', in P. Ackers, C. Smith and P. Smith (eds) *The New Workplace and Trade Unionism*, London: Routledge.

—— (1998) *Rethinking Industrial Relations: Mobilization, Collectivism and Long Waves*, London: Routledge.

—— (2004) 'Social partnership agreements in Britain', in M. Stuart and M. Martinez Lucio (eds) *Partnership and Modernization in Employment Relations*, London: Routledge.

Kelly, J. and Heery, E. (1994) *Working for the Union*, Cambridge: Cambridge University Press.

Kelso, P. (2002) 'Angry women find a voice over pay that doesn't add up', *The Guardian*, 18 July.

Kennedy, P. (1998) *A Guide to Econometrics* (4th edition), Malden, MA: Blackwell.

Kessler, I. and Heron, P. (2001) 'Steward organization in a professional union: the case of The Royal College of Nursing', *British Journal of Industrial Relations*, 39(3): 367–91.

Klandermans, B. (1997) *The Social Psychology of Protest*, Oxford: Blackwell.

Kochan, T. (1980) *Collective Bargaining and Industrial Relations*, Homewood, IL: Irwin.

—— (2003) 'A US perspective on the future of trade unions in Britain', in H. Gospel and S. Wood (eds) *Representing Workers: Trade Union Recognition and Membership in Britain*, London: Routledge.

Kochan, T. and Katz, H. (1988) *Collective Bargaining and Industrial Relations* (2nd edition), Homewood, IL: Irwin.

Lawler, J. (1984) 'The influence of management consultants on the outcome of union certification elections', *Industrial and Labor Relations Review*, 38(1): 38–51.

Levitt, M.J. and Conrow, T. (1993) *Confessions of a Union Buster*, New York: Crown.

Lister, J. (2003) *The PFI Experience: Voices from the Frontline*, London: UNISON.

Logan, J. (2002) 'Consultants, lawyers, and the "union free" movement in the USA since the 1970s', *Industrial Relations Journal*, 33(3): 197–214.

LRD (2001) 'Building unions in call centres', *Labour Research*, 90(7): 9–12.

McBride, A. (2001) *Gender Democracy in Trade Unions*, Aldershot: Aldgate.

McGregor, D. (2001) 'Jobs in the public and private sectors', *Economic Trends*, 571: 35–50.

Machin, S. (2000) 'Union decline in Britain', *British Journal of Industrial Relations*, 38(4): 631–45.

Martin, D.L. (1980) *An Ownership Theory of the Trade Union*, Berkeley, CA: University of California Press.

Mason, R. and Bain, P. (1993) 'The determinants of trade union membership in Britain: a survey of the literature', *Industrial and Labor Relations Review*, 46(2): 332–51.

Metcalf, D. (1991) 'British unions: dissolution or resurgence?', *Oxford Review of Economic Policy*, 7(1): 18–32.

—— (2001) 'British unions: dissolution or resurgence revisited', in R. Dickens, J. Wadsworth and P. Gregg (eds) *The State of Working Britain: Update 2001*, London: LSE, Centre for Economic Performance.

—— (2003) 'British unions: what future?', in D. Metcalf (ed.) *Future of Unions in Modern Britain, Mid-Term Report on Leverhulme Trust-Funded Research Programmes 2000–2002*, London: LSE, Centre for Economic Performance.

Milburn, A. (2003) 'New instruments for health', in *Progressive Politics – 21st Century Public Services*, Progressive Governance, London, 11–13 July, 2003.

Millward, N., Bryson, A. and Forth, J. (2000) *All Change at Work?*, London: Routledge.

Milne, S. (2000) 'Unions aim to swallow Amazon', *The Guardian*, 7 December.

Mitchell, D.J. (1972) 'Union wage policies: the Ross–Dunlop debate reopened', *Industrial Relations*, 11(1): 46–61.

Monger, J. (2003) 'International comparisons of labour disputes in 2000', *Labour Market Trends*, 111(1): 19–28.

Moore, S., Wood, S. and Davies, P. (2000) 'Recognition of trade unions – consultation over the Access Code and method of bargaining', *Industrial Law Journal*, 29: 406–15.

Morris, G. (2000) 'Employment in public services: the case for special treatment', *Oxford Journal of Legal Studies*, 20(2): 167–83.

Murray, A. (2003) *A New Labour Nightmare: The Return of the Awkward Squad*, London: Verso.

NGH (2002) *Organising Homeworkers in the UK: An NGH Interim Report on Trade Union Policies and the Collective Organisation Needs of UK Homeworkers*, Leeds: National Group on Homeworking.

Nolan, P. and Slater, G. (2003) 'The labour market: history, structure and prospects', in P. Edwards (ed.) *Industrial Relations* (2nd edition), Oxford: Blackwell.

Offe, C. and Wiesenthal, H. (1980) 'Two logics of collective action: notes on social class and organizational form', *Political Power and Social Theory*, 1: 67–115.

Oxenbridge, S. and Brown, W. (2002) 'The two faces of partnership? An assessment of partnership and cooperative employer/trade union relationships', *Employee Relations*, 24(3): 262–76.

Palloix, C. (1976) 'The labour process: from Fordism to neo-Fordism', in CSE (ed.) *The Labour Process and Class Strategies*, London: Conference of Socialist Economists and Stage 1 Books.

Pendleton, A. (1997) 'What impact has privatisation had on pay and employment? A review of the UK experience', *Relationnes Industrielles*, 52(3): 554–79.

Perrons, D. (2003a) 'The new economy, labour market inequalities and the work life balance', in R. Martin and P. Morrison (eds) *Geographies of Labour Market Inequality*, London: Routledge.

—— (2003b) 'The new economy and the work life balance: conceptual explorations and a case study of new media', *Gender, Work and Organisation*, 10(1): 65–93.

Prentis, D. (2003) 'Is the future of the NHS at stake?', *The Observer*, 4 May.

Prism Research (2000) *Homecare Workers Recruitment and Retention Study: Draft Final Report*, Brighton: Prism Research.

Public Administration Select Committee (2002) *The Public Service Ethos: Seventh Report of Session 2001–02, Volume 1*, London: HMSO.

Quah, D. (1996) 'The invisible hand and the weightless economy', Occasional Paper No. 12, London: LSE, Centre for Economic Performance.

—— (2003) 'Digital goods and the new economy', unpublished MS, available online at http://econ.lse.ac.uk/staff/dquah.

RCN (2001) *Widening Membership to Health Care Assistants and Nurse Cadets*, London: Royal College of Nursing.

Rogers, S. (2002) 'Fired over saucy email', *Evening Argus*, 22 November.

Rubery, J., Ward, K., Grimshaw, D. and Beynon, H. (2003) 'Time and the new employment relationship', Paper presented at the Second ESRC Seminar on Work Life and Time in the New Economy, University of Manchester, February.

Rundle, J. (1998) 'Winning hearts and minds in the era of employee-involvement programs', in K. Bronfenbrenner, S. Friedman, R.W. Hurd, R. Oswald and R. Seeber (eds) *Organizing to Win: New Research on Union Strategies*, Ithaca, NY: ILR Press.

Sapper, S. (1991) 'Do members' service packages influence trade union recruitment?', *Industrial Relations Journal*, 22(1): 63–78.

Sennett, R. (1998) *The Corrosion of Character: The Personal Consequences of Work in the New Capitalism*, New York: Norton.

Skinner, C. (2003) *Running Around in Circles: Coordinating Childcare, Education and Work*, Bristol: The Policy Press with the Joseph Rowntree Foundation.

Soskice, D. (1990) 'Wage determination: the changing role of institutions in advanced industrialized countries', *Oxford Review of Economic Policy*, 6(4): 36–61.

Spector, R. (2000) *Amazon.com: Get Big Fast*, New York: Random House.

Strategy Unit (2002) *Delivering for Children and Families: Inter-departmental Childcare Review*, London: Strategy Unit.

Streeck, W. and Visser, J. (1997) 'The rise of the conglomerate union', *European Journal of Industrial Relations*, 3(3): 305–32.

Stuart, M. and Martinez Lucio, M. (eds) (2004) *Partnership and Modernization in Employment Relations*, London: Routledge.

Taylor, P. and Bain, P. (2003) 'Call center organizing in adversity: from Excell to Vertex', in G. Gall (ed.) *Union Organizing: Campaigning for Trade Union Recognition*, London: Routledge.

Taylor, P. and Ramsay, H. (1998) 'Unions, partnership and HRM: sleeping with the enemy?', *International Journal of Employment Studies*, 6(2): 115–43.

Terry, M. (1996) 'Negotiating the government of UNISON: union democracy in theory and practice', *British Journal of Industrial Relations*, 34(1): 87–110.

Terry, M. and Smith, J. (2003) *Evaluation of the Partnership Fund at Work*, London: Department of Trade and Industry, Employment Relations Research Series No. 17.

Tilly, C. (1978) *From Mobilization to Revolution*, New York: McGraw Hill.

Towers, B. (2003) 'Comparisons and prospects: industrial relations and trade unions in North America and Britain', in G. Gall (ed.) *Union Organizing: Campaigning for Trade Union Recognition*, London: Routledge.

TUC (1995) *Your Voice at Work: TUC Proposals for Rights to Representation at Work*, London: Trades Union Congress.

—— (1996) *Congress Report 1996*, London: Trades Union Congress

—— (1998) *Take your Partners: The Business Case for a Union Voice*, London: Trades Union Congress.

—— (2002a) *Today's Trade Unionists,* London: Trades Union Congress.

—— (2002b) *About Time: A New Agenda for Shaping Working Life*, London: Trades Union Congress.

—— (2003) *Submission to the Government on the Review of the Employment Relations Act 1999*, London: Trades Union Congress.

Undy, R. (1999) 'New Labour's industrial relations settlement: the Third Way?', *British Journal of Industrial Relations*, 37(2): 315–36.

—— (2002) 'New Labour and new unionism 1997–2001: but is it the same old story?', *Employee Relations*, 24(6): 638–55.

Undy, R., Ellis, V., McCarthy, W.E.J. and Halmos, A.M. (1981) *Change in Trade Unions: The Development of UK Unions since 1960*, London: Hutchinson.

Undy, R., Fosh, P., Morris, H., Smith, P. and Martin, R. (1996) *Managing the Unions*, Oxford: Clarendon Press.

UNISON (2000) *Contracting-Out and the Two Tier Workforce*, London: UNISON.

—— (2003) *Duty of Care Handbook*, London: UNISON.

Verma, A., Wood, S. and Kochan, T. (2002) 'Introduction: special issue on union decline and prospects for revival', *British Journal of Industrial Relations*, 40(3): 373–85.

Visser, J. (1990) *In Search of Inclusive Unionism*, Deventer: Kluwer.

Voos, P. (1984) 'Union organizing: costs and benefits', *Industrial and Labor Relations Review*, 36(4): 576–91.

Waddington, J. (2003a) 'Trade union organisation', in P. Edwards (ed.) *Industrial Relations: Theory and Practice*, Oxford: Blackwell.

—— (2003b) 'Heightening tension in relations between trade unions and the Labour Government in 2002', *British Journal of Industrial Relations*, 41(2): 335–58.

Waddington, J. and Kerr, A. (2000) 'Towards an organising model in UNISON?', in M. Terry (ed.) *Redefining Public Sector Unionism: UNISON and the Future of Trade Unions,* London: Routledge.

Webb, S. and Webb, B. (1907) *The History of Trade Unionism,* London: Longman Green.

Williamson, O.E. (1975) *Markets and Hierarchies,* Glencoe, IL: Free Press.

—— (1985) *The Economic Institutions of Capitalism: Firms, Markets, Relational Contracting,* New York: Free Press.

—— (1991) 'Comparative economic organization: the analysis of discrete structural alternatives', *Administrative Science Quarterly,* 36(2): 269–98.

Willman, P. (1982) 'Opportunism and labour contracting: an application of the organisational failures framework', *Journal of Economic Behaviour and Organisation,* 2(1): 83–98.

—— (1989) 'The logic of market share unionism: is membership decline inevitable?', *Industrial Relations Journal,* 20(3): 260–71.

—— (1996) 'Merger propensity and merger outcomes among UK unions, 1986–1995', *Industrial Relations Journal,* 27(4): 331–39.

—— (2001) 'The viability of trade union organisation: a bargaining unit analysis', *British Journal of Industrial Relations,* 39(1): 97–117.

Willman, P. and Morris, T. (1995) 'Financial management and financial performance in British trade unions', *British Journal of Industrial Relations,* 33(2): 289–98.

Willman, P., Bryson, A. and Gomez, R. (2003) *Why Do Voice Regimes Differ?,* London: LSE, Centre for Economic Performance, Discussion Paper 591.

—— (2004) 'The sound of silence: determinants of no voice among British employers', unpublished MS, London: LSE, Centre for Economic Performance.

Willman, P., Morris, T.J. and Aston, B. (1993) *Union Business: Trade Union Organisation and Financial Reform in the Thatcher Years,* Cambridge: Cambridge University Press.

Wills, J. (2001) *Mapping Low Pay in East London,* London: UNISON.

—— (2002) *Union Futures: Building Networked Trade Unionism in the UK,* London: Fabian Society.

Wood. S. and Godard, J. (1999) 'The statutory union recognition procedure in the Employment Relations Bill: a comparative analysis', *British Journal of Industrial Relations,* 37(2): 203–45.

Wood, S., Moore, S. and Ewing, K. (2003) 'The impact of the trade union recognition procedure under the Employment Relations Act, 2000–2', in H. Gospel and S. Wood (eds) *Representing Workers: Trade Union Recognition and Membership in Britain,* London: Routledge.

Wood, S., Moore, S. and Willman, P. (2002) 'Third time lucky for statutory union recognition in the UK', *Industrial Relations Journal,* 33(3): 215–33.

Index

Note: Tables in the text are indicated
  by (*table*) after the page number,
  e.g. 24(*table*), and Figures by (*Fig.*),
  e.g. 42(*Fig. 2.1*)

Academy Organisers 153–4
Ackers, P. and Payne, P. 110
activists: and ballot surveys 28–9;
  importance of 24–6, 29, 164, 165;
  and membership recruitment 40–1,
  43, 44, 45–6, 155; and public sector
  modernization 91, 98; and the
  statutory recognition process 8;
  victimization of 19–20
AEEU (Amalgamated Engineering and
  Electrical Union) 16, 75
agency 33, 133
agency workers 54, 55, 61–2, 65–6, 70
Aidt, T.S. and Sena, V. 85
Amalgamated Engineering and
  Electrical Union (AEEU) 16, 75
Amazon on-line 34–5, 44–8, 167, 168
AMICUS 16, 75
AMO (Association of Magisterial
  Officers) 112, 113
Armstrong, G. 110
ASDA 127
Association of Magisterial Officers
  (AMO) 112, 113
Association of Teachers and Lecturers
  (ATL) 100–1
Association of University Teachers
  (AUT) 34, 35–8, 49
Aston, B. 80
Atkinson, P. 92
ATL (Association of Teachers and
  Lecturers) 34, 35–8, 49
Audia, G. *et al.* 78

Audit Commission 64–5, 65–6, 93, 98,
  102
Australian unions 154, 159
AUT (Association of University
  Teachers) 34, 35–8, 49
Autolost 10(*table*), 15–16, 18, 23, 25,
  26

Bach, S. 89, 92; and Givan, R.K. 76;
  and Winchester, D. 94, 96, 112
Bacon, N. and Storey, J. 111
ballots *see* recognition ballots
BALPA 12
Barber, B. 150
bargaining: power 165; units 20, 81–2,
  see also collective bargaining
Bassett, P. and Cave, A. 78
Baumol, W. 53
Beck, U. 51, 52, 70
Becker, B. *et al.* 85
Behrens, M. *et al.* 165
Best Value 66–7, 96
'bitstrings' 52
Black and Decker 16
Blanchflower, D. and Bryson, A. 78,
  138
BMA (British Medical Association) 107
book publishing sector 156
Boraston, I. 82
Boxall, P. and Haynes, P. 77
Brightex 60, 61–2
Brighton and Hove 55–70
British Medical Association (BMA) 107
British Worker Representation and
  Participation Survey (BWRPS) 3, 127
Bronfenbrenner, K. *et al.* 34
Bronfenbrenner, K. and Juravich, T. 8,
  18–19, 21, 47, 105

Brook, K. 35, 78, 89, 127
Bryson, A. *et al.* 168
Bryson, A. and Gomez, R. 87
Buchanan, R. 74
Burchill, F. 98, 99, 106
Burke Group 152
Burke, T. 152
business performance 115
BWRPS (British Worker
    Representation and Participation
    Survey) 3, 127

CAC (Central Arbitration Committee)
    7, 9, 11–16, 23
call-centre 34, 38–44, 49
campaigns: against privatization 104,
    105; local and sector based issues
    60–1; organizing campaigns 34–8,
    40–2, 44–8, 49, 77, 166;
    recognition campaigns 21–2; on
    working conditions 101–2
care workers 51, 53, 55, 67–9
Carvel, J. 120
case studies: employer behaviour and
    union organizing 16–29; new media
    and IT 56–61; social partnership
    112–26; statutory recognition
    procedure 10(*table*)
Castells, M. 51, 52
CCT (compulsory competitive
    tendering) 63, 66, 96
Central Arbitration Committee (CAC)
    7, 9, 11–16, 23
Charlwood, A. 8, 77
CHI (Commission for Health
    Improvement) 124, 125
Child, J. *et al.* 73
childcare provision 54–5, 67–9
City Clean 64
Clark, A. and Oswald, A. 84
Clark, P.F. 33, 38
Clarke, Charles 103–4
Classic (company) 59, 60
Clegg, H. 73
closure threats 17–18, 26–7, 167
Cohen, L. and Hurd, R.W. 8
Cohen-Rosenthal, E. and Burton, C. 111
'collective action frames' 33, 46, 50
collective bargaining 94–5, 94(*table*),
    104, 113, 156, 160, *see also*
    bargaining units
Commission for Health Improvement
    (CHI) 124, 125

community unionism 102, 105,
    159–60
companies *see* employers; management
Compass Catering 157
Comprehensive Performance
    Assessment 96
compulsory competitive tendering
    (CCT) 63, 66, 96
conglomeration 73, 74–6, 81–2
consultation processes 87, 95, 121–2,
    169
consumers 132
Cooke, W. 7, 20
cost, and risk 78–9, 80
costs: of services 64–6; transaction cost
    economics 133–5; and voice 132–3
counter-mobilization 7–8, 16–21, 30,
    46–8, 162, 167–8
Coyle, D. 51, 52
Crosby, M. 154
Cully, M. 35, 93, 95, 106; *et al.* 92,
    115

Daycare Trust 67
Deery, S. *et al.* 110
density: in Europe 165; falling numbers
    152; in the public sector 94,
    94(*table*); and social partnership
    127; in traditional areas 157, *see
    also* membership
Department of Health 112, 116
Department of Trade and Industry
    (DTI): *Fairness at Work* 11, 29, 53,
    93, 95; 'Flexible working' 54
deregulation 53–5
DfES, *21st Century Skills* (White
    Paper) 152
Diamond, W. and Freeman, R. 59, 127,
    145
Digitareel 58
DiMaggio, P.J. and Powell, W.W. 78
disciplinary issues 47, 61–2
dismissals 47, 61–2, 167
Doogan, K. 52
dot.com companies *see* new media
    workers
DTI *see* Department of Trade and
    Industry

earnings *see* pay issues
economy *see* new economy; scale
    economies; transaction cost
    economics

education: TUC programmes 153, 155, 156, 159, *see also* AUT; teaching unions

elections, NLRB certification elections 7, 8

employees: ballots and union access to workforce 22–4; call-centre employees 34, 38–44; childcare workers 51, 53, 55, 67–9; direct employer communication 21; e-retailers 44–8; labour turnover 48; new media workers 51, 52, 56–61, 70; occupational boundaries 99–102; refuse collectors 51, 53, 63–7; representative bodies 26; research workers 34, 35–8; and social partnership 115–19, 122–3; support for unions 48, 59, 66, 68, 158, 166; threats to 17–18, 26–7, 47, 166, 167–8; and union structuring 86, 87, *see also* agency workers; fixed-term contract staff; freelance workers; temporary workers; Workplace Employee Relations Survey

employers: attitudes to unions 59–60, 61, 141(*Fig. 8.5*), 144–5, 160–1, 165–6; counter-mobilization tactics 7–8, 16–21, 30, 46–8, 162, 167–8; disciplinary issues 47, 61–2; equality policies 56; and market dominance 52–3; multinationals 44–8, 62, 64, 152; organizations of 160–1; and organizing campaigns 36, 41–2, 43, 44, 161, 166; and social partnership 114–15, 122–3; support for membership 141–2; and union organization 4, 5; and union recognition 2, 12–16, 45, 129–49, 164; and union structuring 76, 78–9, 86, 87; and voice 129, 132–6, 138, 140, 141–4

employment: employment relations data 93; EU guidelines 53, 54, 61; and new economy 51–5; and union membership 1–3, 32–4, *see also* job security; work–life balance

Employment Relations Act 1999 (ERA) 3, 164, 168; and partnership agreements 112; and statutory recognition procedure 7, 45, 54, 162

equality: employer policies 56; in the new economy 52–3; for women 54–5, 70

ERA *see* Employment Relations Act 1999

ethnic minorities 45–6, 48, 158, 159

Etzioni, A. 92

EU Directives 53, 54, 61, 169; information and consultation 169; Temporary Agency Worker Directive 54, *see also* consultation processes; transparency; website information

Ewing, K. *et al.* 30

exit costs 133

Fairbrother, P. 97

Fairness at Work (DTI) 11, 29, 53, 93, 95

Faith, R.L. and Reid, J.D. 85

Fantasia, R. 47

Farber, H. and Western, B. 7

Fastwon 10(*table*), 20, 22, 24

finance sector 127

Fiorito, J. *et al.* 82, 84

firms *see* employers; management

fixed-term contract staff 35–8, 52

Flanders, A. 87

flexible working 39, 54, 98

Flood, P. *et al.* 80

Folbre, N. and Nelson, J. 53

freelance workers 58

Freeman, R. and Medoff, J. 132, 133; and Pelletier, J. 9

Frege, C. and Kelly, J. 79, 86, 91

fund-raising 38

funding 96, 97

Gall, G. 32, 127, 168

gender issues 52–3, 56; legislation on 54, 70; and union membership 92, 101–2, 158, *see also* women workers

Gibson, O. 44

gifts and bonuses 56–7

Gill, R. 56

GMB: campaigns 104, 161; employer intervention in recognition ballots 14; membership and modernization 99

GMPU (Graphical Paper and Media Union) 38, 40–4, 44–8; and book

publishing sector 156; and new media workers 60, 62
Gomez, R. 60
Gospel, H. and Willman, P. 86, 145
governance costs 132–3
government: funding control 97; lobbying 79; and public service reforms 89; and union organization 4, 5, 152; and union recognition 11, 12, 161–2, 168–9, *see also* Labour government
Grant, R. 78
Graphical Paper and Media Union *see* GMPU
Green, F. 147
'greenfield recruitment' 49, 105–6
Greenhouse, S. 44
grievances 33, 37, 38, 40, 46, 49
Guest, D. and Peccei, R. 110, 111, 113

Hamann, K. and Kelly, J. 169
Hardwidge, C. 127
health sector: funding of 96; unionization in 60, 61–2, 100, *see also* NHS Trusts
Heery, E. 127; *et al.* 21, 24, 28, 32, 45, 153, 154, 164, 166; and Simms, M. 161
Hemingway, J. 82
Hildreth, A.K.G. 138
Hirschman, A. 132
homeworking 158–9
hours of work *see* flexible working; working hours
housing 57(*table*), 65, 68
HSBC Bank 127–8
Huber–White robust variance estimator 147
Hudson, M. *et al.* 111
Hyman, R. 75, 77, 78, 86, 87, 101; categories of union representation 98, 102, 104, 105

ICT technologies 51, 52, 53; case studies 56–61
identity 33
ideology 38
IER survey 54
India 62
individual services 77
industrial action 66, 69, 70–1, 100

industrial relations 123–6, *see also* social partnership
industrial sector unions 89, 157, 161
inequality 53, 70
'infill recruitment' 49
interests, representation of 102, 104, 115
Internet *see* website information
Ironside, M. and Siefert, R. 101

Javeline, D. 33
JCC (Joint Consultation Committee) 125
job security 17–18, 26–7; and the new economy 52, 58(*table*), 70; and social partnership 114, 120–1, *see also* work satisfaction; work–life balance
Johnston, P. 91, 105
Joint Consultation Committee (JCC) 125
Joyce, P. *et al.* 92

Kelly, J. 7, 8, 27, 33, 111, 127; and Heery, E. 83, 154
Kelso, P. 67, 69
Kennedy, P. 147
Kessler, I. and Heron, P. 98, 99
Klandermans, B. 33
knowledge work and goods 51, 52–3
Kochan, T. 7, 129; and Katz, H. 82

labour force *see* employees
Labour government: decentralization and partnership 111–12; and modernization agenda 103, 108, 169; and public service reforms 89, 91, 92, 96, 97; and union recognition 11, *see also* government
labour–management partnerships *see* partnership agreements
Lawler, J. 7, 20
leadership 156, 169
legal system 112
legislation: gender issues 54, 70; racial issues 54; recognition legislation 7–31, 161–2, 165; working hours 54
Levitt, M.J. and Conrow, T. 43, 46
linear probability estimation of union voice 146–7, 148(*table*)
Lister, J. 104

litigation, and union membership 68
lobbying 79
Logan, J. 17, 19
LRD 34

McGregor, D. 91
Machin, S. 76
Magisterial Courts Committees
    (MCCs) 112–23, 125–7
management (of companies): and
    employee well-being 61; and
    organizing campaigns 39–40, 41–2,
    43; public sector relationships 95,
    96, 97, 98; US ownership of UK
    companies 17, 18, 19, 44–8, 152
Mason, R. and Bain, P. 77
MCC see Magisterial Courts
    Committees
media workers see new media workers
membership: 1975–2002 1–3; of
    agency workers 66; and bargaining
    power 165; of care workers 68;
    employers' support for 141–2; loss,
    and restructuring 73, 76–9, 151–2;
    membership trends 1–3, 32–4,
    43–4, 48, 74; of new media workers
    60; non-joiners 37–8, 47; non-
    members 34, 157, 164; and
    organizing campaigns 49; and public
    service restructuring 98–102; of
    public service unions 89, 90(table),
    92, 94, 96; and recognition ballots
    11–16, 42–3; and social partnership
    127; subscriptions 68–9, 78, see also
    representation
membership recruitment 33, 37, 38,
    154; and activists 40–1, 43, 44,
    45–6; campaigns 34–8, 40–2, 44–8,
    49, 157–8; and professional identity
    100; public sector unions 95
mergers 73, 74–6
Metcalf, D. 32, 34, 49
Milburn, A. 111
Millward, N. et al. 74, 76, 94, 95, 98,
    131, 136, 138
Milne, S. 44
minimum wage 54, 71
minorities: and economic constraints
    53; ethnic 45–6, 48, 158, 159;
    union membership of 153, 157,
    158, 159
Mitchell, D.J. 84
mobilization theory 8, 33–4, 48

Monger, J. 138
Monks, J. 150
Moore, S. et al. 22
Morris, G. 91
multi-unionism 95, 96
multinationals 44–8, 62, 64, 152
Murray, A. 169

NAHT (National Association of Head
    Teachers) 101
NASUWT 101
National Association of Head Teachers
    (NAHT) 101
National Group on Homeworking
    (NGH) 158–9
National Labour Relations Board
    (NLRB) 7, 8
National Union of Teachers (NUT) 101
negotiation: employee/employer 60;
    employer/union 43
new economy 51–5; and job security
    52, 58(table), 70
new media workers 51, 52, 56–61, 62,
    70
New Unionism 150–1, 153–60, 162,
    167; Task Group 150, 153
NGH (National Group on
    Homeworking) 158–9
NHS Trusts: and Foundation Trusts 96;
    social partnership 112–25; and
    union membership 60, see also
    health sector
NLRB (National Labour Relations
    Board) 7, 8
'no-voice' workplaces 136–8, 169
Nolan, P. and Slater, G. 52
NUT (National Union of Teachers) 101

occupational boundaries 99–102
Offe, C. and Wiesenthal, H. 80
officials (trade union) 91, 154, 155–6,
    see also activists; representatives
on-line information 55, 60, 62, 69
one-to-ones 18–19
organizers (trade union) see activists;
    officials
Organizing Academy 21, 22, 45, 153
organizing campaigns 34–8, 40–2,
    44–8, 49, 155–6; and employers 36,
    41–2, 43, 44, 161, see also union
    organizing
outcomes 4–5
Oxenbridge, S. and Brown, W. 111

parental leave 54
parents, support for 54, 55
part-time work 54
partnership agreements 60, 71, 77, 97,
    110–28, 160; six principles of 111,
    113–15
pay issues 43, 47, 48, 56–8; and costs
    133; and minimum wage 54, 71;
    and public sector modernization
    94–5, 94(table); representation of
    interests 102, 104; responsibility
    and low pay 67–9; and union
    structuring 87; and working time
    64–5
pay review bodies 94, 104
Pendleton, A. 89
performance measures 84–5, 85(table)
Perrons, D. 52, 56, 78, 92
PFI see Private Finance Initiative
portfolio workers 52
PPP see Public Private Partnerships
Prentis, D. 111
Prism Research 69
Private Finance Initiative (PFI) 55, 96,
    97, 104–5, 111, 169
private sector: and childcare provision
    55; membership and public service
    restructuring 98–102, 104; and
    partnership 127; and public
    service reforms 89, 94(table), 95,
    96, 97; temporary workers in 17,
    52; unionization in 140, 141,
    165
productivity 63
professional unions 89, 92, 95, 98;
    membership 99–102; and
    modernization 104–5; workplace
    representation of 99, 106–7
Public Administration Select
    Committee 93
Public Private Partnerships (PPP) 97,
    111, see also partnership agreements
public sector 55, 69, 89–109;
    bargaining and membership 165;
    membership and the private sector
    98–102, 104; modernization of
    96–107; public service trade unions
    91–3, 169; reforms, and the private
    sector 89, 94(table), 95, 96, 97, see
    also AUT; Magisterial Courts
    Committees (MCCs); NHS Trusts;
    teaching unions
Public Services Forum 162

Quah, D. 51, 52, 53
quality of life see work–life balance

racial issues 45–6, 48, 54, 62
RCN (Royal College of Nursing) 100,
    102, 104
recognition agreements 151, 157, 160,
    161, 164, 166
recognition ballots 7, 9, 11–16; and
    bargaining units 20; and employer
    tactics 20–1, 152, 167; and
    organizing campaigns 42–3, 47–8;
    survey of 28–9; and union access to
    workforce 22–4
recognition campaigns 21–2, 157
recognition legislation 7–31, 161–2,
    165
recruitment agencies see agency
    workers
recruitment campaigns 34–8, 40–2,
    44–8, 49, 165, see also membership
    recruitment
refuse collectors 51, 53, 63–7
relocation threats 17–18, 26–7, 167
representation: on bodies 152; under-
    representation 153, 157, 158,
    159–60; in the workplace 99,
    102–7, 123–6, 144–6
representatives: and non-union
    employers 144; in public sector
    workplaces 94, 96, 97; and social
    partnership 119–20, 123–6; women
    as 158, 159, see also activists;
    officials
research workers 34, 35–8
resources 4–5
retail sector 127, 159
rights, and membership 33, 77
Rogers, S. 62
Royal College of Nursing (RCN) 100,
    102, 104
Rundle, J. 27

sacking 47, 61–2, 167
salaries see pay issues
Sapper, S. 78
scale economies 74, 80–1
Secondary Heads Association (SHA)
    101
'Senior Leaders Programme' (TUC)
    156
Sennett, R. 51, 52
service provision 92–3

SHA (Secondary Heads Association)
101
shift work 40, 65
shipbuilding industries 161
SITA 64
Skinner, C. 54, 55
social divisions 52–3
social mobility 53
social partnership 112–28, 162; and
non-partnership organization 118,
126, 127, see also partnership
agreements
Spector, R. 44
staff forums 41, 47, 166, 168, see also
employees; freelance workers
statutory recognition 7–31, 161–2,
164; the procedure 9–12, 15(Fig.
2.1)
strategy: conglomeration 81–2;
effectiveness of 84–6; options for
77–9; and resource allocation 82–4
Strategy Unit 54
Streeck, W. and Visser, J. 81, 82
street cleaning 63–7
strike action 66, 69, 70–1, 100
Stuart, M. and Martinez Lucio, M. 111
sub-contracting 55, 62
subscriptions (union membership)
68–9, 78
superstar effect 53
supervisors 18–21, 46–7
surgeries 22, 23, 28

Taylor, P.: and Bain, P. 39; and Ramsay,
H. 127
teaching unions 100–1, 104–5, 106–7
Telco 105
temporary workers 17, 35–8, 52, see
also agency workers
Terry, M. 99; and Smith, J. 128
Tilly, C. 33
Towers, B. 9
Trades Union Congress see TUC
training (TUC programmes) 153, 155,
156, 159
transaction cost economics 133–4
transparency 115, 121–2
TUC: affiliated and non-TUC unions
74; education programmes 153, 155,
156, 159; on employer counter-
mobilization 30; and government
modernization agenda 1, 103;
lobbying co-ordination 79; 'one

movement' approach of 162–3;
publications quoted 7, 11, 106, 110,
150, 158; six principles of
partnership 111, 113–15, see also
New Unionism; Organizing Academy
Tyneside Maritime Group 161

Undy, R. 92, 108, 112; et al. 79, 80, 82
unemployment: and union membership
trends 2(table), 32, see also
employment
union agency see agency
Union Learning Reps 159
union organizing 5, 21–9, 32–50,
105–6, 165–9; the New Unionism
approach 150–1, 153–60, 162, 167;
objectives of 164
unions: decline of 73, 74, 140; density
94, 94(table), 127, 152, 157, 165;
employers attitudes to 59–60, 61,
141(Fig. 8.5), 144–5, 160–1, 165–6;
governance 99, 100, 108; growth
mechanisms 83(table); influence on
government policies 92; presence in
the workplace 130–1, 139–41; and
recognition 2–3; responses to public
service modernization 90–1,
98–107; revitalization of 86–7,
151–2, 157–9, 165; structure and
strategies 4, 73–87, 80–6, 97, 106,
150–63, 164, 166–7; tactics 8, 48;
TUC membership 153–4; voice 129,
133–6; and workplace representation 99, 102–7, 119–20, 123–6,
see also activists; membership;
TUC; union organizing
UNISON 99, 101–2, 108; and
conglomeration 75; NHS Trust
partnership 113, 124; organizing
initiatives 155; Positively Public
Campaign 104; and union
organizing 60, 103
United States: community unionism in
160; employer tactics 14, 17, 19,
152; NLRB certification elections 7,
8; ownership and management of
UK companies 17, 18, 19, 44–8;
and union organizing 105, 164; and
union resource allocation 82; union
success and failure 7
university research workers 34, 35–8

Van den Noord, P. 92

Verma, A. *et al.* 74
victimization 19–20
Video Duplicating Company 28
voice: decline of in unions 144; of
    employers 129, 132–6, 138, 140,
    141–4; mechanism 76, 85(*table*),
    86; 'no-voice' workplaces 136–8,
    169; regimes 136–9; theory 132–6,
    146–7; union/non-union voice 131,
    141–4, 168
Voos, P. 82

Waddington, J. 75, 91, 92, 108
wages *see* pay issues
website information 55, 60, 62, 69
WERS *see* Workplace Employee
    Relations Survey
Williamson, O.E. 82, 132, 134
Willman, P. 74, 81, 82, 83, 136; *et al.*
    74, 76, 78, 79, 80; and Morris, T.J.
    76, 81
Wills, J. 96, 105
Winning the Organised Workplace
    (*WOW*) (TUC) 155
win–win partnership 115

women: as Academy Organisers 153;
    earnings of 58; and union
    membership 92, 101, 158, 159;
    workers 54–5, 67–9, 70
Wood, S.: *et al.* 11; and Godard, J. 7,
    14
work satisfaction 58(*table*)
workers *see* employees
workers' representation *see* activists;
    officials; representatives
working hours 39, 40, 56–7; legislation
    on 54; and pay 64–5, 67, *see also*
    flexible working
workplace: 'no-voice' workplaces
    136–8; public sector representatives
    in 94, 96, 97; union representation
    in 99, 102–7, 119–20, 123–6,
    144–6
Workplace Employee Relations Survey
    (WERS) 3, 91, 93–6, 136, 141
work–life balance 54, 58(*table*), 68,
    114, *see also* job security; work
    satisfaction
WOW (*Winning the Organised
    Workplace*) (TUC) 155